# GOD'S GUARANTEE

The Divine Plan for Victorious Christian Living

**Courtney Jackson**

World rights reserved. This book or any portion thereof may not be copied or reproduced in any form or manner whatever, except as provided by law, without the written permission of the publisher, except by a reviewer who may quote brief passages in a review.

The author assumes full responsibility for the accuracy of all facts and quotations as cited in this book. The opinions expressed in this book are the author's personal views and interpretations, and do not necessarily reflect those of the publisher.

This book is provided with the understanding that the publisher is not engaged in giving spiritual, legal, medical, or other professional advice. If authoritative advice is needed, the reader should seek the counsel of a competent professional.

The website references in this book have been shortened using a URL shortener and a redirect service called 1ref.us, which ASPECT Books manages. If you find that a reference no longer works, please contact us and let us know which one is not working so that we can correct it. Any personal website addresses that the author included are managed by the author. ASPECT Books is not responsible for the accuracy or permanency of any links.

Copyright © 2022 Courtney Jackson
Copyright © 2022 ASPECT Books
ISBN-13: 978-1-4796-0494-4 (Paperback)
ISBN-13: 978-1-4796-0495-1 (ePub)
Library of Congress Control Number: 2022905182

Unless otherwise indicated, all Scripture quotations are from the King James Version (KJV).

Scripture quotations marked ARV are from the American Revised Version (also called the American Standard Version), issued in 1900–1901.

Scripture quotations marked R.V. are from the English Revised Version, issued in 1881–1885.

Boldfacing and underlining in quotations throughout the book are for emphasis and were supplied by the author. Emphasis through italics is from the original.

Published by

www.ASPECTBooks.com

# Contents

*Introduction* . . . . . . . . . . . . . . . . . . . . . . . . . . . . . . . . . . . *v*

Chapter 1:   The Struggle in Obtaining the Character of Christ . . . . . . 7

Chapter 2:   Encouragement to Go Forward . . . . . . . . . . . . . . 23

Chapter 3:   God's Guarantee . . . . . . . . . . . . . . . . . . . . . . 45

Chapter 4:   The New Birth in the New Covenant . . . . . . . . . . . 63

Chapter 5:   God's Promise to Israel . . . . . . . . . . . . . . . . . . . 85

Chapter 6:   What Makes the New Covenant New? . . . . . . . . . . 105

Chapter 7:   A Shadow of Things to Come . . . . . . . . . . . . . . . 129

Chapter 8:   The Immense Cost in Securing Salvation . . . . . . . . . 151

Chapter 9:   God's Justice in Our Redemption . . . . . . . . . . . . . 167

Chapter 10:  Security through Dependence . . . . . . . . . . . . . . . 185

Chapter 11:  The Spirit of Prophecy on the Covenant . . . . . . . . . 203

Chapter 12:  Utilizing the Covenant for Victory . . . . . . . . . . . . . 217

Chapter 13:  Sanctification by Faith . . . . . . . . . . . . . . . . . . . 251

Chapter 14:  Faith to Follow . . . . . . . . . . . . . . . . . . . . . . . 297

*Bibliography* . . . . . . . . . . . . . . . . . . . . . . . . . . . . . . . *311*

# Introduction

We admire athletes who have worked hard to overcome adversity and accomplish great results. These would be athletes like Tom Dempsey, who kicked a winning 63-yard field goal for the New Orleans Saints in 1970 with half a foot; or like asthma sufferer Amy Van Dyken, who is a six-time Olympic swimmer gold medalist; or like Wilma Rudolph, who was sickly as a child and wore a brace on her left leg but went on to be the first American woman to win three gold medals at a single Olympic games. We admire such people for their achievements even while most of us do not possess their physical stamina or even the stamina that our grandparents once had. While Nike commercials encourage activity with the slogan, "Just do it," many other commercials say, "Indulge yourself." Most Americans do the latter, and our children spend much more time indoors than out. Schools promote self-esteem often to the neglect of self-discipline. The media report that college students have difficulty balancing academic and social demands.

The Christian church is not much better. Christians have become spiritual weaklings who glory in God's forgiveness. Twenty-first-century megachurches have flourished under the philosophy of "It's all about me as I sing about Him." Great Christian leaders of past generations would have difficulty recognizing twenty-first century Christianity. These giants of faith encouraged Bible study, the discipline of one's personal habits, active service and fulfilling the Ten Commandments rather than glorying in weakness and forgiveness.

Dr. Courtney Jackson swims against the current of modern trends, taking seriously the high moral expectations of the New Testament and Adventist writer and pioneer Ellen G. White. As such, he promotes biblical teachings that modern Christianity does not usually emphasize. We can best understand these teachings if we take them in the spirit of an athlete who achieves great results by exercising the will to bring the physical body into line with his or her goals. Success in spiritual matters belongs to those who bend the will to apply this insight spiritually.

CHAPTER 1

# The Struggle in Obtaining the Character of Christ

> Teach me, Father, what to say;
> Teach me, Father, how to pray;
> Teach me all along the way
> How to be like Jesus.
> —A. D. Ellington[1]

Mankind has been set in the center of a battle that knows no end until the second coming of Christ. The outcome of the battle for each soul will be determined individually. There is no greater struggle, nor greater attainment than eternal life and the development of the character of Christ, which is the character of God. But many are almost clueless regarding the severity of the conflict and the discipline required to reach this high and holy goal. They are caught off guard by Satan's attacks and do not recognize the value of the struggle in the Christian life. Even those who have professed the "straight truth" believe that, because we are saved by grace obtained by righteousness by faith, there should not be much of a struggle. They read the Word of God and the Testimony of Jesus with scales on their eyes blind to that which is inconvenient.[2]

---

[1] A. D. Ellington, "Like Jesus," 1931, Hymnary, https://1ref.us/1kt (accessed February 17, 2021).
[2] Throughout this book, the author uses the term "the Testimony of Jesus" to refer to the gift of prophecy (also called "the spirit of prophecy") that God promised His people in the last days (see Rev. 12:17; 19:10). The phrase is capitalized because it designates the counsel of the Holy Spirit in the writings of Ellen G. White.

Dear reader, you know that every time you look in the mirror you have to face your faults—the thoughts, words, actions, intentions, and motives that you know must change. You struggle with pride, covetousness, and lust among the multitude of temptations you face day by day, and even moment by moment. Though you know that salvation comes by grace and that you are righteous by faith, your life is sadly lacking in the evidence of your profession. And faithful to His work, the Lord Jesus promised and sent the Holy Spirit to reprove "the world of sin, and of righteousness, and of judgment" (John 16:8). In the back of your mind, the outcome of judgment is an uncertainty, and you believe that your only chance of salvation is to slip into heaven by grace. But the Word of God, faithful to its work, continues to say the same thing, testifying over and over in different ways and in words too clear to ignore.

> This I say then, Walk in the Spirit, and ye shall not fulfil the lust of the flesh. For the flesh lusteth against the Spirit, and the Spirit against the flesh: and these are contrary the one to the other: so that ye cannot do the things that ye would. But if ye be led of the Spirit, ye are not under the law. Now the works of the flesh are manifest, which are these; adultery, fornication, uncleanness, lasciviousness, idolatry, witchcraft, hatred, variance, emulations, wrath, strife, seditions, heresies, envyings, murders, drunkenness, revellings, and such like: of the which I tell you before, as I have also told you in time past, that <u>they which do such things shall not inherit the kingdom of God</u>. But the fruit of the Spirit is love, joy, peace, longsuffering, gentleness, goodness, faith, meekness, temperance: against such there is no law. And <u>they that are Christ's have crucified the flesh with the affections and lusts</u>. (Gal. 5:16–24)

You recognize these works of the flesh and see many that you are giving into, or you may recognize even more obviously that you are lacking in the fruit of the Spirit. You see your frustration, irritation, impatience, and anger repeatedly, causing you to react badly to those around you seemly nonstop. How can you obtain the victory? You call yourself a Christian, but you have not seen Christ in your heart. After all that you have tried, Satan appears stronger than Christ, and he often wins in the struggle of the moment. To make matters worse, you sense the strength of your temptations increasing. Where is the corresponding increase of Christ's power in your life?

## Encouragement in the Struggle

We have been placed in this world to help one another as brothers and sisters in the struggle, for only someone with an experience like yours can really understand you when you talk of the circumstances you are going through. Therefore, the Bible was written in its manner to share examples of people who overcame huge character defects and misconceptions of applying the truth. The Bible was written especially for the last generation who will have the greatest struggles in overcoming sin. If I were Gabriel, the highest angel in the order of heaven, even though holy and sinless, I would not be qualified to help you in the struggle with overcoming sin by nature. Only humans are qualified to help other humans because we share the same weakness in our human nature. Brother and sister, we face a struggle of immense proportions to overcome sin in this world. Yet, we must not give up. Don't give in—believe with all your heart and all your experience that Jesus Christ is omnipotent and that He can deliver you from all types of temptations. At the same time, we must also recognize that, even with the power of God, it will require a struggle. Why? In this world of sin, the effort of struggling is what makes us stronger in our nature.

It may seem odd that I have emphasized the struggle in obtaining the character of Christ by the power of God at the outset of this book, but I have done so because many seem to think that there shouldn't be a battle since we are saved by grace and we obtain righteousness by faith. The reason that we need to focus on this very real battle is so that we will understand how to approach it and so that we will grow in faith in the midst of this monumental struggle. Why does it require such a huge struggle? Because we must overcome every sin and every temptation, not just the "really bad ones," for all sin is hateful to God. All this we must do in a body that, by nature, insatiably craves the things of the world.

To establish our bases, let us turn to Scripture and the Testimony of Jesus. In the beginning, God created man perfect in a perfect world, with Eden to be kept as man's home as long as man obeyed the command of God. So logic would reveal that, to return to Eden, we must return to a life without sin which the Lord declares to us in the statement, "He that overcometh shall inherit all things; and I will be his God, and he shall be my son" (Rev. 21:7). Furthermore, we have this encouragement about the struggle:

> Wrongs cannot be righted, nor can reformations in conduct be made by <u>a few feeble, intermittent efforts</u>. Character building is

the work, not of a day, nor of a year, but of a lifetime. The struggle for conquest over self, for holiness and heaven, <u>is a lifelong struggle</u>. **Without continual effort and constant activity, there can be no advancement in the divine life, no attainment of the victor's crown.**

The strongest evidence of man's fall from a higher state is the fact that **it costs so much to return**. The way of return can be gained only by <u>hard fighting</u>, <u>inch by inch</u>, <u>hour by hour</u>. In one moment, by a hasty, unguarded act, we may place ourselves in the power of evil; **but it requires <u>more than a moment to break the fetters and attain to a holier life</u>**. The purpose may be formed, the work begun; but its accomplishment will require **toil, time, perseverance, patience,** and **sacrifice**.

We cannot allow ourselves to act from impulse. **We cannot be off guard for a moment.** Beset with temptations without number, we must resist firmly or be conquered. <u>Should we come to the close of life with our work undone, it would be an eternal loss.</u> (*The Ministry of Healing*, p. 452)

If I were to poll one hundred people for the names of those whom they most admire, among the top names on the list would have to be Bill Gates, who was at one time the richest man in the world. He would be on the list because of the benefit that his computer programs have brought human beings. Yet, Bill Gates is only a weak and feeble man of flesh who gets sick, tired, and hungry. So, was it easy to accomplish what he has done? No, if it were, everybody would have done it. That what he has accomplished is unique tells us that it must not be easy. By simple reasoning, once again, we can see that what he has accomplished is unique and therefore must be difficult. Yet, all that he has accomplish is simply to engineer computer products and make lots of money. Aside from this, his character, spiritually speaking, may be very defective.

How much greater is God the Creator of the infinite universe than a mere human being who is only a particle in this great universe? God is presenting to us the opportunity to be like Him, to have His character. Do we grasp the magnitude of what He has offered? This is all the more immense because, in human flesh with fallen natures, we must struggle to become like God. Yet, this is our purpose: we were created to be like God! Genesis says, "So God created man in his own image, in the image of God created he him: male and female created he them" (Gen. 1:27). Think about what that includes. We were created to think, talk, and act like God Himself. We were to be holy, pure, perfect, and loving in every circumstance.

## The Discipline and Science of Being a Christian

In the New Testament, Paul compared the Christian life to a race in which runners direct all their energies toward gaining the prize (Heb. 12:1–3).[3] Paul also compared the Christian life to combat and urged the Christian to put on armor to face the devil's attacks (Eph. 6:11, 12). The Testimony of Jesus compares the Christian life to combat but also calls it a science:

> The Christian life is **a battle and a march.** In this warfare there is no release; the effort must be continuous and persevering. It is by unceasing endeavor that we maintain the victory over the temptations of Satan. Christian integrity must be sought with resistless energy and maintained with a **resolute fixedness of purpose**.
>
> **No one** will be borne upward without stern, persevering effort **in his own behalf**. All must engage in this warfare for themselves; no one else can fight our battles. Individually we are responsible for the issues of the struggle; though Noah, Job, and Daniel were in the land they could deliver neither son nor daughter by their righteousness.
>
> There is a **science** of Christianity to be mastered—a science as much deeper, broader, higher than any human science as the heavens are higher than the earth. **The mind is to be disciplined, educated, trained; for we are to do service for God in ways that are not in harmony with inborn inclination. Hereditary and cultivated tendencies to evil must be overcome.** Often the education and training of a lifetime must be discarded, that one may become a learner in the school of Christ. Our hearts must be educated to become steadfast in God. **We are to form habits of thought that will enable us to resist temptation**. We must learn to look upward. The principles of the word of God—principles that are as high as heaven, and that compass eternity—**we are to understand** in their bearing upon our daily life. **Every act, every word, every thought,** is to be in accord with these principles. All must be brought into harmony with, and subject to, Christ. (*The Ministry of Healing*, pp. 453, 454)

---

[3] Throughout this book, the author assumes the Pauline authorship of the Epistle to the Hebrews.

Science, by definition, is an established system of study and methodology based on facts and laws, which, when carried out, yields the same product without fail. That is what we are searching for in relation to our salvation when we study and apply the Word of God. The Word of God has already been verified by millions, but, as students in a chemistry class must do, each of us must repeat the experiments himself to see the working out of the methodology that we may base our own belief in verified facts and laws, which produce a specific product without fail every time. As professed Christians, the product we are instructed to produce with God's power is the character of Christ (Eph. 2:10; Col. 1:27, 28; 2 Cor. 3:18).

Look at the order of duty we are called to perform: "The mind is to be disciplined, educated, and trained." We must "form habits of thought that will enable us to resist temptation." Keep in mind this process is a science. That's fantastic! Why a science? A science is an appropriate description because science requires following a particular method or procedure that, when completed, will produce the expected consistent results every time without fail. Amen! That is why the "Word of God" is such a fitting name for the Bible because every time it is followed the expected results are accomplished.

Reader, with this being the case, let us therefore go about finding out the method of victory because victory is guaranteed. If you wanted to market and sell computer software like Bill Gates, you would do well to ask him (if he would ever tell you) what to do because he is successful at it, right? So look at what the Word says about the guaranteed method of success, "For we have not an high priest which cannot be touched with the feeling of our infirmities; but was in all points tempted like as we are, yet without sin" (Heb. 4:15). Our High Priest was tempted like we are in all points but without sin. Therefore, He obviously knows how to obtain victory over sin in human flesh. Note the significance of the words immediately after "yet without sin": "Let us therefore." What do these three simple words mean? Because of what was done by Christ before, we can do the same thing. Therefore, let us follow in like manner the pattern of the One who went before us. Putting this into a practical example, if someone were to come to you and say, "For 25 cents I bought materials and learned to build a house that is worth $12 million," you could turn to your neighbor or friend and say, "Wow! I will therefore go build a house and make a profit like he did"? In the same way, should we not have confidence in following the admonition of verse 16? "Let us therefore come boldly unto the throne of grace, that we may obtain mercy, and find grace to help in time of need." Why do we need mercy? Because of sin. What is the purpose of grace? (1) To receive unmerited favor and (2) to receive power for achieving victory (see also Eph. 2:8, 9; 1 Thess. 1:12).

When, in the midst of temptation, are you utilizing these resources? Are you praying until you get the victory, or are you just struggling in your own power? There are two types of struggling Christians. The first struggles to maintain victory through prayer (see James 1:12). The second struggles with falling into sin knowing that he should have gained the victory but doesn't endure the temptation and eventually gives into it. Consider the following:

> The precious graces of the Holy Spirit **are not developed in a moment**. Courage, fortitude, meekness, faith, unwavering trust in God's power to save, are acquired by the experience of years. By a life of holy endeavor and firm adherence to the right the children of God are to seal their destiny. (*The Ministry of Healing*, p. 454)

Many who are young in their conversion experience fall easy prey to Satan through inexperience. They fall away, not maintaining their position in the battle while under the intensified constant assault. Then discouragement sets in, which is one of Satan's favorite tools, and he overcomes them by simple persistence. The occasional fall eventually becomes a return to the old life of sin. This pattern does not need to be.

> Minds that have been given up to **loose thought** need to change. "Gird up the loins of your mind, be sober, and hope to the end for the grace that is to be brought unto you at the revelation of Jesus Christ; as obedient children, not fashioning yourselves according to the former lusts in your ignorance: but as He which hath called you is holy, so be ye holy in all manner of conversation; because it is written, Be ye holy; for I am holy." 1 Peter 1:13–16.
>
> The thoughts must be **centered** upon God. We must put forth **earnest effort** to overcome the evil tendencies of the natural heart. Our efforts, our self-denial and perseverance, **must be proportionate to the infinite value of the object of which we are in pursuit**. Only by overcoming as Christ overcame shall we win the crown of life….
>
> It is not only at the beginning of the Christian life that this renunciation of self is to be made. At every advance step heavenward it is to be renewed. All our good works are dependent on

> a power outside of ourselves; therefore there needs to be **a continual reaching out of the heart after God**, a constant, earnest confession of sin and humbling of the soul before Him. Perils surround us; **and we are safe only as we feel our weakness and cling with the grasp of faith to our mighty Deliverer.** (*The Ministry of Healing*, pp. 455, 456)

Many, many people profess to be Christians to some extent because it is popular. However, the Christian life is more than profession. It is actually practical living exactly as Jesus lived. You are not to yield to temptation under any circumstance, nor to perform only sufficient benevolent acts to be deemed a good person at your funeral, as if the performance of a few more good deeds than one's neighbor is enough to grant a person entrance into heaven. Everything that Christ did was good. When we look at Genesis chapter 1, we see God the Creator, Christ (see John 1:3; Heb. 1:2). Christ surely could not make a mistake as God. And because He does not change, He surely did not make a mistake as a man. His life as a human being shows you how to live a godly life in the body of a man with human nature.

> [Christ] laid aside His glory, His dominion, His riches, and sought after those who were perishing in sin. He humbled Himself to our necessities, that He might exalt us to heaven. Sacrifice, self-denial, and disinterested benevolence characterized His life. He is our pattern.... He is a perfect and holy example, given for us to imitate. We cannot equal the pattern; but we shall not be approved of God if we do not copy it and, according to the ability which God has given, resemble it. Love for souls for whom Christ died will lead to a denial of self and a willingness to make any sacrifice in order to be co-workers with Christ in the salvation of souls. (*Testimonies for the Church*, vol. 2, p. 549)

## The Necessity of Godly Living

Funerals are sad but strange services because Christians continually profess, "Grace, grace, not by our own merits, but by faith only—it is this that gives us entrance into heaven." However, at a funeral, friends and family members make a long list of all the good deeds the deceased has committed, thereby declaring the loved one righteous before God, fit to live for eternity right next to God. Deep down inside, all people—including the unchurched—know that there is a judgment. How do they know? It is through the Holy Spirit, who reproves of sin, righteousness, and judgment (John 16:8). While we live, we will do well to listen to the Holy Spirit and ignore the loud professions of preachers and church members alike who say, "Only believe."

Do not forget that we are talking about righteousness by faith in the power of God to deliver from all our temptations and trials of life. That is what an omnipotent God can do. "Now unto him that is able to keep you from falling, and to present you faultless before the presence of his glory with exceeding joy" (Jude 24). Those who do not believe that Jesus can keep them from falling in this present world, living like Christ, will be cast into the lake of fire as unbelievers.

"He that overcometh shall inherit all things; and I will be his God, and he shall be my son. But the fearful, and unbelieving, and the abominable, and murderers, and whoremongers, and sorcerers, and idolaters, and all liars, shall have their part in the lake which burneth with fire and brimstone: which is the second death" (Rev. 21:7, 8). "Jesus came into Galilee, preaching the gospel of the kingdom of God, and saying, The time is fulfilled, and the kingdom of God is at hand: repent ye, and believe the gospel" (Mark 1:14, 15). "For the grace of God that bringeth salvation hath appeared to all men, teaching us that, denying ungodliness and worldly lusts, we should live soberly, righteously, and godly, in this present world" (Titus 2:11, 12).

To have victory like Christ is to live like God in this present world. "For the grace of God that bringeth salvation hath appeared to all men, Teaching us that, denying ungodliness and worldly lusts, we should live soberly, righteously, and **godly**, in this present world" (Titus 2:11, 12). Real belief results in godly actions in one's life.

> The **greatest deception** of the human mind in Christ's day was that a mere assent to the truth constitutes righteousness. In all human experience a theoretical knowledge of the truth has been proved to be insufficient for the saving of the soul. It does not bring forth the fruits of righteousness. A jealous regard for what is termed theological truth often accompanies **a hatred of genuine truth as made manifest in life**. The darkest chapters of history are burdened with the record of crimes committed by bigoted religionists. The Pharisees claimed to be children of Abraham, and boasted of their possession of the oracles of God; yet these advantages did not preserve them from selfishness, malignity, greed for gain, and the basest hypocrisy. They thought themselves the greatest religionists of

the world, but their so-called orthodoxy led them to crucify the Lord of glory.

**The same danger still exists.** Many take it for granted that they are Christians, simply because they subscribe to certain theological tenets. But they have not brought the truth into practical life. They have not believed and loved it, therefore **they have not received the power and grace** that come through sanctification of the truth. Men may profess faith in the truth; but if it does not make them **sincere, kind, patient, forbearing, heavenly-minded**, it is a curse to its possessors, and through their influence it is a curse to the world.

**The righteousness which Christ taught** is conformity of heart and life to the revealed will of God. Sinful men can become righteous only as they have faith in God and maintain a vital connection with Him. Then true godliness will elevate the thoughts and ennoble the life. Then the external forms of religion accord with the Christian's internal purity. Then the ceremonies required in the service of God are not meaningless rites, like those of the hypocritical Pharisees. (*The Desire of Ages*, pp. 309, 310)

Make sure your profession includes a practical application of the balm of Gilead. Don't settle for being just another "good person." Be satisfied only when you reflect the qualities of the Creator, as David when he expressed his desire to be satisfied only with likeness to God upon his own resurrection. "As for me, I will behold thy face in righteousness: I shall be satisfied, when I awake, with thy likeness" (Ps. 17:15). Paul wrote: "Knowing this, that our old man is crucified with him that the body of sin might be destroyed, that henceforth we should not serve sin.... Let not sin therefore reign in your mortal body, that ye should obey it in the lusts thereof" (Rom. 6:6, 12). Crucify the "old man," that "body of sin," and be resurrected by the power of Jesus that you may awake in His likeness.

David was a man we know who had great struggles with his human nature, yet he overcame. David had an exceptional life only because he made God his trust and dependence. Every true Christian will live as an exception to the surrounding degradation of the world. Did you notice that the words "the greatest deception" of "the human mind" is "that a mere assent to the truth constitutes righteousness"? Are you deceived, reader? Live the life of Christ; don't just profess it. Be clear on this point. When you in your heart decide to put away sin, you will enter a fierce battle of intense proportions with your flesh and the forces outside of you, which include people, the world, and demons. The Bible clearly states: "Forasmuch then as Christ hath suffered for us in the flesh, arm yourselves likewise with the same mind: for he that hath suffered in the flesh hath ceased from sin" (1 Peter 4:1). You will suffer when you have ceased from sin, there is no doubt about it. Did you know that? You live in human flesh. When you decide in your heart, in the closet of your soul hidden from human sight, to stop sinning, you will have intense urges to break God's law at home with nobody looking and all the more when you leave your home and mingle with human society under constant coercion. Therefore, you need to be ready to deal with the inevitable. Everyone gets to this point, but what you do about it and how you handle it will determine whether you go to heaven or to hell.

In the parable of the seed and the sower, there are four types of responses of heart to the seed sown. Only one of these is depicted as producing salvation. From this parable we can also learn what to expect in our circumstances that may hinder us, helping us to give the appropriate response to the Word of God. The second response to the seed has very significant meaning for our current study because it indicates what occurs when someone is not prepared for or expecting temptation. Either situation is fraught with failure. "But he that received the seed into stony places, the same is he that heareth the word, and anon with joy receiveth it; yet hath he not root in himself, but dureth for a while: for when tribulation or persecution ariseth because of the word, by and by he is offended" (Matt. 13:20, 21). Jesus did not say, "if" tribulation comes, nor "if" persecution comes, He said, "when it comes." Through the parable Jesus indicates that we are to expect temptation and prepare for it. Otherwise we will be offended and leave the truth, the Church. Oh, what a fearful position to be in! Most will be surprised by the second coming of Christ because they have not remained vigilant and steadfast (see Heb. 10:37, 38).

I urge you to heed the counsel regarding preparation for the second coming of Christ and apply it in regard to your daily consecration, for no man knows when he will be severely tempted. Watch and pray as the Lord has said, "And take heed to yourselves, lest at any time your hearts be overcharged with surfeiting, and drunkenness, and cares of this life, and so that day come upon you unawares. For as a snare shall it come on all them that dwell on the face of the whole earth. Watch ye therefore, and pray always, that ye may be accounted worthy to escape all these things that shall come to pass, and to stand before the Son of man" (Luke 21:34–36). To "pray without ceasing" (1 Thess. 5:17) is not a suggestion. Let this become a daily, constant exercise. You will be tempted daily, but facing the temptation in prayer fortifies the soul with Christ. "For my name's sake will I defer mine anger, and for my praise will I refrain for thee, that I cut thee not off. Behold, I have refined thee, but not with silver; I have chosen thee in the furnace of affliction. For mine own sake, even for mine own sake, will I do it: for how should my name be polluted? and I will not give my glory unto another" (Isa. 48:9–11).

## Answering Satan's Charges against God

Were you aware that God has a point to prove in having weak and degenerate, sinful flesh gain the victory over the once perfect being who has accused God that a created being doesn't have the capability to keep the law? The psalmist wrote: "Nevertheless he saved them for his name's sake, that he might make his mighty power to be known" (Ps. 106:8). "I will instruct thee and teach thee in the way which thou shalt go: I will guide thee with mine eye" (Ps. 32:8). If you have never been to a friend's house and do not know how to get there, you ask for directions, follow him home, or accompany him on the way. Whichever way you choose, you are guaranteed to still get to the destination. In like manner, we must walk with God, and follow Him home.

> Of the Spirit Jesus said, "He shall glorify Me." The Saviour came to glorify the Father by the demonstration of His love; so the Spirit was to glorify Christ by revealing His grace to the world. The very image of God is to be reproduced in humanity. The honor of God, the honor of Christ, is involved in the **perfection of the character of His people**. (*The Desire of Ages*, p. 671)

This statement accepted will bring you much courage and comfort. The honor of God is at stake in the development of your perfection of character as His child. It was one thing for Christ to live in a human body with human nature and not sin, it is another thing for God to do the same in the bodies of those who have tasted of the fruit of the tree of knowledge of good and evil.

> As yet the disciples were unacquainted with the Saviour's unlimited resources and power. He said to them, "Hitherto have ye asked nothing in My name." John 16:24. He explained that **the secret of their success would be in asking for strength and grace in His name.** He would be present before the Father to make request

for them. The prayer of the humble suppliant He presents as His own desire in that soul's behalf. Every sincere prayer is heard in heaven. It may not be fluently expressed; but if the heart is in it, it will ascend to the sanctuary where Jesus ministers, and He will present it to the Father without one awkward, stammering word, beautiful and fragrant with the incense of His own perfection. (*The Desire of Ages*, p. 667)

## The Secret to Growing in Grace

The Lord beckons you to get acquainted with His power through experience that you may become a seasoned warrior, valiantly gaining victories through His grace. Here is the secret to growing in grace:

> The path of sincerity and integrity is <u>not a path free from obstruction</u>, **but in every difficulty we are to see a call to prayer**. There is no one living who has any power that he has not received from God, and <u>the source whence it comes is open to the **weakest human being**</u>. "Whatsoever ye shall ask in My name," said Jesus, "that will I do, that the Father may be glorified in the Son. If ye shall ask anything in My name, I will do it." (*The Desire of Ages*, p. 667)

Open your eyes, reader. "In every difficulty we are to see a call to prayer." How many opportunities have you missed to talk with the Lord of heaven? Let the Lord be near and dear to you in the experiences of life. Share everything with Him rather than with your fellow man who, in the weakness of the flesh, cannot sustain you.

> <u>The Lord is disappointed when His people place a low estimate upon themselves.</u> He desires His chosen heritage to value themselves according to the price He has placed upon them. God wanted them, else He would not have sent His Son on such **an expensive errand** to redeem them. **He has a use for them**, and <u>He is well pleased when they make the **very highest demands** upon Him, that they may glorify His name</u>. **They may expect large things if they have faith in His promises.** (*The Desire of Ages*, p. 668)

How large a victory do you need? How large an obstacle is the trial, the affliction, or that temptation that you are under? Let all these burdens be cast on the Lord. "Casting all your care upon him; for he careth for you. Be sober, be vigilant; because your adversary the devil, as a roaring lion, walketh about, seeking whom he may devour: Whom resist stedfast in the faith, knowing that the same afflictions are accomplished in your brethren that are in the world. But the God of all grace, who hath called us unto his eternal glory by Christ Jesus, **after** that ye have suffered a while, **make you perfect**, stablish, strengthen, settle you" (1 Peter 5:7–10). The suffering serves a purpose in the purifying of the soul and ultimately increases strength. Through suffering, we realize our need of constant dependence upon God's grace (Heb. 4:16).

> A noble character is not the result of accident; it is not due to special favors or endowments of Providence. It is the result of **self-discipline**, of subjection of the lower to the higher nature, of the surrender of self to the service of God and man. (*Prophets and Kings*, p. 488)

What are the conditions most favorable to the development of a noble character? The answer to this question gives us a better understanding of why God permits circumstances **to develop us into His image. Recognizing, then, that God has put us in the best environment for development, we need not be surprised by experiences that** come our way. The prophet Isaiah revealed God's vindication through the furnace of circumstance:

> For my name's sake will I defer mine anger, and for my praise will I refrain for thee, that I cut thee not off. Behold, I have refined thee, but not with silver; I have chosen thee in the **furnace of affliction**. For mine own sake, even for mine own sake, will I do it: for how should my name be polluted? and I will not give my glory unto another. (Isa. 48:9–11)

When you follow the Lord's admonition, you will be ready for the coming storm. Jesus said: "Therefore whosoever heareth these sayings of mine, and doeth them, I will liken him unto a wise man, which built his house upon a rock: and the rain descended, and the floods came, and the winds blew, and beat upon that house; and it fell not: for it was founded upon a rock" (Matt. 7:24, 25). It is not a matter of *whether* the storm will come but *when* it will come and what type of storm it will be. Will it be rain or hail, or will it be snow, ice, sleet, or a blizzard?

> Christ was the only sinless one who ever dwelt on earth; yet for nearly thirty years He lived among the wicked inhabitants of Nazareth. **This fact is a rebuke** to those who think themselves dependent upon place, fortune, or prosperity, in order to live a blameless life. **Temptation, poverty, adversity**, is the very discipline needed to develop **purity** and **firmness**. (*The Desire of Ages*, p. 72)

Christ lived amongst the wicked inhabitants of the world, showing that victory is not dependent upon place, fortune, or prosperity but upon watching and praying without ceasing as we recognize the source of our strength. Temptation, poverty, and adversity are the main things we try to avoid in this life. However, these are the very things that God uses to form our character into His image. Think about it. The Bible says, "And we know that all things work together for good to them that love God, to them who are the called according to his purpose" (Rom. 8:28). Not just a few things or some things or most things, but *all things* work together to develop us into the image of our pure, holy, and sinless God. "All things" includes every experience. Amen to that!

If you are looking to join a team and know that one team has the strongest and most capable players, and prophecy showed that they would ultimately win, would it not be wise to join them? We have just such an opportunity under Michael, the Captain of the Lord's host. Regardless of your circumstances, you can call upon the Father to send you Michael's "team" of holy angels to encircle you and give you strength. Throughout the Bible are inspiring examples of victory over the apparently overwhelming host of evil. No fully surrendered soul has ever been lost. As the angel declared to Mary: "For with God nothing shall be impossible" (Luke 1:37).

CHAPTER 2

# Encouragement to Go Forward

> And though this world, with devils filled,
> Should threaten to undo us,
> We will not fear, for God hath willed
> His truth to triumph through us.
> —Martin Luther[4]

If you look at your past life, there could be many memories of failure. However, God in His great mercy and grace wants you to be encouraged and to know that you have actually everything to look forward to because of the victory He will empower you to gain.

> Many are inquiring, "*How* am I to make the surrender of myself to God?" You desire to give yourself to Him, but you are weak in moral power, in slavery to doubt, and controlled by the habits of your life of sin. Your promises and resolutions are like ropes of sand. You cannot control your thoughts, your impulses, your affections. The knowledge of your broken promises and forfeited pledges weakens your confidence in your own sincerity, and causes you to feel that God cannot accept you; but <u>you need not despair</u>. **What you need to understand is the true force of the will. This is the governing power in the nature of man, the power of decision,**

---

[4] Martin Luther, "A Mighty Fortress," 1529, Hymnary, https://1ref.us/1ku (accessed February 17, 2021).

> **or of choice.** Everything depends on the right action of the will. <u>The power of **choice** God has given to men; it is theirs to exercise.</u> You cannot change your heart, you cannot of yourself give to God its affections; but you can *choose* to serve Him. You can give Him your will; He will then work in you to will and to do according to His good pleasure. Thus your whole nature will be brought under the control of the Spirit of Christ; your affections will be centered upon Him, your thoughts will be in harmony with Him. (*Steps to Christ*, p. 47)

Mankind was given a will to reason and choose. However, as a child you must learn to exercise and keep it resolved. The past need not be a prognostication of the future. Your will and resolve were given to you to exercise and strengthen by your election and usage. "Let not sin therefore reign in your mortal body, that ye should obey it in the lusts thereof. Neither yield ye your members as instruments of unrighteousness unto sin: but <u>yield yourselves unto God</u>, as those that are alive from the dead, and your members <u>as instruments of righteousness unto God. For sin shall not have dominion over you</u>" (Rom. 6:12–14). Surrender is something learned and, like a physical muscle, gains strength by exercise and practice. "<u>Submit yourselves therefore to God.</u> Resist the devil, and he will flee from you. <u>Draw nigh to God, and he will draw nigh to you.</u> Cleanse your hands, ye sinners; and purify your hearts, ye double minded" (James 4:7, 8). Notice as James says, when you "resist the devil," he will flee, not because he is scared of you, but because he trembles at the presence of God drawing nigh to you. Keep the following words in mind and let them encourage you:

> There are those who have known the pardoning love of Christ and who really desire to be children of God, yet they realize that their character is imperfect, their life faulty, and they are ready to doubt whether their hearts have been renewed by the Holy Spirit. To such I would say, Do not draw back in despair. We shall often have to bow down and weep at the feet of Jesus because of our shortcomings and mistakes, but we are not to be discouraged. Even if we are overcome by the enemy, we are not cast off, not forsaken and rejected of God. No; Christ is at the right hand of God, who also maketh intercession for us. Said the beloved John, "These things write I unto you, that ye sin not. And if any man sin, we have an advocate with the Father, Jesus Christ the righteous." 1 John 2:1.

And do not forget the words of Christ, "The Father Himself loveth you." John 16:27. He desires to restore you to Himself, to see His own purity and holiness reflected in you. **And if you will but yield yourself to Him**, <u>He that hath begun a good work in you will carry it forward to the day of Jesus Christ</u>. Pray more **fervently**; believe more **fully**. As we come to distrust our own power, **let us trust the power of our Redeemer**, and we shall praise Him who is the health of our countenance.

<u>The closer you come to Jesus, the more faulty you will appear in your own eyes</u>; for your vision will be clearer, and your imperfections will be seen in broad and distinct contrast to His perfect nature. **This is evidence that Satan's delusions have lost their power**; that the vivifying influence of the Spirit of God is arousing you. (*Steps to Christ*, pp. 64, 65)

<u>In the whole Satanic force</u> **there is not power to overcome one soul** <u>who in simple trust casts himself on Christ</u>. "He giveth power to the faint; and to them that have no might He increaseth strength." Isa. 40:29.

"If we confess our sins, He is faithful and just to forgive us our sins, and to cleanse us from all unrighteousness." The Lord says, "Only acknowledge thine iniquity, that thou hast transgressed against the Lord thy God." "Then will I sprinkle clean water upon you, and ye shall be clean; from all your filthiness and from all your idols will I cleanse you." 1 John 1:9; Jer. 3:13; Eze. 36:25. (*Christ's Object Lessons*, pp. 157, 158)

The widow's prayer, "Avenge me"—"do me justice" (R.V.)—"of mine adversary," represents the prayer of God's children. Satan is their great adversary. He is the "accuser of our brethren," who accuses them before God day and night. (Rev. 12:10.) He is continually working to misrepresent and accuse, to deceive and destroy the people of God. And **it is for deliverance from the power of Satan and his agents that in this parable Christ teaches His disciples to pray**.

In the prophecy of Zechariah is brought to view Satan's accusing work, and the work of Christ in resisting the adversary of His people. The prophet says, "He showed me Joshua the high priest standing before the angel of the Lord, and Satan standing at his right hand to resist him. And the Lord said unto Satan, The Lord rebuke thee, O Satan; even the Lord that hath chosen Jerusalem rebuke thee: is not this a brand plucked out of the fire? Now Joshua was clothed with filthy garments, and stood before the angel." Zech. 3:1–3.

The people of God are here represented as <u>a criminal on trial</u>. Joshua, as high priest, is seeking for a blessing for his people, who are in great affliction. While he is pleading before God, Satan is standing at his right hand as his adversary. <u>He is accusing the children of God, and making their case appear as desperate as possible</u>. He presents before the Lord their evil doings and their defects. He shows their faults and failures, <u>hoping they will appear of such a character in the eyes of Christ that He will render them no help in their great need</u>. Joshua, as the representative of God's people, stands under condemnation, clothed with filthy garments. Aware of the sins of his people, he is weighed down with discouragement. <u>Satan is pressing upon his soul a sense of guiltiness that makes him feel almost hopeless</u>. Yet there he stands as a suppliant, with Satan arrayed against him.

<u>The work of Satan as an accuser began in heaven</u>. This has been his work on earth ever since man's fall, and **it will be his work in a special sense as we approach nearer to the close of this world's history**. <u>As he sees that his time is short</u>, **he will work with greater earnestness to deceive and destroy**. <u>He is angry when he sees a people on the earth who</u>, <u>even in their weakness and sinfulness</u>, **have respect to the law of Jehovah. He is determined that they shall not obey God**. He delights in their unworthiness, and has devices prepared for every soul, that all may be ensnared and separated from God. He seeks to accuse and condemn God and all who strive to carry out His purposes in this world in mercy and love, in compassion and forgiveness.

**Every manifestation of God's power for His people arouses the enmity of Satan.** Every time God works in their behalf, <u>Satan with his angels works with renewed vigor to compass their ruin</u>. He is jealous of all who make Christ their strength. His object is to instigate evil, and when he has succeeded, <u>throw all the blame upon the tempted ones</u>. He points to their filthy garments, their defective characters. He presents their weakness and folly, their sins of ingratitude, their unlikeness to Christ, which have dishonored their Redeemer. All this he urges as an argument proving his right to work his will in their destruction. **He endeavors to affright their souls with the thought that their case is hopeless, that the stain of their defilement can never be washed away.** <u>**He hopes so to destroy their faith that they will yield fully to his temptations, and turn from their allegiance to God.**</u> (*Christ's Object Lessons*, pp. 166–168)

The Testimony of Jesus is clear. You can know what Satan is doing in your life to discourage you, attempting to have you release your hold on the Lord. You don't need to let go. Even though you have been bruised and afflicted by the battle and sometimes have fallen, take courage. One of the oldest tricks of the devil is frustration and discouragement because of continual battle. After the devil tempts you through continual harassment and you fall, then he pushes your face in the mud, reminding you of what you have done wrong, and then he grinds your face in further through the consequences you reap, attempting to discourage you and get you to believe that God has forsaken you. This was the trick he used on the angels who fell with him from heaven. They believed his lies and later found out that, until they consented to go with Lucifer, they could have returned to God. Yet, by then they had passed the point of no return. If the devil can get you to feel your case is hopeless and get you to give up, he has you. You will go to hell without a fight. However, if you fight with the Lord's host on your side, the devil is unable to match the power of Heaven, and it will be his case that is hopeless.

We have already established that only those with Christ's character enter heaven. So, if you are going to be like Christ, should not your experience be like His? Then, what is it like to experience such development of character?

> **Christ is our example** <u>in all things</u>. In the providence of God, his early life was passed in Nazareth, where the inhabitants were of that character that <u>he was **continually** exposed to temptations</u>, and <u>**it was necessary for him to be guarded** in order to remain pure and spotless amid so much sin and wickedness</u>. Christ did not select this place himself. His Heavenly Father **chose** this place for him, **where his character would be tested and tried in a variety of ways**. <u>The early life of Christ was subjected to severe trials, hardships, and conflicts, that he might develop the **perfect character**</u> which makes him **a perfect example** for children, youth, and manhood. (*The Youth's Instructor*, March 1, 1872, par. 2)

God the Father chose the environment in which to place Jesus, and He has also chosen your environment that He might perfect your character traits, whether or not your defects of character are hereditary or cultivated. He will use the circumstances around you to reveal the weaknesses that you possess. It is up to you to choose to call on Him and depend on Him for strength to overcome. Many times we look at someone else's life and think that they have an easy life. So it may seem to us. Yet, we should not be deceived. While their life might seem easy to us, our life might seem easy to someone else. Nonetheless, it is God who gives to each his or her circumstances, perfectly calculated to develop character. An easy life does not develop a character in His image.

The Lord in His divine patience will heal your wounds if you allow Him. Accept the balm of Gilead, not because you are worthy, but because of the covenant privilege made available by the name of the Lord, who receives all who call on Him for victory.

As you come closer to the Lord, the contest will intensify. We are brands plucked from the fire. That is not a lawn chair, lemonade-sipping experience. You will need a large spiritual beach towel to wipe off the sweat that the experience causes us to produce.

Having heard the Testimony of Jesus, let us also hear the Word as it encourages us to *strive* for victory in the battle. Note that many of its encouragements are from the pen of the "apostle of grace," Paul.

> And I am sure that, when I come unto you, I shall come in the fulness of the blessing of the gospel of Christ. Now I beseech you, brethren, for the Lord Jesus Christ's sake, and for the love of the Spirit, that ye strive together with me in your prayers to God for me. (Rom. 15:29, 30)
>
> Know ye not that they which run in a race run all, but one receiveth the prize? So run, that ye may obtain. And every man that striveth for the mastery is temperate in all things. Now they do it to obtain a corruptible crown; but we an incorruptible. I therefore so run, not as uncertainly; so fight I, not as one that beateth the air: but I keep under my body, and bring it into subjection: lest that by any means, when I have preached to others, I myself should be a castaway. (1 Cor. 9:24–27)

Paul paints no picture of ease. So why do so many think that grace makes the Christian life easy? It comes from the traditions of man adding to the selective reading of Scripture under the hellish torch of Satan. Let the Word speak for itself. It reveals to us what is ahead so that we are not deceived by the realities we encounter but can bravely face them in the power of the Lord.

> Thou therefore, my son, be strong in the grace that is in Christ Jesus. And the things that thou hast heard of me among many witnesses, the same commit thou to faithful men, who shall be able to teach others also. Thou therefore endure hardness, as a good soldier of Jesus Christ. No man that <u>warreth</u> entangleth himself with the affairs of this life; that he may please him who hath chosen him to be a soldier. And if a man also <u>strive</u> for masteries, yet is he not crowned, except he <u>strive</u> lawfully. (2 Tim. 2:1–5)
>
> Even the mystery which hath been hid from ages and from generations, but now is made manifest to his saints: To whom God would make known what is the riches of the glory of this mystery among the Gentiles; which is Christ in you, the hope of glory: Whom we preach, warning every man, and teaching every man in all wisdom; that we may present every man perfect in Christ Jesus: Whereunto I also <u>labour</u>, <u>striving</u> according to his working, which worketh in me mightily. For I would that ye knew what <u>great conflict</u> I have for you, and for them at Laodicea, and for as many as have not seen my face in the flesh; that their hearts might be comforted, being knit together in love, and unto all riches of the full assurance of understanding, to the acknowledgement of the mystery of God, and of the Father, and of Christ; in whom are hid all the treasures of wisdom and knowledge. <u>And this I say, lest any man should **beguile** you with **enticing** words</u>. (Col. 1:26–2:4)

All who are saved will be perfectly surrendered to God and obeying God's commandments before the second coming of Christ. This is the message to be preached, alerting the world that we need to learn how to obtain this victory in the wisdom of the Lord. Paul says first, "I also labour." Does labor require more or less effort than work? In context, we usually place labor as more intensive than work. Yet, Paul goes further. He says that he is "striving according to [Jesus'] working." Is this not a step above labour in the amount of effort expended? Paul also uses the word "mightily," an indication of conquering in the strength we have through the Holy Spirit. Paul then goes further in talking about the conflict in Asia Minor, leaving me to ask: Of the seven church periods of Revelation, dear reader, which church do you live in? Is it not the last one—Laodicea? Applied spiritually, this message is especially for those of us living at the end of time. In being the last church, Laodicea will have the most intense battle, for it will signal the end of Satan's life. He will fight all the more vehemently. Paul even finishes this statement admonishing us not to let anyone beguile us. Beguile us into what? The context indicates that Paul is talking about being beguiled into the belief that the strait and narrow path has no struggle or victory.

> Wherefore seeing we also are compassed about with so great a cloud of witnesses, let us lay aside every weight, and the sin which doth so easily beset us, and let us run with patience the race that is set before us, looking unto Jesus the author and finisher of our faith; who for the joy that was set before him endured the cross, despising the shame, and is set down at the right hand of the throne of God. For consider him that endured such contradiction of sinners against himself, lest ye be wearied and faint in your minds. Ye have not yet resisted unto blood, <u>striving</u> against sin. (Heb. 12:1–4)

So then, great are the promises of victory! Pray them; strive under them. In this way, Christ was victorious, and He is our example to follow. In no other way will we be able to obtain the victory. Note David's prayer speaks of deliverance:

> Plead my cause, O LORD, with them that <u>strive</u> with me: <u>fight</u> against them that <u>fight</u> against me. Take hold of shield and buckler, and stand up for mine help. Draw out also the spear, and stop the way against them that persecute me: say unto my soul, I am thy salvation. Let them be confounded and put to shame that seek after my soul: let them be turned back and brought to confusion that devise my hurt. Let them be as chaff before the wind: and let the angel of the LORD chase them. Let their way be dark and slippery: and let the angel of the LORD persecute them. For without cause have they hid for me their net in a pit, which without cause they have digged for my soul. Let destruction come upon him at unawares; and let his net that he hath hid catch himself: into that very destruction let him fall. And my soul shall be joyful in the LORD: it shall rejoice in his salvation. All my bones shall say, **LORD, who is like unto thee, which deliverest the poor from**

**him that is too strong for him**, yea, the poor and the needy from him that spoileth him? (Ps. 35:1–10)

Dear reader, why is it that people are willing to give almost life and limb for what the world considers accomplishments, with toil, effort, sweat, and perseverance, yet they consider obtaining the character of God to be some easy, light achievement? We climb the academic ladder for a better job, the career ladder for money, the societal ladder for friends, and we struggle financially to live in an upscale house so that others will perceive us as being successful. These things, however, are not eternal. By the time most people studying for a profession get through school, they are in their mid-twenties. When I was in dental school, I averaged about five hours of sleep for four years, studying about fourteen hours a day to qualify myself for a career that would last until I reached sixty-five. That is only forty years. So how much effort should a person put into preparing for eternity and developing a godly character?

My purpose in writing this book is to emphasize that the Christian life requires a struggle even though we are living by faith. The benefit of knowing that it will be a struggle is that it gives us the opportunity to have the right mindset in facing the task ahead and to understand what is so valuable that it is worth the struggle. When a person is oblivious to the battle, they are easy prey for Satan. That's what the parable of the seed and the sower teaches us.

As we continue in our study, we will see that, if we follow the prescribed path, victory is guaranteed—just as surely as the sky is blue. "But thanks be to God, which giveth us the victory through our Lord Jesus Christ. Therefore, my beloved brethren, be ye stedfast, unmoveable, always abounding in the work of the Lord, forasmuch as ye know that your labour is not in vain in the Lord" (1 Cor. 15:57, 58). "And let us not be weary in well doing: for in due season we shall reap, if we faint not" (Gal. 6:9).

## Biblical Parallels for the Struggle with Human Flesh

Did Jesus live by faith in the power of God the Father? Most certainly. Was He striving in human nature? Definitely. If He lived by faith, why did He sweat blood in Gethsemane? The correct answer is that it was literally, specifically, and particularly because of my sin and your sin. Jesus struggled with every negative component that comes with sin, that He could give you and I power to overcome our own sins. In addition, He was suffering under the full wrath of God which grace delivers you from during the time of probation.

Jesus knows the fullest results of your sins, though you have not had that experience. It is because the strength of character that fallen humans need to develop comes from learning to depend on power from above and outside themselves. It comes from connecting the weakness of human flesh with the power of God the Father and depending on Him to sustain us. The struggle that Jesus had in Gethsemane is the anti-type of the struggle that Jacob had beside the River Jabbok.

One may wonder, *What was the purpose of that struggle? Was Jesus not omnipotent as God?* To answer, we need to consider who the second most powerful individual in the universe was, for, when the two strongest powers in a given realm collide, it cannot help but result in the greatest of battles. Knowing this, we can expect certain things to take place and not jump to faulty conclusions. Add to this the will of man in its weakness struggling to decide which side to choose and needing to be strengthened to maintain his decision.

In this last section, we will end with what I call, "the greatest struggle in the universe." We will finish this chapter with the Spirit of Prophecy regarding the strait and narrow way, which will explain why Jacob struggled so much at the River Jabbok and what that struggle accomplished. You can be sure that, if you are to enter the kingdom of God, you will have a garden of Gethsemane/River Jabbok experience. "Who are kept by the power of God through faith unto salvation ready to be revealed in the last time. Wherein ye greatly rejoice, though now for a season, if need be, ye are in heaviness through manifold temptations. That the trial of your faith, being much more precious than of gold that perisheth, though it be tried with fire, might be found unto praise and honour and glory at the appearing of Jesus Christ" (1 Peter 1:5–7). Jacob understood by experience what Peter described, as all Jacob's children will. That is why we the redeemed will be called, "Children of Israel," so that, in our sole dependence on God's power, we will have the victory even though the temptations and the struggle are severe.

What is your greatest spiritual need? It is victory—victory over temptation. All who enter the kingdom of God will have to struggle in gaining the victory. Consider these comments on Jesus' promise in Matthew 7:

> *"Ask, and it shall be given you; seek, and ye shall find; knock, and it shall be opened unto you."* Matthew 7:7.
>
> To leave no chance for unbelief, misunderstanding, or misinterpretation of His words, the Lord repeats the thrice-given promise. He longs to have those who would seek after God believe in

Him who is able to do all things. Therefore He adds, "For everyone that asketh receiveth; and he that seeketh findeth; and to him that knocketh it shall be opened."

The Lord specifies no conditions except that **you hunger for His mercy, desire His counsel**, and **long for His love**. "Ask." The asking, makes it manifest that you realize your necessity; and if you ask in faith you will receive. The Lord has pledged His word, and **it cannot fail**. If you come with true contrition **you need not feel that you are presumptuous in asking for what the Lord has promised**. When you ask for the blessings you need, **that you may perfect a character after Christ's likeness**, the Lord assures you that you are asking according to a promise that will be verified. That you feel and know you are a sinner is sufficient ground for asking for His mercy and compassion. The condition upon which you may come to God is not that you shall be holy, **but that you desire Him to cleanse you from all sin and purify you from all iniquity**. The argument that we may plead now and ever is our great need, our utterly helpless state, that makes Him and His redeeming power a necessity.

"Seek." Desire not merely His blessing, but Himself. "Acquaint now thyself with Him, and be at peace." Job 22:21. Seek, and you shall find. God is seeking you, and the very desire you feel to come to Him is but the drawing of His Spirit. Yield to that drawing. Christ is pleading the cause of the tempted, the erring, and the faithless. He is seeking to lift them into companionship with Himself. "If thou seek Him, He will be found of thee." 1 Chronicles 28:9.

"Knock." We come to God by special invitation, and He waits to welcome us to His audience chamber. The first disciples who followed Jesus were not satisfied with a hurried conversation with Him by the way; they said, "Rabbi, ... where dwellest Thou? ... They came and saw where He dwelt, and abode with Him that day." John 1:38, 39. So we may be admitted into closest intimacy and communion with God. "He that dwelleth in the secret place of the Most High shall abide under the shadow of the Almighty." Psalm 91:1. Let those who desire the blessing of God knock and wait at the door of mercy with firm assurance, saying, For Thou, O Lord, hast said, "Everyone that asketh receiveth; and he that seeketh findeth; and to him that knocketh it shall be opened." (*Thoughts from the Mount of Blessing*, pp. 130, 131)

How hungry are you for victory, for mercy, for counsel, and for the love of God? The only prerequisites for receiving these gifts of God is that you recognize your need and ask for them in faith. The Lord is not like a man to turn away His pleading child whose need bears eternal consequences. The honor of His name is at stake in hearing every contrite prayer. Do not hurry away from your communion with the Lord. Let His Spirit dwell with you in your secret place of prayer, in your home, in the street, in the city, in the country, and at work or school. Take out special time morning, noon, and evening to be in communion with the Lord so that His angels can continually abide with you, forming a wall of fire around you against temptation. Abide with the Lord where He dwells.

> Jesus looked upon those who were assembled to hear His words, and earnestly desired that the great multitude might appreciate the mercy and loving-kindness of God. As an illustration of their need, and of God's willingness to give, He presents before them a hungry child asking his earthly parent for bread. "What man is there of *you*," He said, "whom if his son ask bread, will he give him a stone?" He appeals to the tender, natural affection of a parent for his child and then says, "If ye then, being evil, know how to give good gifts unto your children, how much more shall your Father which is in heaven give good things to them that ask Him?" No man with a father's heart would turn from his son who is hungry and is asking for bread. Would they think him capable of trifling with his child, of tantalizing him by raising his expectations only to disappoint him? Would he promise to give him good and nourishing food, and then give him a stone? **And should anyone dishonor God by imagining that He would not respond to the appeals of His children?**
>
> If ye, then, being human and evil, "know how to give good gifts unto your children: how much more shall your heavenly Father give the Holy Spirit to them that ask Him?" Luke 11:13. The Holy Spirit, the representative of Himself, is the greatest of all gifts. All "good things" are comprised in this. **The Creator Himself can give us nothing greater, nothing better.** When we beseech the Lord to pity us in our distress, and to guide us by His Holy Spirit, He will never turn away our prayer. It is possible even for a parent to turn away from his hungry child, but **God can never reject the cry** of the needy and longing heart. With what wonderful tenderness He has described His love! To those who in days of darkness feel that God

is unmindful of them, this is the message from the Father's heart: "Zion said, The Lord hath forsaken me, and my Lord hath forgotten me. Can a woman forget her sucking child, that she should not have compassion on the son of her womb? Yea, they may forget, yet will I not forget thee. Behold, I have graven thee upon the palms of My hands." Isaiah 49:14–16.

**Every promise** in the word of God furnishes us with subject matter for prayer, presenting the pledged word of Jehovah as our assurance. Whatever spiritual blessing we need, **it is our privilege to claim through Jesus**. We may tell the Lord, with the simplicity of a child, exactly what we need. We may state to Him our temporal matters, asking Him for bread and raiment as well as for the bread of life and **the robe of Christ's righteousness**. Your heavenly Father knows that you have need of all these things, and you are invited to ask Him concerning them. It is through the name of Jesus that every favor is received. God will honor that name, and will supply your necessities from the riches of His liberality. (*Thoughts from the Mount of Blessing*, pp. 131–133)

Character is our greatest personal necessity, which is why we will discuss it throughout this book. Can you doubt God after reading such wonderful promises? Live not by your feelings or what you see and hear from other human beings but by His Word:

But do not forget that in coming to God as a father you acknowledge your relation to Him as a child. You not only trust His goodness, but in **all** things yield to His will, knowing that His love is changeless. You give yourself to do His work. It was to those whom He had bidden to seek first the kingdom of God and His righteousness that Jesus gave the promise, "Ask, and ye shall receive." John 16:24.

The gifts of Him who has all power in heaven and earth are in store for the children of God. Gifts so precious that they come to us through the costly sacrifice of the Redeemer's blood; gifts that will satisfy the **deepest craving** of the heart, gifts lasting as eternity, will be received and enjoyed by all who will come to God as little children. Take God's promises as your own, **plead them before Him as His own words**, and you will receive fullness of joy. (*Thoughts from the Mount of Blessing*, pp. 133, 134)

We can use every promise of God in prayer. Pray, yes, pray God's Word directly back to Him, asking Him to give you what He has already pledged. Doing this is the key to powerful prayers that move the hand of God. Such prayers will not fail, for God has already guaranteed them, they are His will. Now that you see and understand that you can depend on God to fulfill His promises given to you, be mindful of the strait and narrow path that He has asked you to travel. God knows the difficulty of the journey, but He assures you that you will have victory as you use the prescribed method of access to these promises. Remember that God allows the struggle that gives you strength, and this is what develops in you a character that holds firmly onto the Saviour.

## Character Development, an Uphill Journey

Jesus emphasized the nature of the spiritual journey:

> *"Strait is the gate, and narrow is the way, which leadeth unto life." Matthew 7:14.*
>
> In the time of Christ the people of Palestine lived in walled towns, which were mostly situated upon hills or mountains. The gates, which were closed at sunset, were approached by steep, rocky roads, and the traveler journeying homeward at the close of the day often had to press his way in eager haste up the difficult ascent in order to reach the gate before nightfall. The loiterer was left without.
>
> The narrow, upward road leading to home and rest furnished Jesus with an impressive figure of the Christian way. The path which I have set before you, He said, is narrow; the gate is **difficult** of entrance; for the golden rule excludes all pride and self-seeking. There is, indeed, a wider road; but its end is destruction. If you would climb the path of spiritual life, you must constantly ascend; for it is an upward way. You must go with the few; for the multitude will choose the downward path. (*Thoughts from the Mount of Blessing*, p. 138)

We must press forward and not loiter, leaving behind anything that would hinder our speedy entrance into the kingdom of God in these last days. You are in a constant uphill battle. Dear reader, your growth must be continuous and not sporadic. In nature we see this lesson every year.

Even the grapevines which appear barren and lifeless during winter are transporting life-giving sap bearing nutrients in preparation for spring.

> In the road to death the whole race may go, with all their worldliness, all their selfishness, all their pride, dishonesty, and moral debasement. There is room for every man's opinions and doctrines, space to follow his inclinations, to do whatever his self-love may dictate. In order to go in the path that leads to destruction, there is no need of searching for the way; for the gate is wide, and the way is broad, and the feet naturally turn into the path that ends in death.
>
> But the way to life is narrow and the entrance strait. If you cling to any besetting sin you will find the way too narrow for you to enter. <u>Your own ways, your own will, your evil habits and practices</u>, **must be given up if you would keep the way of the Lord**. <u>He who would serve Christ cannot follow the world's opinions or meet the world's standard.</u> Heaven's path is too narrow for rank and riches to ride in state, too narrow for the play of self-centered ambition, too steep and rugged for lovers of ease to climb. <u>Toil, patience, self-sacrifice, reproach, poverty</u>, the contradiction of sinners against Himself, was the portion of Christ, and <u>it must be our portion</u>, **if we ever enter the Paradise of God**. (*Thoughts from the Mount of Blessing*, pp. 138, 139)

Because truth is singular and there is only one way to get there you must search for it. To live righteously with our human nature is not natural. That is why we must fight our natural inclinations at every step, thus developing our strength of character. You must set aside all sin, or it will weigh you down especially as the pace of our journey must be hastened. Opinions have no value, only facts matter with truth. The world's advice cannot be trusted, and the world's values must be set aside: rank, riches, and self-centered ambition. The love of ease must be exchanged for toil, patience, self-sacrifice, reproach, poverty, and the "contradiction of sinners against" Christ. (Heb. 12:3). Don't subscribe to what I call, "third grade theology." When elementary children become rebellious and convince their fellow classmates not to do their school assignment, they believe that the teacher will just let it pass and has no option but to not require the work. But the Judge of all the earth is more like a university professor, the most difficult one, who could fail all his students knowing they can only retake the course and face him a second time or not graduate. "In the road to death the whole race may go, with all their worldliness, all their selfishness, all their pride, dishonesty, and moral debasement." It is extremely dangerous to follow the crowd in matters of righteousness.

> Yet do not therefore conclude that the upward path is the **hard** and the downward road the **easy** way. <u>All along the road that leads to death there are pains and penalties, there are sorrows and disappointments, there are warnings not to go on.</u> **God's love has made it hard for the heedless and headstrong to destroy themselves.** It is true that Satan's path is made to appear attractive, but it is all a deception; in the way of evil there are bitter remorse and cankering care. We may think it pleasant to follow pride and worldly ambition, but the end is pain and sorrow. Selfish plans may present flattering promises and hold out the hope of enjoyment, but we shall find that our happiness is poisoned and our life embittered by hopes that center in self. In the downward road the gateway may be bright with flowers, but thorns are in the path. The light of hope which shines from its entrance fades into the darkness of despair, and the soul who follows that path descends into the shadows of unending night.
> 
> "The way of transgressors is hard," but wisdom's "ways are ways of pleasantness and all her paths are peace." Proverbs 13:15; 3:17. <u>Every act of obedience to Christ, every act of self-denial for His sake, every trial well endured, every victory gained over temptation, is a step in the march to the glory of *final* victory.</u> If we take Christ for our guide, He will lead us safely. **The veriest sinner need not miss his way.** <u>***Not one trembling seeker need fail of walking in pure and holy light***</u>. Though the <u>path is so narrow, so holy that sin cannot be tolerated therein, yet **access has been secured for all**</u>, and not one doubting, trembling soul need say, "God cares nought for me."
> 
> The road may be rough and the ascent steep; there may be pitfalls upon the right hand and upon the left; we may have to endure toil in our journey; when weary, when longing for rest, we may have to toil on; when faint, we may have to fight; when discouraged, we must still hope; but with <u>Christ as our guide</u> we shall not fail of reaching the desired haven at last. Christ Himself has trodden the rough way before us and has smoothed the path for our feet.

And all the way up the steep road leading to eternal life are well-springs of joy to refresh the weary. Those who walk in wisdom's ways are, even in tribulation, exceeding joyful; for He whom their soul loveth, walks, invisible, beside them. At each upward step they discern more distinctly the touch of His hand; at every step brighter gleamings of glory from the Unseen fall upon their path; and their songs of praise, reaching ever a higher note, ascend to join the songs of angels before the throne. "The path of the righteous is as the light of dawn, that shineth more and more unto the perfect day." Proverbs 4:18, R.V., margin. (*Thoughts from the Mount of Blessing*, pp. 139–141)

So far, we have emphasized the struggle in obtaining the character of Christ. The good news is that, in letting the Lord help you in the struggle, you will have "exceeding joy," inner peace, rest of soul from the burden of sin, and joy in seeing the development of the image of God manifest through your flesh, having crucified the "old man," or "the flesh," and being born again a "new man," living "godly in this present world" in Christ Jesus. (See Jude 24; John 14:27; Matt. 11:29; Rom. 6:6; 7:5; Gal. 2:20; 1 Peter 1:23; Col. 3:10; Titus 2:12.)

## Cooperation of the Human Will

Jesus called attention to the intensity of the spiritual battle and march of faith. He did not preach that you are only forgiven with grace covering you while continuing in sin:

> *"Strive to enter in at the strait gate." Luke 13:24.*
>
> The belated traveler, hurrying to reach the city gate by the going down of the sun, could not turn aside for any attractions by the way. **His whole mind was bent** on the one purpose of entering the gate. The same **intensity** of purpose, said Jesus, is required in the Christian life. I have opened to you **the glory of character**, which is the true glory of My kingdom. It offers you no promise of earthly dominion; **yet it is worthy of your supreme desire and effort**. I do not call you to battle for the supremacy of the world's great empire, but **do not therefore conclude** that there is no battle to be fought nor victories to be won. I bid you **strive, agonize**, to enter into My spiritual kingdom.

> The Christian life is a battle and a march. But the victory to be gained is not won by human power. The field of conflict is the domain of the heart. The battle which we have to fight—**the greatest battle that was ever fought by man**—is the surrender of self to the will of God, the yielding of the heart to the sovereignty of love. The old nature, born of blood and of the will of the flesh, cannot inherit the kingdom of God. The hereditary tendencies, the former habits, must be given up. (*Thoughts from the Mount of Blessing*, p. 141)

The Almighty God of Heaven cannot and will not force anyone. All must surrender to Him voluntarily. The battle of the will is the greatest battle man will ever fight. Your continual development throughout eternity is dependent on the exercise of your free will choosing holiness. In the struggle, the question is not: Who is the most powerful? Satan is no match for the Almighty's power. The question is: Can weak flesh, submitting its will to the will of God, keep the law of God?

> He who determines to enter the spiritual kingdom will find that **all the powers and passions of an unregenerate nature, backed by the forces of the kingdom of darkness**, are arrayed against him. Selfishness and pride will make a stand against anything that would show them to be sinful. We cannot, of ourselves, conquer the evil desires and habits that strive for the mastery. We cannot overcome the mighty foe who holds us in his thrall. God alone can give us the victory. He desires us to have the mastery over ourselves, our own will and ways. But He cannot work in us without our consent and co-operation. The divine Spirit works through the faculties and powers given to man. **Our energies are required to co-operate with God.** (*Thoughts from the Mount of Blessing*, pp. 141, 142)

Selfishness and pride will do their best to deceive people into the complacency of thinking that they are not a manifestation of sin but are, rather, an advantage wherever present. Satanic genius covers the worst traits of sin's manifestation. Its results are soul-destroying. Yet, God has given you the literal presence of holy angels and their protection to defend you from Satan's angels when you choose righteousness. (See Ps. 35:1–10.)

> The victory is not won without **much earnest prayer**, without the humbling of self at every step. Our will is not to be forced into co-operation with divine agencies, but it must be **voluntarily**

> **submitted**. <u>Were it possible to force upon you with a hundredfold greater intensity the influence of the Spirit of God, it would not make you a Christian, a fit subject for heaven</u>. The stronghold of Satan would not be broken. **The will must be placed on the side of God's will.** You are not able, of yourself, to bring your purposes and desires and inclinations into submission to the will of God; <u>but if you are</u> **"willing to be made willing,"** God will accomplish the work for you, even "casting down imaginations, and every high thing that exalteth itself against the knowledge of God, and bringing into captivity every thought to the obedience of Christ." 2 Corinthians 10:5. Then you will "work out your own salvation with fear and trembling. For it is God which worketh in you both to will and to do of His good pleasure." Philippians 2:12, 13. (*Thoughts from the Mount of Blessing*, pp. 142, 143)

God only makes human beings into faithful Christians through the voluntary and personal co-operative exercise of their will. This is a principle that God Himself has set, and He will not go against it. Human co-operation is required for us to accept God, His law, and His will. Only when we surrender the will to God does He accept us. Yet, we can do so only with much earnest prayer.

> But many are attracted by the beauty of Christ and the glory of heaven, who yet <u>shrink</u> from the conditions by which alone these can become their own. There are many in the broad way who are not fully satisfied with the path in which they walk. They long to break from the slavery of sin, and in their own strength they seek to make a stand against their sinful practices. They look toward the narrow way and the strait gate; but selfish pleasure, love of the world, pride, unsanctified ambition, place a barrier between them and the Saviour. To renounce their own will, their chosen objects of affection or pursuit, requires a sacrifice at which they hesitate and falter and turn back. Many "will seek to enter in, and shall not be able." Luke 13:24. They desire the good, they make some effort to obtain it; but <u>they do not choose it</u>; <u>they have not a settled purpose</u> to **secure it at the cost of all things**.
> 
> The <u>only hope</u> for us if we would overcome is to unite our will to God's will and work in co-operation with Him, hour by hour and day by day. <u>We cannot retain self</u> and yet enter the kingdom of God. If we ever attain unto holiness, it will be through the

renunciation of self and the reception of the mind of Christ. Pride and self-sufficiency must be crucified. Are we willing to pay the price required of us? <u>Are we willing to have our will brought into perfect conformity to the will of God?</u> **Until we are willing, the transforming grace of God cannot be manifest upon us.** (*Thoughts from the Mount of Blessing*, p. 143)

Do you shrink from the conditions of being a Christian? The peace and true happiness that you desire only exist on the side of the fence that the grass is greener and does not wither. Settle it in your mind this day to live holy at all costs. The price is not so expensive as the devil would have you imagine. Paul wrote: "For our light affliction, which is but for a moment, worketh for us a far more exceeding and eternal weight of glory; while we look not at the things which are seen, but at the things which are not seen: for the things which are seen are temporal; but the things which are not seen are eternal" (2 Cor. 4:17, 18). In the light of eternity, our affliction in this world is worth whatever it costs us. When you are willing, then a transforming spirit of grace will come into your life to bring you victory in the struggle.

In my study, I have come to understand that the human brain actually changes physiologically over time based upon the action of the will. I'm speaking specifically about the diligence, perseverance, and endurance that we bring to bear upon the brain when we desire something and have not obtained it but continue to strive or agonize for it. Recognizing what is required helps explain why our prayers are not always answered immediately. The Lord Himself operates within the laws of physiology, which He created, causing the physical organ of the brain to develop along pre-ordained pathways according to desire and experience. By this means does He produce within us a spirit and actions that are in harmony with His law and will. When the mind has not completely developed in this way, the spirit may have wholesome desires while we act completely the opposite. In other words, we may have the Romans 7 experience of doing what we do not want to do (Rom. 7:15). Put another way, God is performing the greatest miracle of miracles but by using ordinary means He accomplishes a supernatural feat.

## Lessons from Jacob's Night of Wrestling

Jacob's wrestling with the angel, Christ, helps us understand that even when you have decided to surrender your will to God and ask for transformation of character. It does not come without a mighty struggle.

The warfare which we are to wage is the "good fight of faith." "I also labor," said the apostle Paul, "striving according to His working, which worketh in me mightily." Colossians 1:29.

Jacob, <u>in the great crisis of his life</u>, turned aside to pray. **He was filled with one overmastering purpose—<u>to seek for transformation of character</u>**. But while he was pleading with God, an enemy, as he supposed, placed his hand upon him, and all night he wrestled for his life. But the purpose of his soul was not changed by peril of life itself. When his strength was nearly spent, the Angel put forth His divine power, and at His touch Jacob knew Him with whom he had been contending. Wounded and helpless, he fell upon the Saviour's breast, pleading for a blessing. He would not be turned aside nor cease his intercession, and Christ granted the petition of this helpless, penitent soul, according to His promise, "Let him take hold of My strength, that he may make peace with Me; and he shall make peace with Me." Isaiah 27:5. Jacob pleaded with determined spirit, "I will not let Thee go, except Thou bless me." Genesis 32:26. This spirit of persistence was inspired by Him who wrestled with the patriarch. It was He who gave him the victory, and He changed his name from Jacob to Israel, saying, "As a prince hast thou power with God and with men, and hast prevailed." Genesis 32:28. <u>That for which Jacob had vainly wrestled in his own strength was won through self-surrender and steadfast faith.</u> "This is the victory that overcometh the world, even our faith." 1 John 5:4. (*Thoughts from the Mount of Blessing*, pp. 143, 144)

All the redeemed in the kingdom of God are represented in Jacob prophetically. His change of name to "Is-ra-el" signaled the transformation of his character. After Jacob had been a supplanting, lying, and cheating sinner, his victory was memorialized that night to represent the pattern for every human who will walk through the gates of the New Jerusalem. Everyone who will be saved is a child of Abraham and a child of Israel, because by experience, all of God's children will have had a transformation of character (see John 1:12). The struggle of Christ in Gethsemane signified the willingness of a soul to surrender their will, though it is a struggle to the will of God. Calvary therefore signifies the death of the "old man" or "the body of sin" (Rom. 6:6).

The experiences of Jacob and Jesus were no small events. They were recorded to show us that we too can have victory as we follow their example by submitting as they submitted. Both Jacob and Jesus had peace following their decision. Reader, isn't that what you want? Do not let the devil's suggestions fool you that surrender brings drudgery without joy. "But be ye doers of the word, and not hearers only, deceiving your own selves" (James 1:22). When we do not do the will of God, when we do not live by His word, we are deceived. In order to escape the devil's deceptions we must live by God's Word. This is why it is at times very difficult to see the blessing of coming fully into the fold of the Lord, for self-deception blinds those who are not doers of the Word. Yes, it is true that the devil makes the world look appealing. All that looks so appealing now will soon be consumed in the lake of fire, but you do not have to burn with it.

Keep in mind what Jacob went through in his struggle and its significance. Jacob prayed all night long. I encourage you to hold on. I will say it again: hold on in prayer, until you receive the blessing of character transformation. To let go means succumbing to sin and death. We who are alive at this time are now considered to be living in the night prophetically and symbolically. As we prepare for the great Day of Atonement, our entire life must be one continuous battle in prayer. When the morning dawns, we will see the Sun of Righteousness, even Jesus Christ, coming in the clouds of glory.

CHAPTER 3

# God's Guarantee

> Turn your eyes upon Jesus,
> Look full in His wonderful face,
> And the things of earth will grow strangely dim,
> In the light of His glory and grace.
> —Helen H. Lemmel[5]

We all know from personal experience that living the life of a Christian—being like Christ—is not easy. Yet, for some reason, the smooth doctrines preached about salvation being easy are so appealing that we forget our experience and listen to delusive concepts that ultimately cause us great loss. How can this be? Either we accept them completely and enjoy the delusion, or we look in the mirror, examine our "inner man," and clearly see the lie. When we do not accept them completely, confusion sets in, then comes disillusionment, and many leave the church saying, "Christianity doesn't do anything. There's no power there." Of course, both of these paths lead to hell. Nowhere does the Bible say that salvation is easy. Jesus gives no such encouragement. Even in the rest that He promised, what is "easy" is His yoke (Matt. 11:28–30), a symbol of laboring with Him, and labor takes effort. Jesus was speaking relatively because the broad road is easy at first, but the bondage to sin is dreadful in the end. He does talk about the "strait ... gate" and the "narrow ... way" (Matt. 7:14) and that He will help you, "For with God nothing shall be impossible" (Luke 1:37). He does not say, "For with

---

[5] Helen H. Lemmel, "Turn Your Eyes Upon Jesus," 1922, Hymnary, https://1ref.us/1kv (accessed February 17, 2021).

God salvation is easy." We will thoroughly study, at this point, the most important thing we as Christians need.

The covenant plan for our redemption is the document that shows the way to victory. So many, though baptized into the church for many years, struggle without any sign of victory and remain clueless about how to obtain victory over the "old man," which is the sinful nature of humanity. Dear reader, knowing this, I urge you to prayerfully consider anew the science of salvation. I urge you to pray even now because you will benefit the most as you are receptive to the work of the Holy Spirit. If you are willing and sincerely want victory, then you will obtain it when—not if—you apply the principles of the covenant in the operation of your life. Because the covenant is God's promise to you, I have entitled this chapter, "God's Guarantee."

God's guarantee is unlike any guarantee made by any human being. Mankind may or may not honor the service they claim to provide or the product they promise to back. Mankind will also put exclusions on their guarantees. For example, the guarantor may include, in small print, a limit of usage, time, or wear and tear. These exclusions leave consumers helpless and very frustrated when the product breaks or malfunctions due to normal usage that is no fault of their own. A product can be poorly engineered, and the manufacturer may not honor the product's warranty. The Almighty does not leave you unprotected. In fact, the guarantee of the gospel is such that everyone will obtain salvation—the gospel's ultimate benefit—when he or she uses the covenant according to its stated conditions. The problem that many Christians have is that they blame God for failures in their life when they have been improperly applying the promises of the covenant or not applying them at all. They can even become angry, have doubt, lose faith, and be frustrated with God for tragedies or over their inability to overcome temptation and over unanswered prayers.

To this point, you may be saying, "Yes, I have heard this all before, but what you are saying doesn't give me much hope." Many are discouraged, shell-shocked, battle-worn, and pinned down without hope as the devil wages successful warfare against them through the continuous bombardment of temptation.

Dear reader, I urge you to pray. Communicate your desire to God for victory, cleansing, hope, faith, courage, and rest. The difference in the four receptions of the seed in the parable of the sower in Matthew 13 is that those represented by the fourth type of soil surrender to God. They are willing to receive the seed. "What does this mean?" you ask. The seed is God's Word. Just as an olive seed will always produce an olive tree, so will the planting of the Word of God in the soil of the human heart always produce a being in the image of God, that is, one possessing the character of Christ. The difference in outcome is not in the seed but in the soil. If you want to be like Jesus, you will be like Him when you receive the Word of God into your heart and let it grow.

Let's think more about this. You determine by choice the hardness of your heart. You determine by choice whether you will be victorious and saved or whether you will be lost and destroyed in the lake of fire. If your desire is sincere and you act to study the truth and live it, I can go so far as to say that God will open your eyes because of your desire. If your desire is sincere while you are studying error, the Lord will somehow produce within you a dislike for error, causing you to move away from error and deception and be led into the truth though you were once deeply deceived. The Lord allows no honest doer of a truth that a person has come to know and receive to remain deceived and deluded.

Though Satan has gotten you to respond with the hardness of unbelief, you can still overcome. If you want truth, the Lord will provide you with truth. When you surrender to the truth that He provides, it will change your life. The problem is that many who read God's Word simply feel warm and fuzzy, yet they never apply its lessons. Pray, dear reader, and ask God to make the change within you today so that you will apply the truth that you learn. To do so requires the surrender of the heart, which means being soft soil so that the Word of God can take deep root within your heart.

God has made a wonderful covenant for us. The study that follows, regarding God's covenant, developed in my mind after I read M. L. Andreasen's book, *The Book of Hebrews*. In the course of our study of the covenant, we will examine many statements from his book and from the Bible and we will demonstrate the omnipotence of God and the omniscient power of the covenant, which, by its structure and nature, could only be from an omnipotent God. To begin our study, we will look to the passages of Scripture that mention the new covenant.

The Bible says regarding Adam and Eve: "… in the image of God created He him; male and female created he them" (Gen. 1:27). Though created in God's image, they fell from holiness in paradise. Immediately after pointing out their sin, God presented the plan of the new covenant to Adam. Genesis 3:15 records God's covenant promise to Adam and his posterity: "And I will put enmity between thee and the woman, and between thy seed and her seed; it shall bruise thy head, and thou shalt bruise his heel." Through this covenant, mankind would be restored and recreated in the image of God.

The first key element in the covenant is enmity, or hatred, between God's human children and Satan. The second element is the bruise on the head of the serpent. In the symbolism of the Bible, a bruise to the head means a fatal wound, and the serpent was a symbol of Satan. Thus, God signaled the complete destruction of sin and Satan.

The Bible mentions the new covenant for the second time concerning Abram: "And I will bless them that bless thee, and curse him that curseth thee: and in thee shall all families of the earth be blessed" (Gen. 12:3). The New Testament describes Abram's call this way: "By faith Abraham, when he was called to go out into a place which he should after receive for an inheritance, obeyed; and he went out, not knowing whither he went. By faith he sojourned in the land of promise, as in a strange country, dwelling in tabernacles with Isaac and Jacob, the heirs with him of the same promise: For he looked for a city which hath foundations, whose builder and maker is God" (Heb. 11:8–10). The key elements mentioned in these passages are: (1) the blessing of the whole world and (2) God's care of those who accept the covenant in His promise to "bless them that bless thee, and curse him that curseth thee." It portrays the heavenly Father taking care of His children. The promise to bless "all families of the earth" through Abram contained a two-fold promise: (1) a son for Abram through whose lineage the Messiah would come and (2) the ultimate reward of inheriting "a city which hath foundations, whose builder and maker is God."

In Genesis 15 and 17 are the third and fourth biblical mentions of the new covenant. These include the details of the covenant. In applying Bible truth, we must always consider the context, for it is crucial in telling the story and in understanding the message that God needs us to grasp to receive His blessing. It also helps to consider yourself as if you are in the story or that the scripture story is about you because, though the Bible is first about Christ, God's primary objective is that you apply the Word to your life. From a spiritual standpoint, the Bible is written about you even though the primary application is about Christ. The submission of Christ, "Then said I, Lo, I come: in the volume of the book it is written of me, I delight to do thy will, O my God: yea, thy law is within my heart" (Ps. 40:7, 8), must be accomplished in everyone who will be saved. You can easily see from the application of verse 7 by itself, without considering its context, that it applies to you. To harness the power of the Word in your personal life, you must understand that the Word of God is written to you personally—to "I" and "me" and not to your family member, friend, neighbor, or stranger. The power of the Word is best seen through the person applying the Word to himself and overcoming in spite of his circumstances, not to change and make your life easy and without headache. In giving victory through adversity, it magnifies the omnipotence of God.

Rightly understood, the entire Bible is the small print of God's covenant with mankind. However, in that small print, the covenant is not worded like the laws of worldly governments, which usually only contain conditions, qualifications, and exemptions. Because God's law is infinite and eternal with implications reaching into eternity, it applies to every person in every era, and it covers a multitude of situations wherever needed or pertinent. Because of a lack of faith, we add qualifications or conditions to the Word of God that are not in the Word itself, and we consider our situation an exception to God's grace when there are no exemptions but those stated in the Bible.

We are to live by "every word that proceedeth out of the mouth of God" (Matt. 4:4). There are no contradictions between the passages in the Word of God. None! We must accept all scriptures, yet we must use them appropriately as the context dictates. One verse does not cancel another because you do not like a verse's conditions for your life. When a second verse is found it does not cancel out the first verse but should be added to your life and applied as it is contextually intended. Likewise it is the same when a third, fourth, fifth, and other additional verses are found. We live by "every word that proceedeth out of the mouth of God."

Keep in mind that Jesus Christ is "the same yesterday, and to day, and for ever" (Heb. 13:8) and that Jesus always spoke in parables—"All these things spake Jesus unto the multitude in parables; and without a parable spake he not unto them" (Matt. 13:34). Applying these together, we infer that "yesterday" means that the Old Testament is entirely made up of parables, some of which are historical object lessons from actual experiences of human beings given for the edification of the greater body (see 1 Cor. 10:11). Relevant to our study, the specific points brought out in the life of Abram are used as a historic parable that illustrate what the Lord would have us understand in order to be saved. Recognizing this, as we define the symbols and events of the story, we find the deeper meaning for our lives.

## Lessons from the Life of Abram

Let us consider the chapter that leads up to Genesis 15. Here, Abram serves as a type of Messiah for his nephew, Lot, and for the four kings of Canaan. Abram, with his 318 servants and his alliance to the kings, redeemed all the people and goods, returning them safely home. Up until this time, Abram had been a man of peace and had never engaged in war. However, after this experience, all the surrounding nations would look at him differently. We understand this even better, in light of the long memory of the people in the Middle East. Abram had good reason to fear, this is the context that helps us to understand the opening statement in Genesis 15: "After these things the word of the LORD came unto Abram in a vision, saying, Fear not, Abram: I am thy shield, and thy exceeding great reward" (Gen. 15:1).

What is the significance of the Lord being Abram's reward? Notice just verses before:

> And the king of Sodom said unto Abram, Give me the persons, and take the goods to thyself. And Abram said to the king of Sodom, I have lift up mine hand unto the LORD, the most high God, the possessor of heaven and earth, That I will not take from a thread even to a shoelatchet, and that I will not take any thing that is thine, lest thou shouldest say, I have made Abram rich. (Gen. 14:21–23)

Abram could have enriched himself by taking a portion of the returned goods. However, he was a man of moral integrity and would not be made rich in this way. Abram was satisfied to wait for his reward from the Lord. The New Testament says: "For he looked for a city which hath foundations, whose builder and maker is God" (Heb. 11:10).

What is the significance of the Lord being Abram's shield? David and Paul answer: "The LORD is my strength and my shield; my heart trusted in him, and I am helped: therefore my heart greatly rejoiceth; and with my song will I praise him" (Ps. 28:7). "For the LORD God is a sun and shield: the LORD will give grace and glory: no good thing will he withhold from them that walk uprightly" (Ps. 84:11). "Above all, taking the shield of faith, wherewith ye shall be able to quench all the fiery darts of the wicked" (Eph. 6:16).

Keep in mind that these verses and all the ones immediately around this story explain the new covenant. They are not included just to tell the story. As a professed Christian in the Lord Jesus Christ, you accept the conditions of the new covenant, allowing it to be as your exceeding great reward, inheritance, and shield. By custom, it was Abram's right to demand and keep the spoil brought back with Lot and the four kings. However, Abram allowed God to provide for him. The Lord's promise to be his shield by faith freed him from having to worry about a continuous battle of retaliatory attacks.

Praying the Word of God in faith is the shield that destroys all the attacks of the devil. We are to employ the same protection provided by the covenant. God promises, "No good thing will he withhold from them that walk uprightly" (Ps. 84:11). His promise is effective for every situation and for every moment we walk with the Lord. With the context of what happened in Genesis 14, we can better understand how Abram felt as he returned home.

> Abraham gladly returned to his tents and his flocks, but his mind was disturbed by harassing thoughts. He had been a man of peace, so far as possible shunning enmity and strife; and with horror he recalled the scene of carnage he had witnessed. But the nations whose forces he had defeated would doubtless renew the invasion of Canaan, and make him the special object of their vengeance. Becoming thus involved in national quarrels, the peaceful quiet of his life would be broken. Furthermore, he had not entered upon the possession of Canaan, nor could he now hope for an heir, to whom the promise might be fulfilled.
>
> In a vision of the night the divine Voice was again heard. "Fear not, Abram," were the words of the Prince of princes; "I am thy shield, and thy exceeding great reward." <u>But his mind was so oppressed by forebodings that he could not now grasp the promise with unquestioning confidence as heretofore. He prayed for some tangible evidence that it would be fulfilled.</u> And how was the covenant promise to be realized, while the gift of a son was withheld? "What wilt thou give me," he said, "seeing I go childless?" (*Patriarchs and Prophets*, p. 136)

So what is the Lord's ultimate object in His reward to man? "Sow to yourselves in righteousness, reap in mercy; break up your fallow ground: for it is time to seek the LORD, till he come and rain righteousness upon you" (Hosea 10:12). "But as it is written, Eye hath not seen, nor ear heard, neither have entered into the heart of man, the things which God hath prepared for them that love him" (1 Cor. 2:9). "For since the beginning of the world men have not heard, nor perceived by the ear, neither hath the eye seen, O God, beside thee, what he hath prepared for him that waiteth for him. Thou meetest him that rejoiceth and worketh righteousness, those that remember thee in thy ways" (Isa. 64:4, 5). The reward of the Lord is righteousness, which fits you to live eternally at peace in His celestial city. Righteousness is one of the provisions of the covenant.

Dear reader, what reward are you looking for? Do you love the things of this world more than the things of the world to come? "For where your treasure is, there will your heart be also" (Matt. 6:21). Ask the Lord to turn your eyes upon Jesus and His reward. In so doing, you will have to go without many things in this life, but they are insignificant when compared to the world to come.

> These all died in faith, not having received the promises, but having seen them afar off, and were persuaded of them, and embraced them, and confessed that they were strangers and pilgrims on the earth. For they that say such things declare plainly that they seek a country. And truly, if they had been mindful of that country from whence they came out, they might have had opportunity to have returned. But now they desire a better country, that is, an heavenly: wherefore God is not ashamed to be called their God: for he hath prepared for them a city. (Heb. 11:13–16)

Keep this in mind as you contemplate the new covenant. In accepting the covenant, you are also renouncing the citizenship of your country of origin, that is, your citizenship in this world. You are saying that you love the God of heaven and that you recognize Him to be just, righteous, holy, and loving. You are also saying that you desire to live by the principles of His kingdom and that you love and accept His qualities as your new culture. With culture comes a distinction of language, work habits, food, dress, entertainment, government, societal order, and economy. Accepting all of these is a part of your agreement to live by the covenant just as a person gaining citizenship to a country, other than the one in which he was born, accepts the constitution of his new country and consents to live by its laws, subject to its leaders. Rather than being a rebellious lawbreaker in the new country, that person will be a better-than-average citizen. Since you are a subject of Christ's kingdom, your allegiance is to heaven, to God, and to God's law. Loyalty to His law makes Christians even better human beings within the society in which they live. Our profession must be backed up by actions. This is a confession, which is a statement of truth or the reality of the matter that we are fit for a certain society. Abraham is our spiritual father. Let us be like him and not return to "Babylon," the land of our origin spiritually. Most people do not understand the seriousness of their accepting the lordship of Christ, but it is infinitely more significant than immigrating from one country to another.

Genesis 12 describes the Lord's first presentation of His covenant promise to Abram. The question in chapter 15, verses 2 and 3, has more significance when you understand that it was nine years after the first mention of the covenant promise in chapter 12.

> And Abram said, Lord GOD, what wilt thou give me, seeing I go childless, and the steward of my house is this Eliezer of Damascus? And Abram said, Behold, to me thou hast given no seed: and, lo, one born in my house is mine heir. (Gen. 15:2, 3)

For nine years, Abram was looking for the fulfillment of the word of the Lord without seeing results. Though faithfully doing his part in having physical relations with his wife, they had no child. Remembering that the whole world is to be blessed through his family and that the Messiah was to come through his lineage to bless the whole world, Abram responded to the Lord, "Lo, one born in my house is mine heir." Abram was so desirous of having an heir that he was willing to accept as his heir a steward who was born in his house. Please let us learn from his lack of faith and then move forward in the grace of God. Salvation is personal and can only be experienced and appreciated directly by the individual. The covenant is a statement of the power of God—His promise to keep His word. This historical object lesson within the context of the covenant is for all future generations. The Lord is revealing His character to us in how He responded to Abram so that we can know how He will respond to us as children of Abraham. We will join with the psalmist who wrote: "I will worship toward thy holy temple, and praise thy name for thy lovingkindness and for thy truth: for thou hast magnified thy word above all thy name" (Ps. 138:2). What a God we serve that puts His word above His name!

## God's Promise Fulfilled Just as He Said

Remember what God promised: "And, behold, the word of the LORD came unto him, saying, This shall not be thine heir; but he that shall come forth out of thine own bowels shall be thine heir" (Gen. 15:4). We are admonished to live by every word that proceeds "out of the mouth of God," not just some of the words or the ones we want to follow or the ones we think we heard. We must be diligent students of the Word, for the purpose of God's word is to infinitely bless the contrite searcher after truth. As we see how Abram's life turned out, we recognize that the Lord kept His word for His name's sake to His glory. Because we can depend on God's promises, we must take the words "out of thine own bowels shall be thine heir" in the letter that God spoke them.

What did the Lord consider "thine own bowels," or his flesh? God had pronounced: "Therefore shall a man leave his father and his mother, and shall cleave unto his wife: and they shall be one flesh" (Gen. 2:24). The husband and wife are one flesh according to the word of the Lord. So Abram was to wait with patience, faithfully maintaining physical relations with his wife, Sarai. The Lord would deliver the promise in His time.

Now let us consider the context of the story in Genesis 17. The events of Genesis 16 take place one year after those in chapter 15. Sarai, having lost faith in the word of the Lord, asked Abram to help fulfill the promise of the Lord by taking her servant Hagar as his wife and the mother of the promised heir. Immediately we see Sarai repentant of her wrong of her lack of faith.

> And Sarai Abram's wife took Hagar her maid the Egyptian, after Abram had dwelt ten years in the land of Canaan, and gave her to her husband Abram to be his wife. And he went in unto Hagar, and she conceived: and when she saw that she had conceived, her mistress was despised in her eyes. And Sarai said unto Abram, My wrong be upon thee: I have given my maid into thy bosom; and when she saw that she had conceived, I was despised in her eyes: the LORD judge between me and thee. (Gen. 16:3–5)

## God's Personal Prophecy

Just one year after the reiteration of the covenant promise, Abram and Sarai had lost faith in the Lord. Yet, by the bitterness of this experience especially for Sarah and then for Abram, they were transformed in heart. This transformation is indicated by Abram's name change to Abraham—"Father of many nations"—before Isaac was born. Because of His foreknowledge, the Lord was able to count them faithful through imputed righteousness, even though they still had more faith to gain in the future. In reality, the name change to Abraham was a personal prophecy from the Lord to Abraham regarding his future transformation of character. Paul wrote:

> What shall we say then that Abraham our father, as pertaining to the flesh, hath found? For if Abraham were justified by works, he hath whereof to glory; but not before God. For what saith the

scripture? Abraham believed God, and it was counted unto him for righteousness. Now to him that worketh is the reward not reckoned of grace, but of debt. But to him that worketh not, but believeth on him that justifieth the ungodly, his faith is counted for righteousness. Even as David also describeth the blessedness of the man, unto whom God imputeth righteousness without works, Saying, Blessed are they whose iniquities are forgiven, and whose sins are covered. Blessed is the man to whom the Lord will not impute sin. (Rom. 4:1–8)

Don't miss the point the Lord is making. Because of His perfect foreknowledge, He could count Abram righteous and He could change His name to Abraham even before Abraham acted in faith. The Lord already knew that Abram would act in faith in due time as he learned to trust God under a change of heart. The Lord knows that a person is committed to follow that which the Lord has said to do, and He also knows that He will not fail to recreate and redeem the person. To the Lord, victory is sure, even though the person must continue to grow in experience as time allows. That is why someone can die repentant and be saved having never committed any righteous acts except for a change of mind. Our actions are a confirmation of what the heart has decided. Thoughts are the seeds. Nonetheless, though God can invariably read the heart, the angels and other unfallen beings in the universe and other humans need to see evidence. The real substance is the merit of Christ's life being accepted, the realization of a belief in Him and His mediation and utilization of the grace given in applying imparted righteousness.

Throughout the unfolding of their roughly twenty-five years of experiences, we see Abraham and Sarah's living out of the realities of the new covenant as the Lord bore patiently with them until He brought Abraham forth purified in the offering of Isaac for a sacrifice. Notice what our faithful God said to Abram, "when Abram was ninety years old and nine," after Abram's previous failure of faith:

> <u>I am the Almighty God</u>; <u>walk before me</u>, and <u>be thou perfect</u>. And <u>I will</u> make my covenant between me and thee, and <u>will multiply thee exceedingly</u>. And Abram fell on his face: and God talked with him, saying, As for me, behold, my covenant is with thee, and <u>thou shalt be</u> a father of many nations. Neither shall thy name any more be called Abram, but <u>thy name shall be</u> Abraham; for a father of

many nations <u>have I made thee</u>. And <u>I will make thee exceeding fruitful</u>, and <u>I will make</u> nations of thee, and <u>kings shall come out of thee</u>. And <u>I will establish</u> my covenant between me and thee and thy seed after thee in their generations for an everlasting covenant, to be a God unto thee, and to thy seed after thee. And <u>I will give unto thee</u>, and to thy seed after thee, the land wherein thou art a stranger, all the land of Canaan, for an everlasting possession; and <u>I will be their God</u>. And God said unto Abraham, <u>Thou shalt keep my covenant</u> therefore, thou, and thy seed after thee in their generations. (Gen. 17:1–9)

Notice that God identified Himself saying, "I am the Almighty God." That name has no qualifier. In fact, it cannot be conditional. It is an all-encompassing name that tells of God's ability to meet any need. Therefore, the covenant, which reflects His ability, covers every aspect of human need, especially regarding redemption from sin. In light of Abram's previous lack of faith, God's mercy, faithfulness, and grace are glaringly apparent as He appeared to Abram before Abram realized his true condition. This God did, not to rebuke Abram but to encourage him to continue in faith.

Dear reader, have you put a qualifier on God's saving grace because you lack faith? Are you trying to deliver yourself out of a situation before you present yourself to God for service? Do not limit the Almighty. That is a fatal mistake.

Notice also that the Lord did not say, "I will add to your seed." He said that He would "multiply" His seed. This clearly implies, in keeping with the promise of bringing "many nations" from him, that those who accept this covenant can be from any nation and not just from the blood lineage of Abraham. I have underlined several points to highlight the encouragement with which the Lord clearly seeded His words to increase the faith of His son Abraham. That same encouragement was intended for us as well that we might know that He will fulfill all the conditions of the covenant, except for a small part He leaves for us. The word of the Lord is creative power and has creative power in it. The covenant as worded is indeed a powerful promise, personally prophetic to Abram but also to you and me as we believe His words before the promise becomes fulfilled.

The first part of the covenant spelled out in detail for Abram is of great significance. God said: "Walk before me, and be thou perfect" (Gen. 17:1). Within the conditions of what He will fulfill, God sandwiched what He required of Abram and what He requires of anyone else who accepts the covenant: "Thou shalt keep my covenant therefore, thou, and thy seed after thee in their generations." Yes, walking with God requires actions—cooperating with Him in perfect obedience by faith in the word of God. "Blessed be the God and Father of our Lord Jesus Christ, which according to his abundant mercy hath begotten us again unto a lively hope by the resurrection of Jesus Christ from the dead, to an inheritance incorruptible, and undefiled, and that fadeth not away, reserved in heaven for you, who are kept by the power of God through faith unto salvation ready to be revealed in the last time" (1 Peter 1:3–5). We will address the keeping power of God further after studying the covenant in greater detail.

In the Lord's spelling out of the details of the covenant, He changed the name of "Abram" to "Abraham" and of "Sarai" to "Sarah" (v. 15), signifying the transformation of their character. This name change is symbolic of all children of Abraham who acquire the character of Christ when they fully accept and live according to the conditions of the covenant. "To him that overcometh will I give to eat of the hidden manna, and will give him a white stone, and in the stone a new name written, which no man knoweth saving he that receiveth it" (Rev. 2:17). Keep in mind that, at this point, they still manifested a lack of faith. Yet, God in His foreknowledge changed their names to symbolize their change of heart because they were already growing in grace.

The Lord responds the same way to you, knowing you are not yet perfect. His grace extends to you, as a seed planted and received in the heart, to be followed by the physical manifestation of the actions that angels and men will witness. Yet, it implies what you will be. Thus, it is God's personal prophecy for you, to give you faith to believe that, in applying the terms of the covenant, you will be perfect. By definition, faith is belief in a future event that has not yet been seen. The experiences of the past—the taste of bitterness resulting from sin—and the anticipation of the heavenly world free us from the consequences and effects of sin lead the mind to crystallize its desire to commit fully to the Lord with unwavering faith. Growth in faith is why the Lord allows us to experience what we do. The end result, in the will of God, is victory, which determines the name each receives that no one else can know because each person's experience is unique. The Lord allows us to experience the consequences and effects of sin, and, by our learning from these imperfections, we are led into perfection. "Who can bring a clean thing out of an unclean?" (Job 14:4). The Almighty can. We will say more about this guarantee later.

In chapter 17 of Genesis, we see that Abraham had believed for thirteen years that the Lord had answered his prayers and that He had fulfilled His promise through the birth of Ishmael. Notice their dialog:

> And God said unto Abraham, As for Sarai thy wife, thou shalt not call her name Sarai, but Sarah shall her name be. And I will bless her, and give thee a son also of her: yea, I will bless her, and she shall be a mother of nations; kings of people shall be of her. Then Abraham fell upon his face, and laughed, and said in his heart, Shall a child be born unto him that is an hundred years old? and shall Sarah, that is ninety years old, bear? And Abraham said unto God, O that Ishmael might live before thee! And God said, Sarah thy wife shall bear thee a son indeed; and thou shalt call his name Isaac: and I will establish my covenant with him for an everlasting covenant, and with his seed after him. And as for Ishmael, I have heard thee: Behold, I have blessed him, and will make him fruitful, and will multiply him exceedingly; twelve princes shall he beget, and I will make him a great nation. But my covenant will I establish with Isaac, which Sarah shall bear unto thee at this set time in the next year. And he left off talking with him, and God went up from Abraham. (Gen. 17:15–22)

Imagine—for thirteen years Abraham thought that he was walking in the will of God, and how he would have witnessed to his friends, saying: "The Lord has blessed me, I have a son." Nonetheless, Abraham was only in the allowed will of God. Have you ever done that? Rather than just being in the *allowed* will of God, you need to be in the *absolute* will of God. The Lord in His mercy is gracious and may bless us, because of His love, even in situations not of His ordering. Yet, how much greater is His blessing when we are in His absolute will with its infinitely greater reach and unleashing of power that comes from doing what the Lord desires and not just from satisfying our own small-minded thinking.

A closer study of this dialogue reveals that, whenever a person converses with the Lord, it is a prayer, and it elicits a response from the Lord. In verse 18, we see that Abraham was so pleased with his son Ishmael that he laughed when the Lord said, "Sarah shall her name be. And I will bless her, and give thee a son also of her: yea, I will bless her, and she shall be a mother of nations; kings of people shall be of her" (Gen. 17:15, 16). Abraham responded as ordinary human beings often do. Satisfied with what we have, it is as if we are telling God, "Oh, don't bother. What I have is fine. Don't put yourself through any more difficulty." In reality, we also really still don't believe. Keep this thought in mind because it is one of the most important points about the Word of God and His covenant. The Lord *must* keep His word for His name's sake. Your prayer is not answered just because God loves you. God loves everyone. However, His answering one person's prayer over another's is not a matter of His love but of His will and covenant. The question is: Have the conditions been met? The Lord does not look down and say, "Wow, I am impressed—this is the prayer of an Adventist. I love Adventists so much that I will favor this prayer above that of a pagan." No, nothing like that! God answers your prayer if it is according to the covenant. "God is no respecter of persons" (Acts 10:34). The power in praying comes from knowing how to pray and what to pray so that you can remain in the absolute will of the covenant of God. In His absolute will, the answer to your petition is sure.

In this converse, or prayer, of Abraham with God, "O that Ishmael might live before thee!" (Gen. 17:18), the response of God to his petition is noteworthy, considering that the request is not in the absolute will of God but only in his allowed will—"And as for Ishmael, I have heard thee: Behold, I have blessed him, and will make him fruitful, and will multiply him exceedingly; twelve princes shall he beget, and I will make him a great nation" (Gen. 17:20). In His gracious willingness to bless, the Lord responded positively to Abraham's petition, though it was not in His absolute will. God told Abraham that Ishmael would beget twelve princes and become a great nation. Nonetheless, he was not the promised child. The Lord could only go so far with this blessing because that was not what God had promised Abram. Yet—even still—what a blessing it was! In knowing that God is so willing to answer our prayers, a prayer in the absolute will of God has the unquantifiable answer of "exceeding abundantly above all that we ask or think," you also know that you are where the Lord wants you to be. He wants to pour out His infinite stores of blessing upon you. Oh, that we would study and learn the will of God! I am sure that you want to experience the absolute will of God, wherein is full infinite blessing, which God has promised.

Looking back at the promise, do you remember the words, "… he that shall come forth out of thine own bowels shall be thine heir"? This is the Word of God to Abraham that he was to depend on waiting in faith. In the common vernacular that was the "word" that God expected him to put faith in. Remember the context in which God will speak to us—that "thine own bowels" included his wife whom the Lord considered to be one flesh with Abraham. The Lord shows here that He can be depended on to keep the letter of His word. The Lord wants you also to trust Him according to His implicit word, knowing that He is always faithful to fulfill it.

His keeping of His word is such a serious and solemn matter to the Lord that, if Abraham and Sarah had died before the Lord had fulfilled His promise, He would have had to resurrect them to produce the promised child so that His word—His covenant—would be faithfully kept. This example teaches that the Lord in His mercy prolongs life, knowing that, in time and through our various experiences, we will come into the fullness of the character that He intends that we have. Remember, one of the names of God is "the Word"—"for thou hast magnified thy word above all thy name" (Ps. 138:2). The seriousness of God's keeping of His name and His word is why the Lord goes on to respond to Abraham, "Sarah thy wife shall bear thee a son indeed; and thou shalt call his name Isaac: and I will establish my covenant with him for an everlasting covenant, and with his seed after him … my covenant will I establish with Isaac, which Sarah shall bear unto thee at this set time in the next year" (Gen. 17:19–21). The Lord was establishing His covenant—His word—with Abraham and with Isaac as Abraham's heir. The implication of this to Abraham and to his seed is that they can depend on the word of the Lord in its exactness. Though humans at times fail, the Lord in His grace remains faithful to His word, truly demonstrating that He redeems by grace, keeping His good name.

The most significant part of this historical parable is its representation of the "born again" experience of Abraham as well as of you. Birth is another part of the object lesson that we should not overlook, for it is essential in understanding what it means to be "born again." Remembering the struggle and labor pains in our being born the first time tells us what is required in obtaining the righteousness of Christ and His character when you are born again. Let's look at this truth through the story of Zacharias and the birth of his son, John the Baptist, of whom we are to be the antitype in preparing the way for Jesus' second coming.

> Zacharias well knew how to Abraham in his old age a child was given <u>because he believed Him faithful who had promised</u>. But for a moment the aged priest turns his thought to the weakness of humanity. He forgets that **what God has promised, He is able to perform**. What a contrast between this unbelief and the sweet, childlike faith of Mary, the maiden of Nazareth, whose answer to

the angel's wonderful announcement was, "Behold the handmaid of the Lord; **be it unto me according to thy word**"! Luke 1:38.

The birth of a son to Zacharias, like the birth of the child of Abraham, and that of Mary, was to teach a great spiritual truth, a truth that we are slow to learn and ready to forget. In ourselves we are incapable of doing any good thing; but that which we cannot do will be wrought by the power of God in every submissive and believing soul. It was through faith that the child of promise was given. **It is through faith that spiritual life is begotten,** and we are enabled to do the works of righteousness. (*The Desire of Ages*, p. 98)

The most important message for mankind is rebirth—being born again as new creatures fit for the kingdom of God. Rebirth is a major provision of the new covenant. That your heir, like Abraham's, must "come forth out of thine own bowels" is God's guarantee to everyone who accepts His words, His covenant of creative power. My joy in reaching the New Jerusalem will be of no value to you, dear reader, unless you are there as well. God is personal to each individual. The "born again" experience is the greatest miracle that can occur, so it necessarily requires an abundant exercise of faith in the Lord. All the lesser experiences of life—the trials, etc.—are given us to strengthen our faith that God can also accomplish this greatest of miracles through and in us. Through the "new birth," we become children of Abraham by faith, and we receive a new name representing the transformation of our character. Paul wrote: "Know ye therefore that they which are of faith, the same are the children of Abraham" (Gal. 3:7). Jesus spoke definitively about this: "Verily, verily, I say unto thee, Except a man be born again, he cannot see the kingdom of God.... Verily, verily, I say unto thee, Except a man be born of water and of the Spirit, he cannot enter into the kingdom of God" (John 3:3, 5). The new birth is the end point of our experience in faith, the Lord's goal for His children's transformation of their character.

## Defining the "Born Again" Experience

What is the biblical definition of being "born again"? We will let the Word of God answer this directly so that we will not be left with any doubt or questions because this experience is our objective, and it is what fits us for heaven. Jesus said, "Except a man be born again, he cannot see the kingdom of God" (John 3:3). Many views of the new birth sound good and have a general correctness, yet they lead people to lose their souls believing that a generally good life is enough. However, that is not what the Bible teaches, nor is it the object of the covenant.

The biblical answer for what it means to be "born again" is found in John's first epistle: "Whosoever is born of God doth not commit sin; for his seed remaineth in him: and he cannot sin, because he is born of God" (1 John 3:9). "We know that whosoever is born of God sinneth not; but he that is begotten of God keepeth himself, and that wicked one toucheth him not" (1 John 5:18). To be born again ultimately means to be victorious over temptation and not sin, thereby fitting us to enter the kingdom of God. Were not Adam and Eve removed from the garden of Eden for the commission of a single sin? It would only be fair and just of God, in returning man to the Garden of Eden, that all sin must be overcome and brought to an end before the redeemed can enter heaven. When properly applied, the new covenant will accomplish this object in your life. Overcoming sin is what God guarantees if you follow the given conditions of the covenant. It is indeed a science and, as with any science, the results never vary. Thus, the object of the seed, as found in the Word of God, is the recreation of fallen, sinful mankind into the full image of God as God said, "I am the Almighty God; walk before me, and be thou perfect. And I will make my covenant between me and thee" (Gen. 17:1, 2). Praise the Lord! Amen!

CHAPTER 4

# The New Birth in the New Covenant

> Have Thine own way, Lord! Have Thine own way!
> Hold o'er my being absolute sway!
> Fill with Thy Spirit till all shall see
> Christ only, always, living in me!
> —Adelaide Pollard[6]

In our first three chapters, we noted the struggle required in obtaining the character of Christ, overcoming sin, reflecting the character of God, and the biblical definition of being born again. Dear reader, as we begin this chapter, I ask you to pray for a heart of understanding and for willingness to receive and live the Word of God, allowing the seed of the Word to penetrate its roots deeply into your soul to make you unmovable in your trust in God.

The purpose of the last chapter was to introduce the new covenant, which is God's guarantee that He will restore you into His full image, despite your fallen human nature. When we study the Bible with the right understanding of what it means to be born again, then, and only then, will we see the fullness of the power of the omnipotent God in His Word. Then, and only then, can we experience His omnipotence in our life. Otherwise, the Christian life is only seen and experienced as an improvement of the old life and not as our being a "new creature," which is a requirement of salvation.

---

[6] Adelaide Pollard, "Have Thine Own Way, Lord," 1906, Hymnary, https://1ref.us/1kw (accessed February 17, 2021).

## What It Means to Be Born of God

Let us review the biblical definition of what it means to be born again as John recorded it in his first epistle: "Whosoever is born of God <u>doth not commit sin</u>; for his seed **remaineth** in him: and he <u>cannot sin</u>, because he is born of God" (1 John 3:9). "We know that <u>whosoever is born of God sinneth not</u>; but <u>he that is begotten of God keepeth himself</u>, and that wicked one toucheth him not" (1 John 5:18). The added emphasis in these verses is because most people fail to see that, if we are born again and the seed—God's Word—has taken root in our heart and continues to influence us, we will "not commit sin." The verb is in present tense. It is ongoing. The seed that "remaineth" will not give way to sin, and it will keep you from sin because "the word of the Lord endureth for ever." "Being born again, not of corruptible seed, but of incorruptible, by the word of God, which liveth and abideth for ever" (1 Peter 1:25, 23). The seed is incorruptible. It never grows fungus; it never rots; it never becomes sterile. Thus, the failure to get a return from the seed sown is not because the seed is bad. It is due to the rejection of the seed, which is the Word of God. Rejecting the seed is what causes a person to fall into sin again. Most certainly when you disregard the seed and push it out of your life, you remove its preserving power, and it does not take long until you will be back in sin.

In a projection of the future, the verse says that people born of God "cannot sin." You may be saying at this point, "Wait a minute—my experience has not been like that." Sure, dear reader, that may well be. Yet, have you applied the covenant as intended? Based on the fact that you are continuing in sin, I can say without reservation that you have not applied the covenant correctly. God's Word does not fail in producing what it was made to produce. The problem is in our learning how to apply the covenant properly. It is our work to see that the "seed remaineth" inside of us. Thus, the fault lies with us and not with God. If we are not honest with ourselves, we will be deceived into the fatal security of thinking that we are acceptable as we are and that grace covers us in continuing to sin, and that the Word of God does not contain power to keep us from sinning.

Later in this book, we will discuss in detail how to use the Word of God in overcoming sin. For now, the important thing to understand is our objective—believing that victory over all temptation and sin is *possible* even though you may not have already achieved it. If you say that you believe that God is omnipotent, yet you do not believe that He is able to give you victory over every temptation, then you are contradicting what you say you believe. Keep in mind what Paul, the apostle of grace, wrote:

> That I may know him, and the power of his resurrection, and the fellowship of his sufferings, being made conformable unto his death; if by any means I might attain unto the resurrection of the dead. Not as though I had already attained, either were already perfect: but I follow after, if that I may apprehend that for which also I am apprehended of Christ Jesus. Brethren, I count not myself to have apprehended: but this one thing I do, forgetting those things which are behind, and reaching forth unto those things which are before, I press toward the mark for the prize of the high calling of God in Christ Jesus. Let us therefore, as many as be perfect, be thus minded: and if in any thing ye be otherwise minded, God shall reveal even this unto you. (Phil. 3:10–15)

We are to know by experience the power of the resurrection in our lives, as well as the sufferings of Christ. Paul wrote: "Not as though I had already attained, either were already perfect: but I follow after, if that I may apprehend" (Phil. 3:12). The word "already" implies that Paul believed that, in the future, he would be perfect. To "apprehend" means "to lay hold of, to grasp, to understand, or to learn." Paul promised: "God shall reveal even this unto you." That is to say that God will teach you where your defects and weaknesses are and will provide for your strength and victory in those areas, teaching you how to walk by His power in the precepts of His Word that you may lay hold, grasp, and understand how to utilize His power. The Lord is committed to rescuing mankind from our fallen nature. Therefore, dear reader, prepare your heart to learn and accept that, with an omnipotent God, rescue from our fallen nature is possible.

Have you followed Paul's admonishment? In the phrase, "being made conformable unto his death," Paul affirmed that he was following Christ. Unless we understand what it means to be dead to sin, we cannot experience victory over sin. To "attain unto the resurrection of the dead" is a life of sanctification, a life of overcoming sin. Notice that Paul also said, "… this one thing I do, forgetting those things which are behind, and reaching forth unto those things which are before, I press toward the mark" (Phil. 3:12). As a professed spiritually resurrected human being, have you done this? Have you forgotten the sins of the past, or do you let the devil continually harass you about the sins you have committed? The Lord calls you to press toward the mark, reaching forward by faith to the fulfilling of His promises. His call requires no ordinary effort. As you follow God's instructions completely, you can depend on the Lord to fulfill His part, obligating Himself to "keep you from falling." Keep in mind the key words studied in the verses above and that the "seed that remaineth" is incorruptible and apprehend the lesson as you read the quotation below. Though the verses are not directly mentioned in the Testimony, they certainly explain how to preserve your conversion.

> To renounce their own will, perhaps their **chosen object of affection or pursuit,** requires an effort, at which many hesitate and falter and turn back. **Yet this battle must be fought by every heart that is truly converted**. We must war against temptations without and within. We must gain the victory over self, crucify the affections and lusts; and then begins the union of the soul with Christ.... After this union is formed, **it can be preserved only by** continual, earnest, painstaking effort. **Christ exercises His power to preserve and guard this sacred tie,** and the dependent, helpless sinner must act his part with untiring energy, or Satan by his cruel, cunning power will separate him from Christ.... (*God's Amazing Grace*, p. 321)

Without a doubt, being born again is the greatest miracle in our human experience. Remember that God calls it the "new birth," telling us explicitly, through the symbolism, that it is a painful, laborious experience. To encourage us to keep going, the Lord blesses us sometimes with miracles—like an experience of the opening of the Red Sea—and most times with smaller miracles—such as the provision of our temporal necessities and the help we receive in achieving success in school, business, marriage, parenthood, and ministry. Yet, any of these—big or small—is a smaller miracle in comparison with the new birth, though serving as evidence for us to believe in the future transformation of our character. Our new birth serves also to allow the Lord to manifest even greater power in our lives that is "exceeding abundantly above all that we ask or think."

## A Startling Multiplication of Seed

"And he brought him forth abroad, and said, Look now toward heaven, and tell the stars, if thou be able to number them: and he said unto him, So shall thy seed be" (Gen. 15:5). This verse comes immediately after the promise, "he that shall come forth out of thine own bowels shall be thine heir." The heirs of the New Jerusalem are the antitype, or the spiritual fulfillment, of this promise, for God showed Abraham that his seed would be as the stars of heaven. That's a startling multiplication of seed. This same promise of the Lord is for you, and it can only be seen after God's primary objective in your life is accomplished—your being born again. Then the seed multiplies by bountifully sowing itself again.

> But this I say, He which soweth sparingly shall reap also sparingly; and he which soweth bountifully shall reap also bountifully. Every man according as he purposeth in his heart, so let him give; not grudgingly, or of necessity: for God loveth a cheerful giver. And God is able to make all grace abound toward you; that ye, always having all sufficiency in all things, may abound to every good work: (As it is written, He hath dispersed abroad; he hath given to the poor: his righteousness remaineth for ever. Now he that ministereth seed to the sower both minister bread for your food, and multiply your seed sown, and increase the fruits of your righteousness;) Being enriched in every thing to all bountifulness, which causeth through us thanksgiving to God. (2 Cor. 9:6–11)

Sow, brother; sow, sister—that you may reap a harvest as plentiful as the stars!

## God Knows Before He Sees

It is of the utmost importance that we understand the next event in Abraham's story, for it has become the signature of his faith and a necessary characteristic of all who will become partakers of salvation through the covenant as part of the family of Abraham, the nation of Israel: "And he believed in the LORD; and he counted it to him for righteousness" (Gen. 15:6). At this point in Abram's relationship with God, nothing had happened materially except that he had taken God at His word, believing that what the Lord promised would be accomplished. The Lord counted His belief as righteousness. Such belief is righteousness by faith. The "faith chapter" begins by saying: "Now faith is the substance of things hoped for, the evidence of things not seen. For by it the elders obtained a good report. Through faith we understand that the worlds were framed by the word of God, so that things which are seen were not made of things which do appear" (Heb. 11:1–3). An omnipotent God can count belief as righteousness because He not only sees the present, but He also sees the future perfectly. Thus, God could in perfect justice count Abraham righteous in recognition of what he would do in the future, even though Abraham had not yet committed the works of righteousness. Because we are created and fallen beings even our future righteousness does not merit us being worthy of salvation. That is the grace and mercy of God, and it is one of the reasons we cannot say that we have earned our salvation. Wow! God is so very gracious in imputing righteousness to us on the basis of Christ's death, which was future to the time of Abraham, and on the basis of our actions that are future to our justification. There is creative power in the words of the covenant. If we follow the words of the covenant, the Lord promises that we will have victory. Let's see this lesson in nature. An apple seed is really only a very small apple tree. It doesn't turn into an apple tree; it is one from its original DNA, though its form is always changing by growth.

These are only two of the factors determining why the Lord can do this. Having said that, I admonish you, dear reader, to believe in your redemption from sin with continual, perpetual victory over temptation and sin, though this has not been your past or present experience. What the Lord needs from you is a change of mind—repentance—and the purposing of your heart to believe and act on the Word of God. The particular command is not as important as the willingness to believe God and to be mentally committed to complete the action at the appropriate time. Once we have made this commitment, the Lord knows that He can ask us to do anything and that we will do it in the future because it is a command that comes from Him. If people die with this state of mind, they will be saved because their future actions, which will be carried out in eternity, will be perfect. Even as sinners in a fallen world, they have made up their mind to follow God no matter what. As a result, the Lord does not need to change their mind or character, for they have already made their choice. The visible manifestation of our actions is not for God but for the benefit of created beings.

Take courage, sinner. Though you have fallen many times, God is patient with you and will give you His grace and mercy. He allows you to grow stronger mentally as you learn how to keep all of His commandments. In this way, the Lord will have living representations of Himself in humanity. The ultimate purpose of the Advent movement is to finish vindicating God's name by showing that human beings can live in a sinful world without succumbing to temptation, living together as a sanctified, harmonious, and united body.

## The Vindication of God's Character

Because many unfortunately misunderstand the doctrine and application of righteousness by faith, we will need to look to the "apostle of grace," in Romans 3, to utilize his inspired statements to better understand righteousness by faith. We read:

> For what if some did not believe? shall their unbelief make the faith of God without effect? God forbid: yea, let God be true, but every man a liar; as it is written, That thou mightest be justified in thy sayings, and mightest overcome when thou art judged. But if our unrighteousness commend the righteousness of God, what shall we say? Is God unrighteous who taketh vengeance? (I speak as a man) God forbid: for then how shall God judge the world? (Rom. 3:3–6)

In verse 3, Paul clears up the notion that it does not matter what a person believes. Whether you believe or not never changes what *God forbids*. It also never changes God's ability and power. Any false belief we have misrepresents God and underlines the deceitfulness of the heart and that man lies but it is impossible for God to lie. Yet, because the Lord knows your heart, He can count you righteous when you declare your belief, for He knows that you would commit the righteous action if given the opportunity.

So, given the context, what would God be accused of lying about? That with the grace of God (the second definition of grace being power), you, a man with sinful flesh, can keep God's holy law perfectly. However, verse 4 points out that God can be justified and overcome His misrepresented character by allowing righteousness to be seen and contrasted against wickedness and sin. When you are judged, God is also judged. Then, in verse 5, if our sinful acts are a representation of God, producing good and only things that are beneficial, then God is unrighteous for condemning us to the destruction of hell because it means that His power has failed to keep us and that he is unjust in condemning something beneficial. How can God condemn the world as sinful if the best that humans can do is to only decrease their sinning in frequency? That wouldn't be just; it wouldn't be fair. Notice how Paul answers this charge:

> For if the truth of God hath more abounded through my lie unto his glory; why yet am I also judged as a sinner? And not rather,

> (as we be slanderously reported, and as some affirm that we say,) Let us do evil, that good may come? whose damnation is just. What then? are we better than they? No, in no wise: for we have before proved both Jews and Gentiles, that they are all under sin; as it is written, There is none righteous, no, not one. (Rom. 3:7–10)

We bear false witness against God if we say that we represent Him while we continue in sin. The logical question to ask if we cannot stop sinning is: "Why yet am I also judged as a sinner?" There would be no reason to call it unrighteousness or sin. The argument is that we can continue to do evil because eventually good will come out of it. When Paul says that we are "under sin" or that we are "under the law," he means that we are under condemnation for breaking the law, and he later states that death is the wages of breaking the law, or sinning. Because we are all sinners and are condemned to die under penalty of breaking the law, we all need a Saviour.

> There is none that understandeth, there is none that seeketh after God. They are all gone out of the way, they are together become unprofitable; there is none that doeth good, no, not one. Their throat is an open sepulchre; with their tongues they have used deceit; the poison of asps is under their lips: Whose mouth is full of cursing and bitterness: Their feet are swift to shed blood: Destruction and misery are in their ways: And the way of peace have they not known; there is no fear of God before their eyes. (Rom. 3:11–18)

Paul is emphasizing why we have the great need of grace and redemption because of our lack of righteousness, such that we don't even have a fear of God or seek to return to Him. We can understand the implication that Abraham was also in need of grace and redemption as we are, though he became a God-fearing man, as will all whom God redeems will be. We can better appreciate and value the grace we have been given having been in that condition.

> Now we know that what things soever the law saith, it saith to them who are under the law: that every mouth may be stopped, and all the world may become guilty before God. Therefore by the deeds of the law there shall no flesh be justified in his sight: for by the law is the knowledge of sin. (Rom. 3:19, 20)

## Righteousness and the Law

The law's purpose is to show the standard of judgment, the character of God, revealing who is guilty and deserving of the penalty for breaking the law. This must be understood because "the wages of sin is death." This is true whether our sin is the first of many sins or whether it is the only sin we have ever committed. The truth is we cannot make restitution for the lost time, or reverse the effects. From the point that we commit sin, we are eternally deserving of death. When we know that we deserve death, we can appreciate the value of grace. Performing good works from the point of the sin forward cannot provide merit in any form or manner because what we have done is done and it cannot be taken back. If there were no knowledge of the law, then there would be no need of justification. If there is no sin, then there would also be no need of grace, and there would be no condemnation. In such a case we would already be righteous or at least not wicked and we would not need Christ for redemption. God desires that we come into the knowledge of the law and act upon it, for when we do we demonstrate that we have been recreated into the image of God. Apparently this reaching out of our soul for the divine standard is immensely important because, with it, we continue our growth eternally.

> But now the righteousness of God without the law is manifested, being witnessed by the law and the prophets; the righteousness of God which is by faith of Jesus Christ unto all and upon all them that believe: for there is no difference: for all have sinned, and come short of the glory of God; being justified freely by his grace through the redemption that is in Christ Jesus: whom God hath set forth to be a propitiation through faith in his blood, to declare his righteousness for the remission of sins that are past, through the forbearance of God; to declare, I say, at this time his righteousness: that he might be just, and the justifier of him which believeth in Jesus. Where is boasting then? It is excluded. By what law? of works? Nay: but by the law of faith. Therefore we conclude that a man is justified by faith without the deeds of the law. (Rom. 3:21–28)

Verse 21 points to the righteousness that the prophets have declared and that is received by belief first, which must actually come first before the action. The action without faith is worthless. The Word of God (through the prophets who were inspired by the Holy Spirit) is able to discern "the thoughts and intents of the heart" (Heb. 4:12). It witnesses righteousness before the action is physically carried out. That righteousness without the law is the belief without the action that God imputes to us.

Remember that it only requires the commission of a single sin to qualify you for the sentence of death. So when the sin of your past record is atoned for, you actually have no past record of sin. By the same token, neither do you have righteousness of your own from the past to go to your credit. From the point of an atoning sacrifice, God can give grace and impute the righteousness of Christ to you. Then, it would be logical that, from that point forward, you should not commit any more sin if you wish to retain "the righteousness of Christ" during the kingdom of grace. In this way, "the righteousness of God which is by faith of Jesus Christ" (Rom. 3:22) is accomplished in those who believe. They have the full "glory of God" and are "justified freely" (Rom. 3:23, 24). This is a critical point here—that Paul spoke of grace as being only "for the remission of sins that are past" (Rom. 3:25); it is not for future sins. During the kingdom of glory, grace is maintained eternally for the past, though no more forgiveness is needed since all the redeemed will have stopped sinning and probation will have closed. Ezekiel 33 clarifies this:

> Therefore, thou son of man, say unto the children of thy people, The righteousness of the righteous shall not deliver him in the day of his transgression: as for the wickedness of the wicked, he shall not fall thereby in the day that he turneth from his wickedness; neither shall the righteous be able to live for his righteousness in the day that he sinneth. When I shall say to the righteous, that he shall surely live; if he trust to his own righteousness, and commit iniquity, all his righteousnesses shall not be remembered; but for his iniquity that he hath committed, he shall die for it. Again, when I say unto the wicked, Thou shalt surely die; if he turn from his sin, and do that which is lawful and right; if the wicked restore the pledge, give again that he had robbed, walk in the statutes of life, without committing iniquity; he shall surely live, he shall not die. None of his sins that he hath committed shall be mentioned unto him: he hath done that which is lawful and right; he shall surely live. (Ezek. 33:12–16)

We cannot boast about our righteousness because our past will always say: You are a sinner but by the grace of God. When you turn from your wickedness and "restore the pledge, give again that [you] had robbed, walk in the statutes of life, without committing iniquity; [you] shall surely live, [you] shall not die. None of [your] sins that [you have] committed shall be mentioned unto [you]: [you have] done that which is lawful and right; [you] shall surely live." Wow! Praise God for His great love! Ezekiel's explanation of righteousness by faith is clearer than Paul's. He shows the principle of how we are looked upon in an act of righteousness followed by a sin and conversely, when in sin followed by repentance and walking in the way of the Lord. How have Christians missed this explanation? Why aren't Christians studying the prophets of the Old Testament and clearly understanding the new covenant of grace?

Knowing this all to be true, we ask: Is the new covenant only to the bloodline children of Abraham? Paul asks: "Is he the God of the Jews only? is he not also of the Gentiles? Yes, of the Gentiles also: Seeing it is one God, which shall justify the circumcision by faith, and uncircumcision through faith. Do we then make void the law through faith? God forbid: yea, we establish the law" (Rom. 3:29–31). Clearly, God and His covenant is for all of mankind, who have all broken the law. God is not the God of only Abraham and his bloodline. Therefore, anyone and everyone who repents will be accepted into the nation and family of Abraham. For the only way to be accepted by God into Israel is through repentance, which acknowledges man's acceptance of God and His law and His righteousness in place of man's own works.

Dear reader, the Holy Spirit asks, "Do we then make void the law through faith?" What does He mean by "make void"? The Greek word for "make void" (*katargeō*) means "to nullify," "to cancel," or "to eliminate." The answer to the Holy Spirit's rhetorical question is a resounding "no!" For those who have any doubt, the Holy Spirit answers His own question: "God forbid: yea, we establish the law" (Rom. 3:31). So, what is it that the Holy Spirit forbids? He forbids nullifying, canceling, or eliminating the law. And what does "establish" mean? The Greek word for "establish" (*histēmi*) means "to ordain," "to put into effect," "to set up," or "to put on a firm base permanently." Thus, we can incontrovertibly say that faith actually brings the law into effect. Though the carnal nature may have dismissed the claims of the law, under the direction of the Spirit, we now acknowledge and keep the law. When we consider that the symbolic sanctuary built by Moses represents the heavenly sanctuary built by God, we recognize that there is only one piece of furniture in the Most Holy Place—the Ark of the Covenant—and that everything within the holy places has played a role in returning man to direct communion with God the Father.

The Ark of the Covenant, which represents the throne of God, contains the "testimony," which is God's Law. His righteous commandments are the foundation of His throne and authority. "Clouds and darkness are round about him: righteousness and judgment are the habitation of his throne" (Ps. 97:2). "My tongue shall speak of thy word: for all thy commandments are righteousness" (Ps. 119:172). Laws are established for the purpose of governing and keeping order. Laws govern every realm of life—even if unspoken or uncodified. Where there is order, there is law, and by nature you will see order.

The general synopsis of the covenant with God is that He is to do right, and we agree to do right, having seen that His actions are just at all times. Thus, the basis of the covenant is righteousness and judgment. Since a covenant is an agreement, it is only standard procedure that the covenant carry terms and conditions—laws, if you will. By its very nature, a covenant cannot exist without law, just as liquid, by its very nature, must be a wet fluid. If a substance is not a fluid and wet, it cannot be a liquid by nature and by definition. God's law, the Ten Commandments, brings perfect order. We can choose to accept or reject it, based on our experience and the type of environment we want to exist in. In this world, God gives us the time and opportunity to try good and evil that we may decide which we want to live by.

## Righteousness by Faith

Having clarified the language of chapter 3, we can better understand the context of Romans 4 and 5, as well as the entire plan of salvation and righteousness by faith. Let's begin:

> Romans 4:1. What shall we say then that Abraham our father, as pertaining to the flesh, hath found?
> 2. For if Abraham were justified by works, he hath whereof to glory; but not before God.
> 3. For what saith the scripture? Abraham believed God, and it was counted unto him for righteousness.

We have already established that the mental assent of belief is what starts our righteousness. We believe in the Saviour and His law, as witnessed in verse 3. Abraham had come to complete confidence in the word of God. This mental step constituted the beginning of his righteousness. As we continue on, we will see how works have no merit in the earning of righteousness. If we could gain righteousness by our works, then we would have no need for God and could give glory to self. Yet, the Scriptures reveal that we are counted righteous in our belief before any action takes place. Continuing with verses 4 through 8, we read:

4. Now to him that worketh is the reward not reckoned of grace, but of debt.
5. But to him that worketh not, but believeth on him that justifieth the ungodly, his faith is counted for righteousness.
6. Even as David also describeth the blessedness of the man, unto whom God imputeth righteousness without works,
7. Saying, Blessed are they whose iniquities are forgiven, and whose sins are covered.
8. Blessed is the man to whom the Lord will not impute sin.

The key thought in these verses is that God's part of the covenant agreement is to make us new—actually righteous by imputing to us Christ's actual works, merit, and record as our record—as we believe in Him because we cannot become righteous by our own efforts. This is not a superficial belief but a belief that acknowledges the one God we worship as the merciful, Almighty Creator who justifies us through the death and blood of Jesus and who now intercedes for us in the heavenly sanctuary. Thus, through belief, we receive grace, which is an actual transformative rebirth accomplished by the power of God and not just the pronouncement of words. It is actual justification, the wages of sin having been paid by the death of Jesus, our Creator and Redeemer. Therefore, God can be called, in truth, a just God because justice was served. Verse 4 describes the one who "worketh" by himself. It is as if to say that you could repay God or give Him something He did not originate. God is, therefore, paying a debt to you, therefore God owes you a reward. Such a person is demonstrating that he believes that he can earn salvation. However, God owes no man anything, and it is impossible for us to repay Him. Recognizing these facts magnifies the value of grace and our need of it. We continue with verses 9 through 13:

9. Cometh this blessedness then upon the circumcision only, or upon the uncircumcision also? for we say that faith was reckoned to Abraham for righteousness.
10. How was it then reckoned? when he was in circumcision, or in uncircumcision? Not in circumcision, but in uncircumcision.

11. And he received the sign of circumcision, a seal of the righteousness of the faith which he had yet being uncircumcised: that he might be the father of all them that believe, though they be not circumcised; that righteousness might be imputed unto them also:
12. And the father of circumcision to them who are not of the circumcision only, but who also walk in the steps of that faith of our father Abraham, which he had being yet uncircumcised.
13. For the promise, that he should be the heir of the world, was not to Abraham, or to his seed, through the law, but through the righteousness of faith.

These verses are the key to understanding righteousness by faith. We must understand that "circumcision," in this context, connotes separation from sin. We see this in verse 9, which says: "Cometh this blessedness then upon the righteous only or upon the sinner also?" Understanding that Paul was speaking of separation from sin clarifies how God has given grace. To better see the separation, I will insert into verses 10 through 13 the definitions derived from the biblical context:

10. How was it then reckoned? when he was in righteousness, or in sin? Not in righteousness, but in sin.
11. And he received the sign of righteousness, a seal of the righteousness *[sanctification]* of the faith which he had yet being a sinner: that he might be the father of all them that believe, though they be still sinners; that righteousness might be imputed unto them also:
12. And the father of the righteous to them who are not of the righteousness only, but who also walk in the steps of that faith of our father Abraham, which he had being yet a sinner.
13. For the promise, that he should be the heir of the world, was not to Abraham, or to his seed, through the law, but through the righteousness of faith *[in God's covenant to give imputed and imparted power that redeems and restores people who choose to leave their sins and follow the law of God]*.

Dear reader, I pray that the "science of salvation" makes more sense to you now. To properly understand the Bible, you must learn to read God's Word using the contextual definitions that proceed from the text. We cannot afford to ignore the spiritual and symbolic language of Scripture, for the God of heaven created us to reason and the exercise of our reason in understanding the implied meaning of each term strengthens our mental powers and ennobles our character, leading us to grow into His image. This is one reason why certain words are used and the text is phrased in a certain way in the original. The explicit (literal) words have limited reach as they are only the words that are quoted, which do not take us any further. The implied language or symbolism is far reaching and can be even infinite in its scope as needed. The contextual definition of a word is how it is used in a specific circumstance. Its further implications are derived from the circumstances under which it is used.

## The Relationship of Faith and Works

To save time and space, I have added contextual definitions to the next verses in the passage as well as a practical application. Here are verses 14 through 16:

14. For if they which are of the law *[those who work to earn salvation]* be heirs, faith is made void, and the promise *[covenant]* made of none effect:
15. Because the law worketh wrath *["the wages of sin is death"]*: for where no law *[no covenant]* is, there is no transgression *[no action against the law or breaking of the covenant and, therefore, no need for justification/forgiveness and no penalty of death]*.
16. Therefore it is of faith, that it might be by grace; to the end the promise *[the covenant]* might be sure to all *[sinners]* the seed; not to that only *[the righteousness]* which is *[of works only]* of the law, but to that also which is of the faith of Abraham *[a man with human nature and sinful flesh]*; who is the father of us all *[keeping the law by faith]*.

The elements of faith and works must not be separated. Both are necessary, as we see in James 2:22, 24: "Seest thou how faith wrought with his works, and by works was faith made perfect? ... Ye see then how that by works a man is justified, and not by faith only." Continuing on in our study of Romans 4, we pick up with verse 17:

17. As it is written, I have made thee a father of many nations, before him whom he believed, even God, who quickeneth *[gives power for a righteous spiritual life]* the dead *[those living in sin]*, and calleth those things which be not *[man's righteousness]* as though they were *[a personal prophecy and a sure promise when a person depends on God]*.

18. Who against hope *[the impossibility of man keeping of the commandments in his own power]* believed in hope *[Jesus' power to keep us keeping the law]*, that he might become the father of many nations, according to that which was spoken, So shall thy seed be. *[So all can have victory like Abraham.]*
19. And being not weak in faith, he considered not his own body now dead *[Abraham now strong in faith having learned to depend on the faithfulness of God's word, did not consider the physical inability of his body or of Sarah's womb]*, when he was about an hundred years old, neither yet the deadness of Sarah's womb:
20. He staggered not at the promise of God through unbelief; but was strong in faith, giving glory *[keeping the law perfectly, now by faith]* to God;
21. And being fully persuaded that, what he *[God]* had promised, he was able *[God is indeed Almighty]* also to perform *[an impossibility to man without dependence on God]*.
22. And therefore *[because of his mental assent in believing in what God could do through him before having carried out the action]* it was imputed *[credited]* to him for righteousness.
23. Now it was not written for his sake alone, that it was imputed *[credited]* to him;
24. But for us also, to whom it shall be imputed *[credited]*, if we believe *[if you believe before an action or experience or event, you also have righteousness like Abraham]* on him that raised up Jesus our Lord from the dead;
25. Who was delivered for our offences, and was raised again for our justification. *[Jesus' resurrection is a necessity for salvation, for without the resurrection, justification is not possible because there would be no mediator.]*

Romans 5:1. Therefore being justified by faith, we have peace *[since there is no wrath or penalty because of God's forgiveness and victorious living by God's grace as we stand before God blameless and faultless]* with God through our Lord Jesus Christ:
2. By whom also we have access by faith into this grace wherein we stand, and rejoice in hope of the glory *[keeping the Ten Commandments with having obtained the character]* of God.
3. And not only so, but we glory in tribulations *[the struggle with the flesh]* also: knowing that tribulation worketh patience *[learning to endure and wait upon God for spiritual growth in due time]*;

4. And patience, experience *[learning how to utilize the covenant's promises, not just receiving imputed righteousness but exercising imparted righteousness];* and experience, hope *[in perpetual obedience, knowing we can trust God though we do not see the full objective]:*
5. And hope maketh not ashamed *[we have nothing to cause us to be ashamed because we are spiritually clothed by Christ when we are not sinning];* because the love of God is shed abroad in our hearts by the Holy Ghost which is given unto us.
6. For when we were yet without strength, in due time Christ died for the ungodly. *[Finally, we see our need of power over the sinful nature and the need for Christ's death to allow the wrath of God to have been exercised on Christ instead of us. We learn that fallen human nature by itself does not give us the necessary strength for godly living. For God to be just, at some point, He must execute the penalty for sins committed. The implication is that God gives power to all who, by trusting in Him and His power, ignore the weakness of their flesh and go forth unto victory, keeping God's commandments.]*

We will consider the principles of victory—the practical application of the covenant—in later chapters, though now, you can begin to understand God's principles of victory before we do.

## Belief Precedes and Requires Action

By biblical definition faith includes belief and action. Without one or the other there is no faith. Belief and action must go together, yet the thought process of belief precedes action, with a separation in time between the origination of the thought and the action that necessarily follows. We must use the conscious brain and actively think before an action can take place.

Let's apply this principle to Abraham and to our own life. Before Isaac was born or even conceived in the womb of Sarah, Abraham believed that God would be faithful in creating a child in the "bowels" of Sarah's dead womb. With this belief, Abraham committed himself to action—the action of intimacy with his wife until the promised child would be conceived. That's righteousness by faith. In like manner, though we have not yet been born again or had victory over sin yet, we are to commit ourselves to God, according to the covenant, and wait for God's power to be manifest when we perform the physical work that He has asked us to do. Both Abraham's belief and our commitment to God's working through us are examples faith as a belief separated in time from the promised fulfillment after an action is accomplished. Because the intended objective is not immediately realized does not give you an excuse to stop your work and simply wait for God to give you a finger-snap miracle, nor is it an excuse to devise some other method of which God does not approve to accomplish the objective. That is sin.

Paul illustrated this same pattern of faith and action in Romans 11. When most people read the Bible, they often fail to consider that they are reading a connected manuscript literally a letter, a series of thoughts in which all the points are connected and must be considered in reference to each singular verse along with the entire biblical canon.

In chapter 11, Paul is stating the conclusions of the matter. Chapter 11 is about the final restoration of Israel, which happens **on earth** before the second coming. Dear sinner, do you believe in this? Did you know this? I pray so, this is our blessed hope, our redemption from sin. Believe, dear reader, and prepare to be counted today among the righteous described as, the "sealed" in Revelation. With a living faith and abiding in Christ, our human frailty is not limited to what we can accomplish:

> "I am the Vine, ye are the branches," Christ said to His disciples. Though He was about to be removed from them, their spiritual union with Him was to be unchanged. The connection of the branch with the vine, He said, represents the relation you are to sustain to Me. The scion is engrafted into the living vine, and fiber by fiber, vein by vein, it grows into the vine stock. The life of the vine becomes the life of the branch. So the soul dead in trespasses and sins receives life through connection with Christ. By faith in Him as a personal Saviour the union is formed. The sinner unites his weakness to Christ's strength, his emptiness to Christ's fullness, his frailty to Christ's enduring might. Then he has the mind of Christ. The humanity of Christ has touched our humanity, and our humanity has touched divinity. Thus through the agency of the Holy Spirit man becomes a partaker of the divine nature. He is accepted in the Beloved. (*The Desire of Ages*, p. 675)

Keep in mind what Paul said about applying the covenant continually in our life: "… but we glory in tribulations also: knowing that tribulation worketh patience; and patience, experience; and experience, hope" (Rom. 5:3, 4). This we will explain in more detail with Romans 11.

## The Saving of All Israel

Now let us review the context of Romans 11 and God's goal for Israel biblically defined as a people of faith. Remember that many of those born of the bloodline of Abraham are not true Israelites unless their relationship to Abraham is made vital through faith and obedience. Nonetheless, many who do not belong to Abraham's bloodline have become Israelites through believing and obeying in Jesus Christ. Please pray and accept the promises in Romans 11, for they describe the fulfillment of God's promise to Abraham. Also consider Paul's strong message, which is the counterpart to John's message in Revelation 14:

> Romans 11:20. Well; because of unbelief they were broken off, and thou standest by faith. Be not highminded, but fear:
> 21. For if God spared not the natural branches, take heed lest he also spare not thee.
> 22. Behold therefore the goodness and severity of God: on them which fell, severity; but toward thee, goodness, if thou continue in his goodness: otherwise thou also shalt be cut off.
> 23. And they also, if they abide not still in unbelief, shall be grafted in: for God is able to graft them in again.
> 24. For if thou wert cut out of the olive tree which is wild by nature, and wert grafted contrary to nature into a good olive tree: how much more shall these, which be the natural branches, be grafted into their own olive tree?
> 25. For I would not, brethren, that ye should be ignorant of this mystery, lest ye should be wise in your own conceits; that blindness in part is happened to Israel, until the fulness of the Gentiles be come in.

That Paul mentioned two groups in verses 24 and 25 is the key to understanding what he meant by his concluding statement about God's objective for those He will redeem:

> 26. And **so all Israel shall be saved**: as it is written, There shall come out of Sion the Deliverer, and shall turn away ungodliness from Jacob:
> 27. For this is my covenant unto them, when I shall take away their sins.

Through the gift of the Holy Spirit the objective of God will be accomplished:

> In describing to His disciples the office work of the Holy Spirit, Jesus sought to inspire them with the joy and hope that inspired His own heart. He rejoiced because of the abundant help He had provided for His church. The Holy Spirit was the highest of all gifts that He could solicit from His Father for the exaltation of His people. The Spirit was to be given as **a regenerating agent**, and without this the sacrifice of Christ would have been of no avail. (*The Desire of Ages*, p. 671)

The gift of the Holy Spirit is essential for salvation, and it would have been unavailable were it not for the resurrection of Christ. Conversely, we cannot be saved only by Jesus' death on the cross as a singular act; other components are necessary for our justification, etc. Yes! The crucifixion of Jesus makes all the other components effective. Without His death the other components would be to no avail for salvation:

> The power of evil had been strengthening for centuries, and the submission of men to this satanic captivity was amazing. Sin could be resisted and overcome only through the mighty **agency of the Third Person of the Godhead,** who would come with no modified energy, but in the fullness of divine power. **It is the Spirit that makes effectual what has been wrought out by the world's Redeemer.** It is by the Spirit that the heart is made pure. Through the Spirit the believer becomes a partaker of the divine nature. Christ has given His Spirit as a divine power to overcome all hereditary and cultivated tendencies to evil, and to impress His own character upon His church. (*The Desire of Ages*, p. 671)

The "all Israel" in Romans 11 are those who died in Christ and those living without sin on the earth, those who "turn away ungodliness" for God knows no sin. O sinner! Do you believe that God the Almighty can do this? For He declares, "this is my covenant unto them," the saving of "all Israel" is conditional upon their believing God's promise—"I shall take away their sins"—on the great and final Day of Atonement (Rom. 11:26, 27). God's promise is His guarantee. What He has promised will take place when you believe and act on the principles stated in the covenant. Remember, the "very image of God is to be reproduced in humanity. The honor of God, the honor of Christ, is involved in the perfection of the character of His people" (*The Desire of Ages*, p. 671).

Consider the magnitude of what the Lord is saying to us in Romans 11: "All Israel shall be saved." This promise is for anyone and everyone who, by faith, accepts Jesus, His divinity, His incarnation, His human nature, His perfect life, His Word, His covenant, His life, His blood, His resurrection, His Spirit and His mediation. No one—absolutely no one—will be lost who accepts and believes in the totality of His redemption. The Lord knows that, when the principles of the Word of God are applied in the life, the result is sure—the one who applies them will develop the character of Christ. That is "God's Guarantee." Dear reader, let us be clear: Only Israelites will be saved, and anyone who is not an Israelite will be cast into the lake of fire. Non-Israelites are, by definition, heathens, pagans, and Gentiles— people without God, without hope and without faith in the name of God and all His work of redemption and restoration in the life of sinful man. Said another way, no Africans, no Americans, no Asians, no Europeans, and no Islanders who retain their distinctive worldly culture will be saved. Everything that is not of God will be renounced. In becoming a true Israelite, we will, by necessity, accept all of that which constitutes being a child of Israel—the faith, thoughts, words, actions, feelings, motives, food, dress, knowledge, education, work, and pleasures of Israel. Some of these things will be an enormous change. However, the Promised Land will not disappoint in the least. Consider that, for God to be a just God, what He provides in replacement of that which He asks you to give up will not only be good for you, no not even only better for you. It must by nature be the absolute best, un-improvable by anybody but God Himself. That is the only way He can righteously claim that He is the God of justice. Beloved, you can trust everything to God—your mind, your body, your life, and your soul.

> This union with Christ, <u>once formed, must be maintained</u>. Christ said, "Abide in Me, and I in you. As the branch cannot bear fruit of itself, except it abide in the vine; no more can ye, except ye abide in Me." This is no casual touch, <u>no off-and-on connection</u>. The branch becomes a part of the living vine. The communication of life, strength, and fruitfulness from the root to the branches is unobstructed and constant. Separated from the vine, the branch cannot live. No more, said Jesus, can you live apart from Me. The life you have received from Me can be preserved only by **continual**

**communion**. Without Me you cannot overcome one sin, or resist one temptation. (*The Desire of Ages*, p. 676)

As a part of the nation of Israel, you gain everything; outside the nation of Israel, you lose everything. It is either life or death. Therefore, we can conclude that an Israelite is by definition a person with faith in God, the Almighty. They are a people that, in faith, continue their actions and works, knowing that God will bring to fruition, in due time, the sought-after objective. God will sift His people to see whether their faith is genuine:

> Behold, the eyes of the Lord GOD are upon the sinful kingdom, and I will destroy it from off the face of the earth; saving that I will not utterly destroy the house of Jacob, saith the LORD. For, lo, I will command, and I will sift the house of Israel among all nations, like as corn is sifted in a sieve, yet shall not the **least grain fall upon the earth** *[the weakest Christian]*. All the sinners of my people shall die by the sword, which say, The evil shall not overtake nor prevent us *[people who say there is no judgment]*. In that day will I raise up the tabernacle of David *[the remnant of God]* that is fallen, and close up the breaches *[all will be commandment keepers]* thereof; and I will raise up his ruins, and I will build it as in the days of old: That they may possess the remnant of Edom *[the world, the unrepentant]*, and of all the heathen, which are called by my name, saith the LORD that doeth this. Behold, the days come, saith the LORD, that the plowman shall overtake the reaper, and the treader of grapes him that soweth seed; and the mountains shall drop sweet wine, and all the hills shall melt. And I will bring again the captivity of my people of Israel [Deliverance from the bondage of sin and the world], and they shall build the waste cities, and inhabit them; and they shall plant vineyards, and drink the wine thereof; they shall also make gardens, and eat the fruit of them. And I will plant them upon their land, and they shall no more be pulled up out of their land which I have given them, saith the LORD thy God. (Amos 9:8–15)

Until then, go in peace and in the grace of Jesus Christ our Lord and Saviour, knowing that you are forgiven, "knowing that tribulation worketh patience; and patience, experience; and experience, hope and hope maketh not ashamed" (Rom. 5:3–5). Amen.

CHAPTER 5

# God's Promise to Israel

> His oath, His covenant, and blood
> Support me in the whelming flood;
> When all around my soul gives way,
> He then is all my hope and stay.
> —Edward Mote[7]

In Chapter 2, we recognized that the honor of God is at stake in His covenant with the people. "The very image of God is to be reproduced in humanity. The honor of God, the honor of Christ, is involved in the perfection of the character of His people" (*The Desire of Ages*, p. 671). Vindicating God's honor is the foremost objective of God in allowing the devil to demonstrate his case against God. The victory of weaker beings, in the last and weakest generation, against the strongest of God's created beings is an undeniable testimony for the vindication of the name of God. We also have come to understand the meaning of Paul's statement, "All Israel shall be saved: as it is written, There shall come out of Sion the Deliverer, and shall turn away ungodliness from Jacob: For this is my covenant unto them, when I shall take away their sins" (Rom. 11:26, 27). The salvation of all Israel must be understood as a necessary clause in His covenant to sustain His name as Almighty God. Why? When all is said and done, by biblical definition a Jew is a person of faith, and these people of faith make up the entirety of the nation of Israel—a nation of people who believe in God. "For he is not a Jew, which is one outwardly; neither is that circumcision, which is outward

---

[7] Edward Mote, "My Hope Is Built on Nothing Less," 1834, Hymnary, https://1ref.us/1kx (accessed February 17, 2021).

in the flesh. But he is a Jew, which is one inwardly; and circumcision is that of the heart, in the spirit, and not in the letter; whose praise is not of men, but of God" (Rom. 2:28, 29). So according to the covenant, "all people of faith in God," all true Jews, will be saved. All unbelievers will end up in the lake of fire. "But the fearful, and **unbelieving**, and the abominable, and murderers, and whoremongers, and sorcerers, and idolaters, and all liars, shall have their part in the lake which burneth with fire and brimstone: which is the second death" (Rev. 21:8). Thus, no Jews will be lost, or, as Paul says, "All Israel shall be saved."

Our object in this study is to cement your faith that this will be the end product of your life when you put it in Christ's hands. Not one person who is saved will fail of this; not one person ever created will be able to say, "God couldn't accomplish this in my life." All who are saved will have "perfection of character" with all their sins repented of and removed before the second coming of Christ. All will be Israelites in the eyes of God. I can say unequivocally that no Americans will be saved; no Europeans will be saved; no Asians will be saved; no Africans will be saved; no Islanders will be saved; only Israelites will be saved. All who will be saved must obtain the citizenship of the New Jerusalem. God only gives entrance into the heavenly city to those who have fulfilled the conditions of the covenant as stated in Genesis through Revelation. In simple terms, the covenant is God's plan to remove all defects of character—whether they be in thought or in action, whether they be hereditary or a cultivated tendency to sin. We are to place our faith in His ability to transform our character. You must voluntarily remove all connections with this world of sin, for God cannot and will not force you to do so before He grants you citizenship. That is one of the purposes of the grace that has been granted you—to empower you to break all connections with sin. Let's see this point in the Scriptures.

"Now the LORD had said unto Abram, Get thee out of thy country, and from thy kindred, and from thy father's house, unto a land that I will show thee:" "So Abram departed, as the LORD had spoken unto him; and Lot went with him: and Abram was seventy and five years old when he departed out of Haran" (Gen. 12:1, 4). "And he said unto him, I am the LORD that brought thee out of Ur of the Chaldees, to give thee this land to inherit it" (Gen. 15:7).

## Applying the Bible to Your Life

When you read the Bible, you must understand that its history is to be made personal to you, a historical parable, an object lesson personal to you, especially where you see the names Abraham, Isaac, and Jacob as the fathers of the chosen people. In taking God at His Word, all who desire to partake of the covenant promises will spiritually experience what Abraham, Isaac, and Jacob experienced. Therefore, you and I are to read the Bible like this: "Now the LORD had said unto [your name here], Get thee out of thy country, and from thy kindred, and from thy father's house, unto a land that I will show thee" (Gen. 12:1). To leave family is no easy calling, but can the home you live in now compare to the mansion God is preparing for you? Dear brother, dear sister, the Bible is clear. If we claim a connection to the kingdoms of the world, we will be destroyed with them as shown in Daniel 2. No Africans will be saved, nor Americans, nor Asians, nor Islanders, nor Europeans—none. Only Israelites—only Hebrews—will be saved. Sure, there will be people in heaven who look African, American, Asian, Islander, or European, but culturally they will all be spiritual Hebrews.

To partake of the complete fulfillment of the promise given Abraham, we also will walk in the footsteps of the faithful of old.

> These all died in faith, not having received the promises, but having seen them afar off, and were persuaded of them, and embraced them, and confessed that they were strangers and pilgrims on the earth. For they that say such things declare plainly that they seek a country. And truly, if they had been mindful of that country from whence they came out, they might have had opportunity to have returned. But now they desire a better country, that is, an heavenly: wherefore God is not ashamed to be called their God: for he hath prepared for them a city. (Heb. 11:13–16)

Dear reader, I implore you to come out of the world and not return to your culture. You are called to be a child of God, a citizen of the New Jerusalem. None will enter that city who continue to live their native worldly culture in their thinking, entertainment, education, dress, diet, or work—or do anything in their lifestyle that violates the commandments of God. By putting the Lord first, we will rightly prioritize the necessities of life.

> Whosoever therefore shall confess me before men, him will I confess also before my Father which is in heaven. But whosoever shall deny me before men, him will I also deny before my Father which is in heaven. Think not that I am come to send peace on earth: I came not to send peace, but a sword. For I am come to set a man at variance against his father, and the daughter against her mother,

and the daughter in law against her mother in law. And a man's foes shall be they of his own household. He that loveth father or mother more than me is not worthy of me: and he that loveth son or daughter more than me is not worthy of me. And he that taketh not his cross, and followeth after me, is not worthy of me. He that findeth his life shall lose it: and he that loseth his life for my sake shall find it. (Matt. 10:32–39)

The message of Matthew 10 is for all believers a section of Scripture seemingly unlike others except for Luke 14. Please think soberly about it, for if you save your life in this world, you will lose eternal life. The Lord is aware that there will be war in your home if you follow Him and the others do not. However, to compromise for peace in the home is to settle for a close-knit but worldly family that will be committed to the lake of fire. Burning in the lake of fire next to your close relative will be a miserable, lonely experience. Let the Lord take care of you here and now. Let God be your Father as He has said. Let Abraham's family be your family. Haven't you always wanted the perfect family? Well, accept the adoption of God. Also, consider that genuine conversion—setting yourself apart for a holy use—is the surest way to help your loved ones. Though your direct influence may be limited, your prayers have power in interceding for them that would be lacking if you were unconsecrated. Listen to the message of a beautiful psalm of David:

> The LORD is my light and my salvation; whom shall I fear? the LORD is the strength of my life; of whom shall I be afraid? When the wicked, even mine enemies and my foes, came upon me to eat up my flesh, they stumbled and fell. Though an host should encamp against me, my heart shall not fear: though war should rise against me, in this will I be confident. One thing have I desired of the LORD, that will I seek after; that I may dwell in the house of the LORD all the days of my life, to behold the beauty of the LORD, and to inquire in his temple. For in the time of trouble he shall hide me in his pavilion: in the secret of his tabernacle shall he hide me; he shall set me up upon a rock. And now shall mine head be lifted up above mine enemies round about me: therefore will I offer in his tabernacle sacrifices of joy; I will sing, yea, I will sing praises unto the LORD. Hear, O LORD, when I cry with my voice: have mercy also upon me, and answer me. When thou saidst, Seek ye my face; my heart said unto thee, Thy face, LORD, will I seek.

> Hide not thy face far from me; put not thy servant away in anger: thou hast been my help; leave me not, neither forsake me, O God of my salvation. <u>When my father and my mother forsake me</u>, **then the LORD will take me up**. (Ps. 27:1–10)

Hear the words of Jesus:

> If any man come to me, and hate not his father, and mother, and wife, and children, and brethren, and sisters, yea, and his own life also, he cannot be my disciple. And whosoever doth not bear his cross, and come after me, cannot be my disciple. So likewise, whosoever he be of you that forsaketh not all that he hath, he cannot be my disciple. (Luke 14:26, 27, 33)

Jesus is clear—we "cannot be" His disciple and we "cannot be" saved until we put the Lord first. When we love God as He has called us to do, our response to others who would subtract from our commitment to our Lord will be as if we hate them. We have seen what happens when a man or woman are in love and everyone else is put in a subordinate position. The change may seem like hate to the person who has been pushed aside. This change in affections is how it should be with our relationship with the Lord. When we place Jesus first in our affections and others take second place, those around us, who at first may feel slighted, will recognize, upon further thought, the joy and righteousness in how we carry out our life, and they will realize that they should follow in like manner. They will also see that this affection for the Lord is actually a benefit to everyone in contact with us and not just to special objects of affection, which is really selfishness. Of course, when properly carried out, those around us will eventually come to understand that we love them, though not as they may wish if they are worldly. The love of God is not a love of compromise. Note also that in Luke 14, quoted above, the clauses connected with "cannot" are "whosoever doth not bear his cross" and "whosoever he be of you that forsaketh not all that he hath." Most of the time, we do not recognize which cross we are to carry. Yet, the cross we must all bear is self-denial—evaluating everything from the perspective of what God desires and what your fellow human being needs. In forsaking all, we usually limit self-denial to the restriction of possessions. We forget that we are to give to God all our thoughts, all our feelings, all our preconceived theological understandings as well as our reputation. Remember, all means *all*, not what you feel like giving up.

The surrender of all is where we bear our cross, and it is then the power of the Holy Spirit can work in our life in His fullness.

Since sin entered the world, there have only been two kingdoms, and only one of these will stand forever. Remember that, in Bible times, if you were not an Israelite and a worshiper of the living God, you were a pagan, a heathen, a Gentile, and a demon worshiper. It is the same today, though it is much harder today to tell the difference between Christians and the world because of the compromising of the people of God and Satan's multiplying of religions and professed Christian churches. Yet, the Word of God is clear that there are still only two classes of people, though human eyes may not discern this distinction. Nonetheless, a person either worships the God of heaven or he worships the god of this world.

> Be ye not unequally yoked together with unbelievers: for what fellowship hath righteousness with unrighteousness? and what communion hath light with darkness? And what concord hath Christ with Belial? or what part hath he that believeth with an infidel? And what agreement hath the temple of God with idols? for ye are the temple of the living God; as God hath said, I will dwell in them, and walk in them; and I will be their God, and they shall be my people. Wherefore come out from among them, and be ye separate, saith the Lord, and touch not the unclean thing; and I will receive you, and will be a Father unto you, and <u>ye shall be **my sons and daughters**</u>, saith the Lord Almighty. Having therefore these promises, dearly beloved, let us cleanse ourselves from all filthiness of the flesh and spirit, perfecting holiness in the fear of God. (2 Cor. 6:14–7:1)

Dear reader, the Holy Spirit is speaking to you: "Come out from among" the world, "touch not," go not near its attractions. Only follow Jesus. I pray that you now have a clear understanding of what Romans 11 implies and teaches: "And so all Israel shall be saved: as it is written, There shall come out of Sion the Deliverer, and shall turn away ungodliness from Jacob: For this is my covenant unto them, when I shall take away their sins" (Rom. 11:26, 27). When God takes away our sins, so also does He take away our love for the world, its work, its education, its food, its entertainment, its thoughts, and its culture. Then you "shall be saved." The promise is definite—not maybe, not possibly, not probably, not hopefully, but rather, assuredly. It is God's guarantee, then, in the eyes of God—you are fully an Israelite, of whom *all* He will save.

## What it Means to Be a "Hebrew"

Let us look at the word "Hebrew" briefly. The word "Hebrew" denotes who we should be. We see this word for the first time in Scripture in Genesis 14: "And they took Lot, Abram's brother's son, who dwelt in Sodom, and his goods, and departed. And there came one that had escaped, and told Abram the Hebrew" (Gen. 14:12, 13). Let's look at some of the words given in the definition of "Hebrew" in *Strong's Concordance:*

> Descendant of Eber, 5680; from a region across, on the opposite side especially of the Jordan River 5676; overcome, deliver, escape, pass over, set apart, cause to make sweet smelling.

Let's put these words that define a "Hebrew" together, in the biblical fashion that Hebrew is used to form a communicative phrase, to understand better what a "Hebrew" is. When you become an Israelite, you are a spiritual descendant of Abraham, who when he entered Canaan was called a Hebrew, which means a person living opposite of the world in culture, one who is from beyond, a region across the Jordan, an overcomer, delivered by Christ having escaped from this world and sin, passing over to heaven, set apart for a holy use, which will cause you to be a sweet-smelling savor unto God. All Hebrews have these character traits, and all Hebrews will be saved—guaranteed! Biblical Hebrew definitions in the Bible are not just one thing or another but can be all inclusive, as you see from the phrase we just structured together.

Let the Holy Spirit impress upon you the role of Abram in saving his nephew Lot from Sodom. In this role, as a type of Christ, Abram saved those around him by his life, by his separation from the world, by his intercession for the wicked and by his integrity in not seeking the reward of the world. All descendants of Abraham, whether they are of the bloodline of Abraham or whether they are his spiritual descendants, are to intercede for others. All spiritual Hebrews live as types of Christ within the sphere of their influence, bringing others into a knowledge of the character of God by their benevolence to those around them and their rescuing them wherever possible from the cruelties of the world. We read:

> The same angel who visited Sodom is sounding the note of warning, "Escape for thy life." The bottles of God's wrath cannot be poured out to destroy the wicked and their works until all the people of God have been judged, and the cases of the living as well

as the dead are decided. And even after the saints are sealed with the seal of the living God, His elect will have trials individually. Personal afflictions will come; **but the furnace is closely watched by an eye that will not suffer the gold to be consumed**. The indelible mark of God is upon them. God can plead that His own name is written there. The Lord has shut them in. Their destination is inscribed—**"God, New Jerusalem."** They are God's property, His possession.

Will this seal be put upon the impure in mind, the fornicator, the adulterer, the man who covets his neighbor's wife? Let your soul answer the question: <u>Does my character correspond to the qualifications essential that I may receive a **passport** to the mansions Christ has prepared for those who are fitted for them?</u> Holiness must be inwrought in our character.

God has shown me that at the very time that the signs of the times are being fulfilled around us, when we hear, as it were, the tread of the hosts of heaven fulfilling their mission, men of intelligence, men in responsible positions, will be putting rotten timbers in their character building—material which is consumable in the day of God, and which will decide them to be unfit to enter the mansions above. They have refused to let go the filthy garments; they have clung to them as if they were of precious value. They will lose heaven and an eternity of bliss on account of them. (*Testimonies to Ministers and Gospel Workers*, pp. 446, 447)

Oh, dear reader, please let go of that filthy garment—the character of the world! At first, it is pretty, yet it is not durable, and it is most definitely flammable. Pray to the Lord for your deliverance "out of Ur of the Chaldees," and purpose in your mind, as Daniel purposed, not to eat the food of the Babylonian lifestyle but only that which the Lord can approve.

By faith Abraham, <u>when he was called</u> to go out into a place which he should after receive for an inheritance, obeyed; and he <u>went out</u>, **not knowing whither he went**.... These all died in faith, not having <u>received the promises</u>, but having seen them afar off, and **were persuaded of them**, and <u>embraced them</u>, and **confessed** that they were strangers and pilgrims on the earth. **For they that say such things declare plainly that they seek a country**. And truly, <u>if they had been mindful of that country from whence they came out,</u>

they might have had opportunity to have returned. But **now they desire a better country**, that is, an heavenly: wherefore God is not ashamed to be called their God: for he hath prepared for them a city. (Heb. 11:8, 13–16)

The word "confess," as used above, is not about admitting to wrongdoing. It is a declaration of truth, a demonstration of the fruition of faith through a life lived as a testimony to one's love for God, a witness that God is indeed the "Almighty" as witnessed in the transformation of a person's character who has overcome every temptation and character defect and who lives victoriously. Such is the confession of the children of Abraham—that God is the Almighty, Christ is the Redeemer and God is a keeper of His word.

Remember that antitypes follow the pattern of the types. So let the Lord guide your mind that you will come out of the world and its culture, allowing only the Word of God and the Testimony of Jesus to establish the customs by which you will live. Though by birth you look Asian, African, American, European, or Islander, you live as an Israelite.

## God's Promise Sealed by an Oath

"Now of the things which we have spoken this is the sum," we are now ready to enter the heart of our study—the covenant as visibly entered by God and Abraham. Returning to Genesis 15, we find Abram talking with God:

> And he said, Lord GOD, whereby shall I know that I shall inherit it *[the land]*? And he said unto him, Take me an heifer of three years old, and a she goat of three years old, and a ram of three years old, and a turtledove, and a young pigeon. And he took unto him all these, and divided them in the midst, and laid each piece one against another: but the birds divided he not. (Gen. 15:8–10)

In answer to Abram's question, "Lord GOD, whereby shall I know that I shall inherit it?" God condescended to enter into the customary covenant ceremony of the times, which man made with man, so that Abram's faith could take hold of the promise. Genesis 15 takes place nine years after Genesis 12 when God first promised Abram that he would have a son and that the Messiah would come through his lineage. Would you still have faith after nine years without seeing the answer to your prayer or the fulfillment of a promise that you understood God had given you? The covenant to which the Lord God and Abram committed themselves was none other than a *blood covenant*. As such, it meant that, if one of the parties entering the covenant failed to fulfill the commitment to which he had agreed, he was to be killed or chopped in pieces as the animals had been.

I cannot overstate the importance of God and man each keeping their respective portion of the covenant because all the promises of the Bible depend on their doing so. A failure on the part of either one is no small matter, for death is the penalty for God as well as for man. When you rightly understand what is at stake for God and how He backs you in applying the covenant, you will understand why I call it: "God's Guarantee." It is His guaranteed commitment that He will fulfill His obligations to His creation.

Again, dear reader, I would ask you to pray and open your heart and mind to the Holy Spirit that He might impress upon you what is needed to bring about your redemption. If you allow Him in, the Lord "is able to do exceeding abundantly above all that we ask or think, according to the power that worketh in us" (Eph. 3:20). God's covenant is so significant that the angels on the Ark of the Covenant have their faces focused steadfastly upon it. Let us join them in bowing in reverence to behold the foundation of God's relationship with mankind.

## The Promise and Oath

The foundation of mankind's relationship with and redemption by God in the Old and New Testaments is the covenant given to Abraham. My prayer for you, dear reader, is that your faith may grow exponentially from the study, understanding, and application of this covenant in your life. It means everything in regard to your salvation because everything that God has given us is calculated to magnify and glorify His image by the increasing of our faith helping us to know Him and that anyone who depends on Him will never fail as He never fails!

Let us now turn to Andreasen's commentary in *The Book of Hebrews* on Abram in Genesis 15 walking through the midst of the divided sacrifices:

> This was a usual way of making a covenant. The animals were taken, and cut in two from head to tail. Then the pieces were placed against each other, each piece opposite and a little distance from the corresponding piece, and the contracting parties walked between the pieces. (See Jer. 34:18, 19.) And so at night, "when the sun went down, and it was dark, behold a smoking furnace, and

a burning lamp that passed between those pieces. In the same day the Lord made a covenant with Abraham, saying, Unto thy seed have I given this land, from the river of Egypt unto the great river, the river Euphrates." Gen. 15:17, 18. The smoking furnace and the burning lamp were symbols of the presence of God....

The ceremony that Abraham had witnessed was the solemn taking of an oath, in which the contracting parties "cut the calf in twain, and passed between the parts thereof." Jer. 34:18. <u>By this act they signified that should they break their covenant</u> **they were worthy of being dismembered as the calf had been**; <u>that is, it was a blood covenant in which</u> **the participants staked their life on the faithful performance of the agreement**....

The covenant that God made with Abraham was, of course, the new covenant. In this all Christians are interested, for it is indeed the Christian's hope; and this "hope we have as an anchor of the soul, both sure and stedfast; and which entereth into that within the veil." Heb. 6:19....

An anchor is an implement fastened to a ship by a cable, which, being cast overboard, lays hold of the earth or the rocks by a kind of hook, and thus holds the ship in place and saves it from being dashed to pieces on the rocks. An anchor cannot fasten itself to the water. **Unless the cable is long enough to reach bottom** <u>so that the prongs of the anchor can fasten themselves to the earth or projecting rocks</u>, **it is of little use**.

This is the picture here presented. The two cables, God's **promise** and **oath**, <u>will hold</u>. But the anchor itself must be fastened to something that is sure and steadfast, that will not slip or permit it to drag, but will hold it securely. And whatever that is, it is "within the veil; whither the forerunner is for us entered, even Jesus." Heb. 6:19, 20. In Christ, as the Rock of Ages, the anchor is fastened. It will surely hold. (Andreasen, pp. 233, 240–242)

Shedding further light on Andreasen's mention of "God's promise and oath," His covenant and word, below is Paul's exposition on the subject in the epistle to the Hebrews. I have inserted italicized explanations in brackets within the passage:

> For when God made promise *[gave His word]* to Abraham, because he could swear by no greater, he sware by himself, Saying, Surely

blessing I will bless thee, and multiplying I will multiply thee. And so, after he had patiently endured, he obtained the promise *[received God's word]*. For men verily swear by the greater: and an oath *[the covenant]* for confirmation is to them an end of all strife. Wherein God, willing more abundantly to show unto the heirs of promise the immutability of his counsel, confirmed it by an oath *[His covenant]:* That by two immutable things *[God's Word and His covenant]*, in which it was impossible for God to lie, we might have a strong consolation, who have fled for refuge to lay hold upon the hope set before us: Which hope we have as an anchor of the soul, both sure and stedfast, and which entereth into that within the veil; whither the forerunner is for us entered, even Jesus, made an high priest for ever after the order of Melchisedec. (Heb. 6:13–20)

Of significance in Hebrews 6 is the fact that God based His conditions to us on two things that are immutable, that is, that are unchangeable. Based on these, it is "impossible for God to lie." As we remember its immutability and consider the giving of the covenant, its significance, and its penalty upon failure, we can with profoundly deep-rooted faith live by God's Word. One of the hundreds of names for God is "the Word." David wrote: "I will worship toward thy holy temple, and praise thy name for thy lovingkindness and for thy truth: for thou hast magnified thy word above all thy name" (Ps. 138:2). John declared: "In the beginning was the Word, and the Word was with God, and the Word was God" (John 1:1). God's word and His name are connected. Even so, He has committed to putting His word above His name. God makes a commitment and then stands by it—even at the expense of His very life. You can depend on it. In fact, God's word is the only thing that you can depend on—the only certainty in the world.

Let us think about this for a bit. The terms that God committed to with Abraham are such that if He failed in keeping His part, He vowed that He would be dismembered into two pieces. Consider that Abraham also consented to be cut in pieces if he failed to uphold his part of the covenant. In writing to the Galatians, Paul revealed that the covenant is not just for Jews but for all who will be saved, necessarily come under this agreement:

> For ye are all the children of God by faith in Christ Jesus. For as many of you as have been baptized into Christ have put on Christ. There is neither Jew nor Greek, there is neither bond nor free, there is neither male nor female: for ye are all one in Christ

Jesus. And if ye be Christ's, then are ye Abraham's seed, and heirs according to the promise. (Gal. 3:26–29)

Moses encouraged the children of Israel, describing the roots of the covenant and included all those who were in the world that were not there that day:

> Keep therefore the words of this covenant, and do them, that ye may prosper in all that ye do. Ye stand this day all of you before the LORD your God; your captains of your tribes, your elders, and your officers, with all the men of Israel, Your little ones, your wives, and thy stranger that is in thy camp, from the hewer of thy wood unto the drawer of thy water: That thou shouldest enter into covenant with the LORD thy God, and into his oath, which the LORD thy God maketh with thee this day: That he may establish thee to day for a people unto himself, and that he may be unto thee a God, as he hath said unto thee, and as he hath sworn unto thy fathers, to Abraham, to Isaac, and to Jacob. Neither with you only do I make this covenant and this oath; but with him that standeth here with us this day before the LORD our God, and also with him that is not here with us this day. (Deut. 29:9–15)

These are two biblical witnesses to the fact that this covenant is the one you make, even being a stranger to ancient Israel and the Lord, though you may not have realized it. I point this out because many are unaware of what they have committed to, and they speak without truly knowing the requirements of God for their personal salvation. Let us go to the Testimony of Jesus to see what was covenanted. Keep in mind that, when we accept the offer of salvation, there is no other way to be saved except through the terms of the covenanted agreement.

> Still the patriarch begged for some visible token as a confirmation of his faith and **as an evidence to after-generations** that God's gracious purposes toward them would be accomplished. The Lord condescended to enter into a covenant with His servant, employing such forms as were customary among men for the ratification of a solemn engagement. By divine direction, Abraham sacrificed a heifer, a she-goat, and a ram, each three years old, dividing the bodies and laying the pieces a little distance apart. To these he

added a turtledove and a young pigeon, which, however, were not divided. This being done, he reverently passed between the parts of the sacrifice, making **a solemn vow** to God of **perpetual obedience**. Watchful and steadfast, he remained beside the carcasses till the going down of the sun, to guard them from being defiled or devoured by birds of prey. About sunset he sank into a deep sleep; and, "lo, a horror of great darkness fell upon him." And the voice of God was heard, bidding him not to expect immediate possession of the Promised Land, and pointing forward to the sufferings of his posterity before their establishment in Canaan. The plan of redemption was here opened to him, in the death of Christ, the great sacrifice, and His coming in glory. Abraham saw also the earth restored to its Eden beauty, to be given him for an everlasting possession, as the final and complete fulfillment of the promise.

As a pledge of this covenant of God with men, a smoking furnace and a burning lamp, symbols of the divine presence, passed between the severed victims, totally consuming them. And again a voice was heard by Abraham, confirming the gift of the land of Canaan to his descendants, "from the river of Egypt unto the great river, the river Euphrates."

When Abraham had been nearly twenty-five years in Canaan, the Lord appeared unto him, and said, "I am the Almighty God; walk before Me, and be thou perfect." In awe, the patriarch fell upon his face, and the message continued: "Behold, My covenant is with thee, and thou shalt be a father of many nations." In token of the fulfillment of this covenant, his name, heretofore called Abram, was changed to Abraham, which signifies, "father of a great multitude." (*Patriarchs and Prophets*, pp. 137, 138)

A concise synopsis of the covenant between God and Abraham is found in the statement, "I am the Almighty God; walk before Me, and be thou perfect" (Gen. 17:1). We find the full version of the covenant from Genesis to Revelation. The Lord is saying, "I give you My word, of which it is impossible for Me to lie, that with Me you 'can do all things.' With Me 'nothing shall be impossible.' Therefore, I the Almighty can ask you—that is, Abraham and anyone believing in Me and desiring salvation—to keep all of My commandments with 'perpetual obedience' because those who believe in Me, I will keep from falling if you live by 'every word that proceedeth out of the mouth of God.' " These are the words the Lord God Almighty is saying to you, dear reader.

"Be thou perfect." There is a huge obligation in accepting the covenant with God, but everyone who is baptized into the church—no matter the denomination that they claim—is covenanting to this objective and is effectively saying to God, "I will be perfect as You, Lord God Almighty, are perfect. I will be holy, as You are holy, and I believe that You can and will keep me from falling, from violating Your covenant." Following His perfect example is what all Christians commit to do. It does not matter whether they do so knowingly or unknowingly. The Word of God is available for all to study. All can familiarize themselves with the details of the covenant. Choosing to be ignorant is no excuse. Peter wrote: "For this they willingly are ignorant of, that by the word of God the heavens were of old, and the earth standing out of the water and in the water: Whereby the world that then was, being overflowed with water, perished" (2 Peter 3:5, 6). Contrary to popular sayings, ignorance is not always bliss, and faith is not completely blind.

Consider that the word "token" in the testimony shows that the name change of Abram was a personal prophecy to Abram that he would one day obtain the victory in the transformation of his character. The Lord knew that Abram would follow His word. The Lord also knew the power of His word and that Abram would be transformed by receiving His word. He knows this about all of us. Yes, you, dear reader, will be transformed when you follow the Word of the Lord. Not possibly transformed, not maybe transformed, but most assuredly you will be transformed. It is a certainty. You have God's personal prophetic guarantee!

Do you remember the healing of Naaman? He was blessed as you will also be when you carry out God's word; he was healed as he washed. Remember the healing and of the ten lepers? They were healed as they accepted Jesus' word and went to show themselves to the priest.

In studying *Patriarchs and Prophets*, pp. 137, 138, I was astonished when I saw, for the first time, that Abraham vowed "perpetual obedience," and then I eventually saw God's statement, "I am the Almighty God; walk before me, and be thou perfect" (Gen. 17:1). How did I miss that? How have we Christians missed seeing that?

We all take this vow when we accept Christ and the plan of salvation. So why is there any debate about a Christian being required to have a perfect character, a character like Christ's? The Word of God is unequivocal: "The wages of sin is death." Mankind has been selectively blind in not seeing what we do not want to see as we go on living as if sin does not matter one way or the other. Dear reader, if you find this to be new information and hard to accept, I would suggest that you stop reading at this point and pray to the Father and let the Holy Spirit lead you, asking the Father to forgive you for doubting Him as well as accepting delusive, short-sighted theology.

Ultimately, if we believe that we cannot keep the Ten Commandments, we are telling God, "You, O God of heaven, are not omnipotent, for the Devil is stronger than You are, in that he can overcome me. You cannot keep me from sinning. You have therefore lied to me. You have given me the impossible task to keep your commandments, which means that it is not a good law." The fearful implication of our lack of belief is on us. Repent!

"He that believeth on him is not condemned: but he that believeth not is condemned already, because he hath not believed in the name of the only begotten Son of God.... He that hath received his testimony hath set to his seal that God is true.... He that believeth on the Son hath everlasting life: and he that believeth not the Son shall not see life; but the wrath of God abideth on him" (John 3:18, 33, 36). "But the fearful, and unbelieving, ... shall have their part in the lake which burneth with fire and brimstone: which is the second death" (Rev. 21:8).

## Aim High

By God's grace we can achieve what we resolve to do with dependence in Him. It's righteousness by faith or achievement by faith. If you believe before you attempt something, with God it is as good as done. Therefore, the only way to achieve great results is to set high goals by God's grace:

> God **will accept only** those who are determined to **aim high**. He places every human agent under obligation to do his best. Moral **perfection** is required of all. **Never** should we lower the standard of righteousness in order to accommodate inherited or cultivated tendencies to wrong-doing. We need to understand that imperfection of character is sin. All righteous attributes of character dwell in God as a perfect, harmonious whole, and every one who receives Christ as a personal Saviour is privileged to possess these attributes....
> 
> **Of every Christian the Lord requires growth in efficiency and capability in every line**. Christ has paid us our wages, even His own blood and suffering, to secure our willing service. He came to our world to give us an example of how we should work, and what spirit

we should bring into our labor. He desires us to study how we can best advance His work and glorify His name in the world, crowning with honor, with the greatest love and devotion, the Father who "so loved the world, that He gave His only begotten Son, that whosoever believeth in Him should not perish, but have everlasting life." John 3:16.

**But Christ has given us no assurance that to attain perfection of character is an easy matter.** A noble, all-round character is not inherited. It does not come to us by accident. A noble character is earned by individual effort **through the merits and grace of Christ.** *God gives the talents, the powers of the mind;* we form the character. **It is formed by hard, stern battles with self.** Conflict after conflict must be waged against hereditary tendencies. We shall have to criticize ourselves closely, and allow not one unfavorable trait to remain uncorrected.

**Let no one say**, I cannot remedy my defects of character. If you come to this decision, you will certainly fail of obtaining everlasting life. The impossibility lies in your own will. If you will not, then you can not overcome. The real difficulty arises from the corruption of an unsanctified heart, and an unwillingness to submit to the control of God.

**Many** whom God has qualified to do excellent work accomplish very little, because they **attempt little.** Thousands pass through life as if they had no definite object for which to live, no standard to reach. Such will obtain a reward proportionate to their works.

**Remember** that you will **never reach a higher standard than you yourself set.** Then set your mark high, and step by step, even though it be by **painful effort**, by **self-denial** and **sacrifice**, ascend the whole length of the ladder of progress. **Let nothing hinder you.** Fate has not woven its meshes about any human being so firmly that he need remain helpless and in uncertainty. **Opposing circumstances should create a firm determination to overcome them. The breaking down of one barrier will give greater ability and courage to go forward.** Press with determination in the right direction, and **circumstances will be your helpers**, not your hindrances.

**Be ambitious, for the Master's glory, to cultivate every grace of character.** In every phase of your character building you are to please God. This you may do; for **Enoch** pleased Him though living

<blockquote>
in a degenerate age. And there are Enochs in this our day. (<i>Christ's Object Lessons</i>, pp. 330–332)
</blockquote>

The phrase, "Enochs in this our day," tell us that there are some living in the world even now who are having complete victory over the devil and his temptations and over trials, sufferings, demons, and men of iniquity. The statement is a rebuke to those who say that such victory is impossible today, and it stands as evidence in God's favor in the coming day of judgment. Be one of the people, who need no excuse. Many do not see the abundant encouragement that the Lord has for them. I can say most decidedly that the Lord has shown me only encouragement to press on to complete victory in the spiritual battle of life. The inspired statements are abounding in encouragement. Be encouraged! Draw faith from them and plead with the Lord to strengthen you in character and faith. Dear reader, this is my prayer for you.

<blockquote>
Stand like Daniel, that faithful statesman, a man whom no temptation could corrupt. Do not disappoint Him who so loved you that He gave His own life to cancel your sins. He says, "Without Me ye can do nothing." John 15:5. Remember this. <u>If you have made mistakes, you certainly gain a victory if you see these mistakes and regard them as beacons of warning.</u> Thus you turn defeat into victory, disappointing the enemy and honoring your Redeemer.

A character formed according to the divine likeness is the only treasure that we can take from this world to the next. Those who are under the instruction of Christ in this world will take every divine attainment with them to the heavenly mansions. And in heaven we are continually to improve. How important, then, is the development of character in this life.

The heavenly intelligences will work with the human agent who seeks with determined faith that perfection of character which will reach out to perfection in action. To everyone engaged in this work Christ says, I am at your right hand to help you. (<i>Christ's Object Lessons</i>, p. 332)
</blockquote>

Jesus is right by your side to ensure your victory. What a Saviour we have! God guarantees His covenant in person.

To put these statements in context, I would like to quote a most powerful statement. No statement is more powerful, though there may be others equal to it. I encourage you to draw faith from it and to seek after the power it portrays as one seeking hidden treasure.

> As the will of man co-operates with the will of God, it becomes omnipotent. Whatever is to be done at His command may be accomplished in His strength. All His biddings are enablings. (*Christ's Object Lessons*, p. 333)

When we keep in mind that the commandments are a transcript of the character of God, we recognize that His name and His glory are in them. When we sin, we cannot say that we are giving God glory, for sinning means constantly coming short of the glory of God (Rom. 3:23) when the last generation is called to proclaim the message, "Fear God and give glory to Him" (Rev. 14:7). We cannot in truth really say we are Christians, who are supposed to be "Christlike," if we are very unlike Christ, when we continue to sin. Christ came to earth and lived as a man in a human body with human nature subject to the same circumstances that we face daily. He achieved victory through His Father's power and not through His own divine power. Thus, He showed all human beings who have a sinful human nature how to live victorious in human nature by becoming "partakers of the divine nature" (2 Peter 1:4). Let God be glorified in your "mortal flesh" (2 Cor. 4:11). Amen!

CHAPTER 6

# What Makes the New Covenant New?

> Up to the hills where Christ is gone
> To plead for all His saints,
> Presenting at His Father's throne
> Our songs and our complaints.
> —Isaac Watts

Let's take a further look at God's covenants with mankind and their relevance to us. In this chapter, we will look at the definition of covenants given by God to man as described in *The Book of Hebrews* by Andreasen. Before we do, let us review some of what we have seen.

## Christ, the Anchor

> The ceremony that Abraham had witnessed was the solemn taking of an oath, in which the contracting parties "cut the calf in twain, and passed between the parts thereof." Jer. 34:18. By this act they signified that should they break their covenant they were worthy of being dismembered as the calf had been; that is, it was a blood covenant in which the participants staked their life on the faithful performance of the agreement....
>
> The covenant that God made with Abraham was, of course, the new covenant. In this all Christians are interested, for it is indeed the Christian's hope; and this "hope we have as an anchor

of the soul, both sure and stedfast; and which entereth into that within the veil." Heb. 6:19....

An anchor is an implement fastened to a ship by a cable, which, being cast overboard, lays hold of the earth or the rocks by a kind of hook, and thus holds the ship in place and saves it from being dashed to pieces on the rocks. An anchor cannot fasten itself to the water. Unless the cable is long enough to reach bottom so that the prongs of the anchor can fasten themselves to the earth or projecting rocks, it is of little use.

This is the picture here presented. The two cables, God's promise and oath, will hold. But the anchor itself must be fastened to something that is sure and steadfast, that will not slip or permit it to drag, but will hold it securely. And whatever that is, it is "within the veil; whither the forerunner is for us entered, even Jesus." Heb. 6:19, 20. In Christ, as the Rock of Ages, the anchor is fastened. It will surely hold. (Andreasen, pp. 240–242)

We will keep the anchor in mind throughout this book. It should be remembered whenever we study the Bible. Another thing to keep in mind is that the entire Bible is a "blood covenant." In a blood covenant, failure on the part of either party has grave consequences. However, the consequences for God are even more catastrophic, for failure on God's part would be the second death for God, a death with no resurrection, the end of God, and His end would mean the end of all things, since He is the Living God, the Creator and Sustainer of the universe. God linked His faithfulness to His covenant in a message to Jeremiah:

> And the word of the LORD came unto Jeremiah, saying, Thus saith the LORD; If ye can break my covenant of the day, and my covenant of the night, and that there should not be day and night in their season; then may also my covenant be broken with David my servant, that he should not have a son to reign upon his throne; and with the Levites the priests, my ministers. As the host of heaven cannot be numbered, neither the sand of the sea measured: so will I multiply the seed of David my servant, and the Levites that minister unto me. Moreover the word of the LORD came to Jeremiah, saying, Considerest thou not what this people have spoken, saying, The two families which the LORD hath chosen, he hath even cast them off? thus they have despised my

people, that they should be no more a nation before them. Thus saith the LORD; If my covenant be not with day and night, and if I have not appointed the ordinances of heaven and earth; then will I cast away the seed of Jacob, and David my servant, so that I will not take any of his seed to be rulers over the seed of Abraham, Isaac, and Jacob: for I will cause their captivity to return, and have mercy on them. (Jer. 33:19–26)

The Lord Himself has given His word, and we have learned from Hebrews 6 that it is impossible for God to lie. You may ask how His word is to be accomplished. Remember that, in Genesis 1, the Creator God established that He created by the power of His word. He simply spoke, and what He spoke came into existence. His spoken word possesses creative power. Therefore, whenever He speaks, things are created. Since it is impossible for Him to lie in His proclamations, if the Lord were to say, "Your eyes are purple," it would not matter that your eyes are another color or that no one has purple eyes. At the sound of His voice, your eyes would turn purple. This power in His word is why the Lord always speaks only the truth. Because whatever He says is so, or it comes into being. The Lord, knowing the power of His own word, has faith, yes, trusts that when fallen, sinful, and unreliable human beings will faithfully listen to His word, they will manifest God's power because the effect of God's word will do what it is supposed to do. It does not vary, as Isaiah declares: "For as the rain cometh down, and the snow from heaven, and returneth not thither, but watereth the earth, and maketh it bring forth and bud, that it may give seed to the sower, and bread to the eater: So shall my word be that goeth forth out of my mouth: it shall not return unto me void, but it shall accomplish that which I please, and it shall prosper in the thing whereto I sent it" (Isa. 55:10, 11).

Dear reader, learn to recognize the voice of God, to listen to His voice and to purpose in your heart to do what He commands you to do. His voice is the power in the Christian life. Then and only then will you be what God intended. When you think about it, it sounds simple—just listen to the voice of God. And it is simple, except that we consider our feelings and five senses, which we are to ignore, these get in the way of our listening to God's voice. However, the Christian life is not to be guided by our subjective senses but by trust—implicit dependence upon what God has spoken. Because we will never be able to see everything as God does, we must cultivate dependence on Him to keep us from having the same problem with sin over and over again, that sin not rise again in the New Earth.

The anchor on the cable must be let down all the way to take hold of a solid immovable rock bottom. This symbol indicates that we must have a connection that reaches all the way to heaven to secure mankind across the deep dark depths of this world of sin in which man has fallen so low. This cable for the anchor between heaven and earth must be long enough to reach the worst and weakest of sinners, entitling Christ to be appropriately called Redeemer, Saviour and Messiah. Mankind cannot be saved without a complete connection from heaven to earth. This symbol is much like the ladder connecting heaven and earth in Jacob's dream:

> And he dreamed, and behold a ladder set up on the earth, and the top of it reached to heaven: and behold the angels of God ascending and descending on it. And, behold, the LORD stood above it, and said, I am the LORD God of Abraham thy father, and the God of Isaac: the land whereon thou liest, to thee will I give it, and to thy seed; and thy seed shall be as the dust of the earth, and thou shalt spread abroad to the west, and to the east, and to the north, and to the south: and in thee and in thy seed shall all the families of the earth be blessed. And, behold, I am with thee, and will keep thee in all places whither thou goest, and will bring thee again into this land; for I will not leave thee, until I have done that which I have spoken to thee of. (Gen. 28:12–15)

In studying the Bible, many—very many—destroy the proper meaning of Scripture in using it out of context or for a purpose for which it was not intended. One such verse with particularly detrimental results is: "I will never leave thee, nor forsake thee" (Heb. 13:5). The evidence that God has forsaken many people is available for any to see in Scripture and in our own experience. But how did this happen? They forsook the Lord, and the Lord will not force Himself on anyone, and thus He will let them go. Thus, they end up discouraged, hopeless, and despondent. Your choice, is the condition for whether or not you are forsaken of the Lord. "… The LORD is with you, while ye be with him; and if ye seek him, he will be found of you; but if ye forsake him, he will forsake you" (2 Chron. 15:2). The Lord will not—cannot—forsake you before you forsake Him! Those who are lost have all forsaken the Lord first. The Lord will not leave an apparently hopeless soul, struggling to obtain victory, to be the prey of the devil. His tender compassion will not allow Him to do so. On this you can depend.

The biblical context includes the verses immediately surrounding a particular verse. Yet, the entire biblical context is also necessary. To gain a proper understanding of God's covenant, we must consider every passage on the subject from Genesis to Revelation. The trick of the devil is to deceive people into first thinking or feeling, based on their circumstance, that the Lord has forsaken them. When they believe like this, they are doomed. The devil deceived the fallen angels into believing that they could not return, as we read in *Patriarchs and Prophets:*

> Still the loyal angels urged him and his sympathizers to submit to God; and they set before them the inevitable result should they refuse: He who had created them could overthrow their power and signally punish their rebellious daring. No angel could successfully oppose the law of God, which was as sacred as Himself. They warned all to close their ears against Lucifer's deceptive reasoning, and urged him and his followers to seek the presence of God without delay and confess the error of questioning His wisdom and authority.
>
> Many were disposed to heed this counsel, to repent of their disaffection, and seek to be again received into favor with the Father and His Son. **But Lucifer had another deception ready**. The mighty revolter now declared that the angels who had united with him had gone too far to return; that he was acquainted with the divine law, and knew that God would not forgive. He declared that all who should submit to the authority of Heaven would be stripped of their honor, degraded from their position. For himself, he was determined never again to acknowledge the authority of Christ. The only course remaining for him and his followers, he said, was to assert their liberty, and gain by force the rights which had not been willingly accorded them.
>
> So far as Satan himself was concerned, it was true that he had now gone too far to return. But not so with those who had been blinded by his deceptions. To them the counsel and entreaties of the loyal angels opened a door of hope; and had they heeded the warning, they might have broken away from the snare of Satan. But pride, love for their leader, and the desire for unrestricted freedom were permitted to bear sway, and the pleadings of divine love and mercy were finally rejected. (*Patriarchs and Prophets*, pp. 40, 41)

## Christ's Ministry of a Better Covenant

Chapter 7 of Hebrews builds on the themes of the previous chapter, which portray Christ as the High Priest of the new covenant and not as a Levitical priest. He is the "hope we have as an anchor of the soul, both sure and stedfast, and which entereth into that within the veil; whither the forerunner is for us entered, even Jesus, made an high priest for ever after the order of Melchisedec" (Heb. 6:19, 20). The Levitical priests were not anointed by an oath as Christ was, and this is significant. The Lord made these solemn vows to secure our trust in Him as we see His commitment to the covenant. Let's look at the mid-portion of Hebrews 7. The "He" in verse 17 is God the Father.

> For he testifieth, Thou art a priest for ever after the order of Melchisedec. For there is verily a disannulling of the commandment going before for the weakness and unprofitableness thereof. For the law made nothing perfect, but the bringing in of a better hope did; by the which we draw nigh unto God. And inasmuch as not without an oath he was made priest: (For those priests were made without an oath; but this with an oath by him that said unto him, The Lord sware and will not repent, Thou art a priest for ever after the order of Melchisedec:) By so much was Jesus made a surety of a better testament. And they truly were many priests, because they were not suffered to continue by reason of death: But this man, because he continueth ever, hath an unchangeable priesthood. Wherefore he is able also to save them to the uttermost that come unto God by him, seeing he ever liveth to make intercession for them. For such an high priest became us, who is holy, harmless, undefiled, separate from sinners, and made higher than the heavens; who needeth not daily, as those high priests, to offer up sacrifice, first for his own sins, and then for the people's: for this he did once, when he offered up himself. For the law maketh men high priests which have infirmity; but the word of the oath, which was since the law, maketh the Son, who is consecrated for evermore. (Heb. 7:17–28)

Why did the old covenant exist? And why was a new covenant given? Hebrews describes the old covenant as "weak," "unprofitable," making "nothing perfect" (Heb. 7:18; 13:17; 7:19). It did not bring us near to God and the priest who administered it died. The new covenant is eternal. Its High Priest, who "ever liveth," "is holy, harmless, undefiled, separate from sinners," and "higher than the heavens." He never needs a sacrifice for Himself and, most important, "is able also to save them to the uttermost that come unto God by him" (Heb. 7:26, 27, 25).

Nonetheless, the old covenant served a very important purpose for God and man. It portrayed in symbols the plan of salvation that would be fulfilled through the new covenant. Even today it guides our study of what is happening in the heavenly sanctuary that we may act in faith, cooperating with the Lord in our redemption. A proper understanding of the symbols gives a detailed lesson on our part in the process of developing the character of God. A thorough study of the sanctuary builds a deep understanding of the faithfulness of God and builds confidence that God's plan will redeem you through the proper ministration and application of the principles that God has given us to guide our lives.

The old covenant was "a shadow of things to come," which "serve" as an "example and shadow of heavenly things, as Moses was admonished of God when he was about to make the tabernacle: for, See, saith he, that thou make all things according to the pattern shewed to thee in the mount" (Col. 2:17; Heb. 8:5). The beauty of the symbolism is that the infinite Lord could say so much about His character through its symbolism and through additional instruction without having to produce an oversized volume to accomplish the same end. How? In this way, the understanding of one point opens the way to understanding another. The sanctuary was not the old covenant. It could not be. It was the model, the pattern of things in heaven, which is where the reality of the new covenant is accomplished. Remember that a covenant is an agreement, not a piece of wood overlaid with gold. Notice below the old covenant spoken by God to the people and the people's response to God, agreeing to keep the covenant, in Exodus 19. Ancient Israel is saved under the new covenant, just as modern Israel is, though God did accept them as they expressed faith through the use of the Levitical priesthood service done in the sanctuary.

> And Moses went up unto God, and the Lord called unto him out of the mountain, saying, Thus shalt thou say to the house of Jacob, and tell the children of Israel; Ye have seen what I did unto the Egyptians, and how I bare you on eagles' wings, and brought you unto myself. Now therefore, if ye will obey my voice indeed, and keep my covenant, then ye shall be a peculiar treasure unto me

> above all people: for all the earth is mine: And ye shall be unto me a kingdom of priests, and an holy nation. These are the words which thou shalt speak unto the children of Israel. And Moses came and called for the elders of the people, and laid before their faces all these words, which the Lord commanded him. And all the people answered together, and said, All that the Lord hath spoken we will do. And Moses returned the words of the people unto the Lord. And the Lord said unto Moses, Lo, I come unto thee in a thick cloud, that the people may hear when I speak with thee, and believe thee for ever. And Moses told the words of the people unto the Lord. (Exod. 19:3–9)

So why do we need a new covenant? Many give a pat answer from tradition without studying the Scriptures for themselves to see what scripture actually gives as the reason. Unfortunately, the traditional answer, as we will demonstrate, is not entirely correct or contextually accurate. The pat answer, "the children of Israel couldn't keep the old covenant," quotes the words of the people, "And all the people answered together, and said, All that the LORD hath spoken we will do" (Exod. 19:8). This pat answer, though true, falsely implies that God commanded the people to keep a covenant—the Ten Commandments—that could never actually be kept. Most acknowledge that the Ten Commandments are the standard to shoot for, yet they leave the impression that it is of no consequence for believers to fall short from time to time. After all, Jesus will cover our defects. They assert that there is no need to worry, for believers will always continue to sin while they are in this world. Hebrews chapters 8 through 10 say nothing like this, but rather, they give the correct contextual reasons for the new covenant. Let's look at the biblical answer to the question of why the new covenant was needed.

"Now of the things which we have spoken this is the sum: We have such an high priest, who is set on the right hand of the throne of the Majesty in the heavens; a minister of the sanctuary, and of the true tabernacle, which the Lord pitched, and not man" (Heb. 8:1, 2). In the first seven chapters of Hebrews, Paul explains who Christ is. He is God incarnate in the flesh from the tribe of Judah. He is also our High Priest after the order of Melchisedec, who now sits at the right hand of God in actual location and position. Paul points out that, with Christ in heaven, we have an intercessor who knows how we feel, who knows the power of temptation and the weakness of the flesh and the pain of suffering. Chapters 3 and 4 of Hebrews are an admonition for modern Israel not to follow ancient Israel but to have faith in the hand of the Lord and be faithful to His covenant in anticipation of our deliverance especially in light of the fact as we can depend on its better promises.

Verse 6 states: "But now hath he obtained a more excellent ministry, by how much also he is the mediator of a better covenant, which was established upon better promises." Christ has a more excellent ministry, based on a better covenant and promises. Verse 7 adds: "For if that first covenant had been faultless, then should no place have been sought for the second." Thus, the biblical record is that the first covenant had faults. Yet, what does the Bible say the fault was? To answer, neither tradition nor opinion will do. Verse 9 says: "Not according to the covenant that I made with their fathers in the day when I took them by the hand to lead them out of the land of Egypt; because they continued not in my covenant, and I regarded them not, saith the Lord."

The Lord Himself says, "they continued not in my covenant." He does not say, "They could not keep the covenant," but, rather, "they continued not in my covenant," implying that, at one point, they were keeping the covenant but then "continued not" in it. God's statement means that they discontinued their observance of the covenant, that they stopped what they were doing and did otherwise, not that they never were able to keep the covenant, which is an answer based on tradition and the opinions of man, handed down from generation to generation without critical examination and without studying for themselves to see how the conclusion was derived. The proper conclusion is that, at one point, they were keeping the covenant. Otherwise, Moses could not have said: "He hath not beheld iniquity in Jacob, neither hath he seen perverseness in Israel: the LORD his God is with him, and the shout of a king is among them" (Num. 23:21). Dare anyone say that Israel never kept the covenant when the Word of God clearly states that Israel was not committing iniquity nor perverseness? We cannot say it enough that we must let the Bible speak in its plainness and not develop doctrines nor form opinions independent of what the Bible explicitly states or implies. When this is done the meanings of entire sections or doctrines are destroyed and buried, hidden from the understanding of the congregation and out of normal reach. Then, what is worse is that when someone finally uncovers the explicit truth, the people have been conditioned to view it as unwelcome heresy or blasphemy. I pray that, as you study this book, you will also learn proper techniques for studying the Bible. For the sake of brevity, we will not go over every verse in Hebrews chapters 8 through 10 but will rather analyze the key verses. Keep in mind that context is critical in properly understanding what the Scriptures are saying. We pick up with verse 10 of Hebrews 8:

> For this is the covenant that I will make with the house of Israel after those days, saith the Lord; I will put my laws into their mind, and write them in their hearts: and I will be to them a God, and they shall be to me a people: And they shall not teach every man his neighbour, and every man his brother, saying, Know the Lord: for all shall know me, from the least to the greatest. For I will be merciful to their unrighteousness, and their sins and their iniquities will I remember no more. In that he saith, A new covenant, he hath made the first old. Now that which decayeth and waxeth old is ready to vanish away. (Heb. 8:10–13)

Here the Lord has continued to lay out His reasons for the new covenant:

"I will put my laws into their mind." We will remember the law.

"Write them in their hearts." The law will be in our heart, not on tables of stone. This is a way of saying that the law will become our nature, that we will partake of the divine nature.

"I will be to them a God." To be a God to them is to sustain, deliver, and redeem them from all temptations, trials, afflictions and problems.

"They shall be to me a people." All the people of Israel will be perpetual law-keepers with the character of their God and be ambassadors of the Lord.

"They shall not teach every man his neighbour." All will have a personal abiding relationship with the Lord. They will all have studied for themselves.

"All shall know the Lord." No more intercession will be needed. They will all know the Father by the continued keeping of the commandments, which is His name and character.

"I will be merciful to their unrighteousness, and their sins and their iniquities will I remember no more." The record of their sins will be blotted out.

## The Transitory Nature of the Old Covenant

The entire epistle of Hebrews was written to support the crucial points in chapters 8 through 10. Paul there stated that the laws about sacrifice were no more, yet nowhere does he say that the Ten Commandments were abolished. Understand that the epistle to the Hebrews was written for the purpose of giving the Hebrews, who were still clinging to an old covenant thought process and looking longingly back to the old covenant services and sacrifices, the reasons that those things were to be done no more and had no value. To continue in the rituals of the sacrificial system of offerings and ceremonies was indeed a denial of the fulfillment of that system through the sacrifice of Jesus Christ, who had come to earth and returned to heaven to prepare a place for those who believe in Him. For the Lord "to be to them a God" means sustaining, delivering, and redeeming them from all problems. The passing nature of the former covenant is encapsulated in three verses:

> For the priesthood being changed, there is made of necessity a change also of the law.... For there is verily a disannulling of the commandment going before for the weakness and unprofitableness thereof.... In that he saith, A new covenant, he hath made the first old. Now that which decayeth and waxeth old is ready to vanish away. (Heb. 7:12, 18; 8:13)

Hebrews 9 continues: "Then verily the first covenant had also ordinances of divine service, and a worldly sanctuary" (Heb. 9:1). We see here that the covenant and the "ordinances of divine service" are separate. We should take special note that the words "ordinances of divine service" point to the observance of feasts (yearly sabbath days) and the offering of sacrifices, which have been abolished. Let's clarify this even more.

Let's say that in the Old Testament times—specifically between 1491 BC (the biblical date for Exodus 12) and the birth of Christ—that an Israelite who anticipated the new covenant's being ratified by the death of Christ decided that he would only keep the ordinances of baptism and communion. In other words, what if he chose to observe the Christian symbols that are the antitype of the Passover, would he be in accordance with the laws for his time that God ordained and used to relate to His people? Would the Lord overlook the individual's failure to observe the Levitical laws, circumcision, or the Day of Atonement? No, the individual would undoubtedly be cut off; he would be killed according to the law of the time. Would the individual's life be in accord with Jesus' example when He observed, with His people, the laws that He ordained? No! Can a person be saved without Christ's being in harmony with the worship they offer? No, he or she cannot!

We know from the time prophecies of Daniel 8 and 9 that the antitypical day of Atonement, began October 22, 1844, is now going on. Where is Jesus, and what is He doing at this time? Jesus is in the Most Holy Place ministering in the service of the final Day of Atonement. If we will be in accord with Jesus, we must continually observe this antitypical feast as a way of life. If an individual is observing the Passover while Jesus is ministering for the Day of Atonement, then that individual is without Christ and without salvation. Notice what the people did under the old covenant while the priest ministered in the sanctuary:

> And it came to pass, that while he executed the priest's office before God in the order of his course, according to the custom of the priest's office, his lot was to burn incense when he went into the temple of the Lord. And the whole multitude of the people were praying without at the time of incense .... And the people waited for Zacharias, and marvelled that he tarried so long in the temple. (Luke 1:8–10, 21)

From the courtyard of the sanctuary, the people followed what the priest was doing. Under the dispensation of the old covenant, his actions represented Christ's ministry. Under the new covenant dispensation, we must follow our heavenly High Priest in like manner, or we will be without a Saviour. The services and symbols of the sanctuary have been given to us so that we would be conscious of what He is now doing for us. God in His goodness wanted us to know exactly what is being done for us according to the plan of salvation.

> Now when these things were thus ordained, the priests went always into the first tabernacle, accomplishing the service of God. But into the second went the high priest alone once every year, not without blood, which he offered for himself, and for the errors of the people: The Holy Ghost this signifying, that the way into the holiest of all was not yet made manifest, while as the first tabernacle was yet standing. (Heb. 9:6–8)

The Lord Himself acknowledges that the observance of the old covenant ordinances was "the service of God" before the way into the "the holiest of all was" "made manifest," that is, while the "first tabernacle"—the sanctuaries made by Moses and Solomon—"was yet standing."[8] The Holy Spirit

---

[8] The term "the holiest of all" refers to the heavenly sanctuary, which is literally "holy places" in the Greek, as the term is translated in Hebrews 9:24.

did not recognize the inauguration of the heavenly sanctuary until after the death of Christ. Therefore, we can see from Hebrews 9 that God Himself acknowledged the old covenant sanctuary as the proper place for worship and ministration, blessing it with His presence. We conclude that those who keep the feasts of the Old Testament are doing so without God, for they act apart from the corresponding blood sacrifices and the sanctuary that pertain to that system, and they deny the antitype, Christ, and His death on the cross with His present ministration in the holy places in heaven. Therefore, the celebrations that they attempt to keep are void of the presence of God who gave the services for the purpose of being with His people. These services were to bring the people back into right relation a literal dwelling in the material presence of God. We see from these verses, and from the ones immediately following, that, in the ministration of the old covenant, God accepted the sacrifices and services just as much as He now accepts our worship through the ministration of the new covenant. Let us follow on to see other reasons the new covenant was needed.

## Perfection and the Covenants

The next verse in the passage says: "Which was a figure for the time then present, in which were offered both gifts and sacrifices, that could not make him that did the service perfect, as pertaining to the conscience" (Heb. 9:9).

Here again, Paul points to the symbolic nature of the old covenant and its services, explaining in detail the reason for the new covenant. It is that the old covenant "could not make him that did the service perfect, as pertaining to the conscience." This passage is the second time in Hebrews that Paul has talked about a man being made perfect. His first reference to perfection was in chapter 7, verse 19, which says: "For the law made nothing perfect, but the bringing in of a better hope did; by the which we draw nigh unto God." Thus, we see that the principal purpose of the law of the new covenant is to make man perfect, for in keeping the law we are drawing near to God. We can only "draw nigh unto God" if He is ministering in the service that we are engaging in, and, if we recognize Christ's example and follow it, we are developing His character within. This is not a symbolic perfection but a living reality that fulfils the antitype.

That we can be perfect is wonderful news! Haven't you really wanted to be perfect? We have suffered remorse far too frequently as we have allowed our sinful nature to direct us despite our knowing better. Yet, our wonderful God has provided a way in which we can be perfect as we draw near to Him.

Verse 9 states that we are made perfect "as pertaining to the conscience." The statement deals with the mind and our guilt and remorse over the sins of the old man that we remember. These plague us and make it very difficult for us to continue in the strait and narrow path. Satan delights in causing us to stumble by bringing our failings to mind. However, our High Priest is continually working to cleanse us of the guilt that poisons our relationship with God. Though God, who is the offended party, has forgiven the repentant ones, we may have feelings that He has not fully accepted us. We may feel like the brothers of Joseph did toward Joseph whom they had wronged. The wonderfulness of the plan of salvation is that God wants you delivered from this too:

> And when Joseph's brethren saw that their father was dead, they said, Joseph will peradventure hate us, and will certainly requite us all the evil which we did unto him. And they sent a messenger unto Joseph, saying, Thy father did command before he died, saying, So shall ye say unto Joseph, Forgive, I pray thee now, the trespass of thy brethren, and their sin; for they did unto thee evil: and now, we pray thee, forgive the trespass of the servants of the God of thy father. And Joseph wept when they spake unto him. And his brethren also went and fell down before his face; and they said, Behold, we be thy servants. And Joseph said unto them, Fear not: for am I in the place of God? But as for you, ye thought evil against me; but God meant it unto good, to bring to pass, as it is this day, to save much people alive. Now therefore fear ye not: I will nourish you, and your little ones. And he comforted them, and spake kindly unto them. (Gen. 50:15–21)

Joseph is a type of Christ, and we see, in his story, a representation of Christ's forgiveness and acknowledgement of sin by seeing its blessing as the means the Father uses to lead to salvation. Though our sins killed Christ, the Father directs us to ask for forgiveness through Christ, and Christ, whom He commanded to die for you and I in order to forgive our wrong and atone for our salvation shows He loves us as much as the Father does. Beautiful! We need to learn where to center our attention:

> When the mind dwells upon self, it is turned away from Christ, the source of strength and life. Hence it is Satan's constant effort to keep the attention diverted from the Saviour and thus prevent the

union and communion of the soul with Christ. <u>The pleasures of the world, life's cares and perplexities and sorrows, the faults of others, or your own faults and imperfections</u>—to **any or all of these he will seek to divert the mind**. Do not be misled by his devices. Many who are really conscientious, and who desire to live for God, he too often leads to dwell upon their own faults and weaknesses, and thus by separating them from Christ he hopes to gain the victory. We should not make self the center and indulge anxiety and fear **as to whether we shall be saved**. All this turns the soul away from the Source of our strength. **Commit the keeping of your soul to God, and trust in Him**. Talk and think of Jesus. Let self be lost in Him. <u>Put away all doubt; dismiss your fears</u>. Say with the apostle Paul, "I live; yet not I, but Christ liveth in me: and the life which I now live in the flesh I live by the faith of the Son of God, who loved me, and gave Himself for me." Galatians 2:20. <u>Rest in God. He is able to **keep** that which you have **committed** to Him. If you will leave yourself in His hands, **He will bring you off more than conqueror** through Him that has loved you.</u> (*Steps to Christ*, pp. 71, 72)

Satan seeks to draw our minds away from the mighty Helper, to lead us to ponder over our degeneration of soul. But though Jesus sees the guilt of the past, He speaks pardon; and we should not dishonor Him by doubting His love. <u>The feeling of guiltiness must be laid at the foot of the cross, or it will **poison** the springs of life</u>. When Satan thrusts his threatenings upon you, turn from them, and comfort your soul with the promises of God. The cloud may be dark in itself, but when filled with the light of heaven, it turns to the brightness of gold; for the glory of God rests upon it. (*Testimonies to Ministers and Gospel Workers*, p. 518)

Andreasen commented on the perfection described in verse 9:

"Could not make him ... perfect." The difficulty which the author points out is the fact that the gifts and sacrifices offered "could not make him that did the service perfect, as pertaining to the conscience." This was a vital fault, which we have discussed elsewhere as the chief objection to the Levitical system.

God requires perfection of His people. In His opening sermon on the mount Christ declared, "Be ye therefore perfect, even as your Father which is in heaven is perfect." Matt. 5:48. Paul's hope for the church was "that ye may stand perfect and complete in all the will of God," so that "we may present every man perfect in Christ Jesus." Col. 4:12; 1:28. That this matter of perfection is a fundamental necessity in religion is clear from the statement that if "perfection were [possible] by the Levitical priesthood, ... what further need was there that another priest should rise after the order of Melchisedec?" Heb. 7:11. "The law made nothing perfect" and "can never with those sacrifices which they offered year by year continually make the comers thereunto perfect." Heb. 7:19; 10:1.

Perfection is God's goal for His people, and this could not be reached by offering gifts and sacrifices. They "could not make him that did the service perfect."

This fault was inherent in the service itself. Surely, no one can believe that the blood of an animal can atone for the sin of the soul. The forgiveness men obtained did not permanently make them any better. Day by day the people brought their sacrifices, and day by day the priest ministered the blood, and the sinner went away with the assurance of sins forgiven. But next day the service was repeated, and so throughout the year; and year after year, an endless round.

Forgiveness does not lead to perfection. A man may be forgiven a thousand times and yet keep on sinning. An Israelite might bring sacrifices to the sanctuary every day of his life, and yet never reach perfection. Even "thousands of rams" could not do this. And as perfection was the goal, something more than forgiveness must be obtained if perfection was to become possible.

There was a hint of perfection in the services of the Day of Atonement. "On that day shall the priest make an atonement for you, to cleanse you, that ye may be clean from all your sins before the Lord." Lev. 16:30. Here cleansing is brought to view. Forgiveness the people had obtained during the year through the services in the first apartment. But now a new day had come, and with that new day the promise "that ye may be clean from all your sins before the Lord." This was more than forgiveness: it was cleansing, cleansing from *all* sins.

But even this service was not satisfactory. As soon as the Day of Atonement was over, the veil again barred the way to the most holy place, and not for another year could anyone enter. Israel was given a glimpse of the possibilities before them, and then the door was closed. This showed that the way was not open, and that perfection could not be obtained by this service. Something better must be provided to reach the goal.

This something better was foreshadowed in the Old Testament. A man might inadvertently have become defiled, or perhaps have spoken unadvisedly with his lips. He confesses his sin and error, offers the appropriate sacrifice, and is forgiven. He is happy; yet he can but feel that there are other and more serious sins that need forgiveness, but which do not and can not come under the heading of unintentional sins. Led astray by his heathen neighbors, he has attended one of their festivals and participated in their Baal worship; he has profaned the Sabbath and not guarded its edges; he has coveted his neighbor's wife; he has taken God's name in vain.

These sins come to his mind and weigh him down. What can he do? Bring an offering? No; the law of sin offerings provided only for unintentional sins—with a few exceptions—and he himself feels that his sin is too great to be atoned for by an animal. Then he remembers David's sin and repentance, and that God does not want animal sacrifices or burnt offerings for such sins. He hears David say, "The sacrifices of God are a broken spirit: a broken and a contrite heart, O God, thou wilt not despise." Ps. 51:17. He bows his heart before God, confesses his sin, and is forgiven. He brings to God a broken and a contrite heart, and God hears his prayer.

David's experience shows conclusively that men in the Old Testament understood the limited value of sacrifices. How else could David say after his great sin, "Thou desirest not sacrifice; else would I give it: thou delightest not in burnt offering." Ps. 51:16. He knew that a broken heart and a contrite spirit counted with God, and not the blood of animals.

While Israel, therefore, in the sacrificial system was taught that even small errors counted, and that without shedding of blood there could be no forgiveness of sin, they also understood that the sacrifices could never make perfect them that brought them. Real forgiveness could be obtained only through confession and

> humbling of soul, as they with a broken heart and contrite spirit came before God. (Andreasen, pp. 331–334, italics in original)

Regarding the blotting out of sin, there are several pertinent biblical statements: "Repent ye therefore, and be converted, that your sins may be blotted out, when the times of refreshing shall come from the presence of the Lord" (Acts 3:19). "I, even I, am he that blotteth out thy transgressions for mine own sake, and will not remember thy sins" (Isa. 43:25). "In those days, and in that time, saith the LORD, the iniquity of Israel shall be sought for, and there shall be none; and the sins of Judah, and they shall not be found: for I will pardon them whom I reserve" (Jer. 50:20). The new earth will not be a place to lament the pain of the past. The good news, the gospel, is that here on earth, before the second coming of Christ, we will have consciences clear of guilt and remorse and that heaven will be just a continuation of the victories gained on earth. "For, behold, I create new heavens and a new earth: and the former shall not be remembered, nor come into mind" (Isa. 65:17). We will read more about this next.

## The Purging of the Conscience

Today we are to rest by faith in God's promise that we are "accepted in the beloved" (Eph. 1:6)—we are accepted in God's Son—until the day that the Lord brings the promise of the new covenant to complete fulfillment (see Heb. 8:10–12). At that time, God will have blotted out our sins from the records of heaven and purged our consciences. Because, in His greatness and grace, God wanted us to grasp these things, He did not mention them only once or twice. Notice also Hebrews 9 continues explaining in greater detail:

> But Christ being come an high priest of good things to come, by a greater and more perfect tabernacle, not made with hands, that is to say, not of this building; neither by the blood of goats and calves, but by his own blood he entered in once into the holy place, having obtained eternal redemption for us. For if the blood of bulls and of goats, and the ashes of an heifer sprinkling the unclean, sanctifieth to the purifying of the flesh: How much more shall the blood of Christ, who through the eternal Spirit offered himself without spot to God, purge your conscience from dead works to serve the living God? (Heb. 9:11–14)

Andreasen appropriately comments on the phrase, "An high priest of good things to come":

> The old ceremonies have been enumerated in the preceding verses. The good things to come are the promises of the gospel: forgiveness, sanctification, victory over sin, everlasting righteousness, holiness; **not merely in figure, but in reality**. (Andreasen, pp. 335, 336)

That sin actually defiles is something little thought of. There is a need for cleansing, so God built a sanctuary in heaven to eliminate sin. The story of Jesus in Gethsemane is not just a great story about God in the flesh overcoming the powers of darkness. The literal physical sins of all who were ever alive on earth and those to be created were literally and physically placed on Jesus. This literal element of the item of sin placed on Him was not simply spiritual. There was a literal, physical placement, a transfer of our sins onto Christ, the sacrifice for you and me. God the Father didn't pretend to separate from Jesus. He had to actually separate from Him because of His position and His holiness. Thus, sin will also be literally and physically destroyed. The sanctuary shows this symbolically but even falls short because this is something mortal man cannot see. The first cleansing is by water, the second by blood, and the final destruction is by fire. This is also represented in the three great dispensations—in the time of Noah, in the time of Moses, and in the final dispensation announced by John the Baptist regarding baptism by fire. Water can clean to a limited extent. The dirt is removed, but it is transferred to another place. Blood covers and signifies the surety, a substitute life for the sinner but doesn't really clean. Fire, however, destroys. Thus, there is finally an actual elimination of sin from the universe.

There is a real need for the sanctuary. So there is a real sanctuary in heaven. Many think that there is no need for a sanctuary because there is nothing to clean in heaven. Well, Jesus really died on the cross because the law was really broken, and there would be no sin if there were no real law. If there were no law, of course you wouldn't really need to be saved because you would already be perfect and holy. But I believe that you're reading this book because you want real and not merely symbolic victory. You can feel real consequences from your sins. Sin will really kill you if its effect and consequences are not removed. Therefore, there is a real need for a sanctuary that has really been defiled.

The sanctuary is a symbolic representation of spiritual realities to give mankind a conception of what God is actually doing in heaven through the life and ministry of Jesus for you. Let's look at some examples of where the spiritual curtain has been removed to allow us to see some of the spiritual realities.

> Then again the scene mentioned above passed before me. I saw that the woman was a true disciple of Christ; her **faith** was that she should be healed. **I saw their prayers**: one was misty, dark, fell downward. The other prayer was mixed with light or specks which looked to me like **diamonds**, and arose upward to Jesus and He sent it up to His Father like sweet incense, and **a beam of light** was immediately sent to the afflicted one and she revived and strengthened under its influence. Said the angel, **God will gather every particle of true, sincere faith; like diamonds shall they be gathered up and will surely bring a return or answer**; and God will separate the precious from the vile. Although He bears long with the hypocrite and sinner, yet he will be searched out. Though he may flourish with the honest a while like the green bay tree, yet the time will come when his folly will be made manifest (Letter 2, 1851). (*Seventh-day Adventist Bible Commentary*, vol. 7, p. 939)

Dear reader, your prayers are not just words or invisible wishes. They are literally gathered and presented to God the Father. The angels are not doing imaginary work, and neither is Jesus doing imaginary work in the heavenly sanctuary. The altar of incense actually receives some physical element of your prayer.

> 88. The same sins exist in our day which brought the wrath of God upon the world in the days of Noah. Men and women now carry their eating and drinking to gluttony and drunkenness. This prevailing sin, the indulgence of perverted appetite, inflamed the passions of men in the days of Noah, and led to general corruption, until **their violence and crimes reached to heaven**, and God washed the earth of its moral pollution by a flood. (*Counsels on Diet and Foods*, p. 60)

The end of the first cleansing dispensation was the Flood. The final cleansing will be with fire. We see above that the sins of the wicked actually reached to heaven.

> Angels were sent to aid the mighty angel from heaven, and I heard voices which seemed to sound everywhere, "Come out of her, My people, that ye be not partakers of her sins, and that ye receive not of her plagues. <u>For her sins have **reached** unto heaven, and God hath remembered her iniquities.</u>" This message seemed to be an addition to the third message, joining it as the midnight cry joined the second angel's message in 1844. The glory of God rested upon the patient, waiting saints, and they fearlessly gave the last solemn warning, proclaiming the fall of Babylon and calling upon God's people to come out of her that they might escape her fearful doom. (*Early Writings*, pp. 277, 278)

It may then be asked, "When do sins reach to heaven?" There are two ways:

The prophet says: "I saw another angel flying." Yes, in reality! Sin has really made us filthy and defiled the heavenly sanctuary, but Christ's ministry in the heavenly sanctuary will really cleanse the sanctuary, and we will really be pure, really be cleansed of all that has defiled us in thought, word, and action. I asked above, "Haven't you ever wanted to be perfect?" or, said another way, "Haven't you wanted to be truly forgiven, sanctified, eternally victorious, and holy?" That we are purified through Christ's ministry is good—really good! The Lord could have left off the rest of the epistle to the Hebrews, but He wanted us to have hope, trust, and faith in His power and determination to save us. We continue with Andreasen's comments on "eternal redemption":

> Eternal redemption is in contrast with the redemption and temporary atonement that the high priest of old obtained for the people. The atonement as well as the forgiveness provided in the sanctuary service was provisional and temporary, and needed to be repeated. Christ's atonement and redemption are everlasting, as is His righteousness. These are the "good things" that Christ came to bring. (Andreasen, p. 347)

The new covenant is eternal. Everything in the old covenant—the sacrifices, the offerings, and the ceremonies—was temporary except for the law of the Ten Commandments, also referred to as "the testimony" inside of the ark of the covenant. Because of their significance, they are the foundation of the throne of God and the transcript of His character. In referring to the new covenant, most Christians forget that the Lord said: "… this shall be the covenant that I will make with the house of Israel; after those days, saith the LORD, I will put my law in their inward parts, and write it in their hearts; and will be their God, and they shall be my people" (Jer. 31:33). The covenant that the Lord has given us combines with the law, He covenants that He will write the law on our hearts. Only when the law is part of our nature are we the people of God and is He our God. Remember Romans 8:7, 8: "Because the carnal mind is enmity against God: for it is not subject to the law of God, neither indeed can be. So then they that are in the flesh cannot please God." Yet, faithful students of the Bible must ask, "To which law is Jeremiah referring?" It must be a law that already existed in the Old Testament, for Jeremiah gives no clue that there will be a different law in the future or that there will be a change in the Ten Commandments that God Himself authorized. We know for certain that the commandments were the standard by which God judged the children of Israel. For God to be just, He would need to maintain the same standard of judgment for all who have had to battle sin in this world. It would not even matter whether He liked the law that He gave. To uphold justice, the same law—the same standard—must be maintained. We will not go into detail about the commandments themselves, for there are many studies on the topic for the honest-hearted seeker.

The focal point of verse 14 is that the blood of the covenant—Christ's blood—will "purge your conscience from dead works to serve the living God." Notice Andreasen's comments:

> "Purge your conscience." Christ's work is here viewed not as a past act but as a present reality. Christ did a definite work on the cross in obtaining redemption for us, but that work and that redemption need to be applied to the individual soul. Our consciences must be purged from dead works to serve the living God; and this is a present, constant work needful in every generation. Those who claim that Christ's work was finished on the cross fail to take into consideration the continued, daily application of the blood necessary to man's salvation. No more than God created the world and set it in motion, and then left it to run by itself, does Christ by one act on Calvary set redemption in motion, and then leave it to work by itself. The slaying of the sacrificial lamb in the sanctuary was a definite act which provided the means of reconciliation, the blood. But the blood had to be ministered to be efficacious, and the ministration was equally vital with the death. The blood shed on Calvary is mighty to the cleansing and purifying of the conscience from dead works, not as a past act merely, but as a living, present reality.

> "To serve." God's work in the soul has a definite end in view. Our lives, our consciences, are purged that we may serve. To have our sins forgiven that we may have a clear conscience is not an end in itself, wonderful though that is. We are saved to serve, purged to serve. (Andreasen, pp. 350, 351)

The purpose of the deliverance of redemption is that we may serve God fully as God intended in our creation and that we may cooperate in the redemption of our fellow human beings. This will be accomplished before the close of probation, though the Lord wishes even today to purge our guilt so we may rest in the comfort of a blessed relationship with Him. He wants us to be free from sin that we might become servants of righteousness. Paul stated this twice in Romans 6: "Being then made free from sin, ye became the servants of righteousness" (Rom. 6:18). "But now being made free from sin, and become servants to God, ye have your fruit unto holiness, and the end everlasting life" (Rom. 6:22). God gave us his covenant which when we choose to live by it, this transforms our mind, as Paul declared: "I beseech you therefore, brethren, by the mercies of God, that ye present your bodies a living sacrifice, holy, acceptable unto God, which is your reasonable service. And be not conformed to this world: but be ye transformed by the renewing of your mind, that ye may prove what is that good, and acceptable, and perfect, will of God" (Rom. 12:1, 2).

## The New Covenant Is Jesus' Will and Testament

Paul goes on in Hebrews to identify the new *covenant* as the new *testament*:

> And for this cause he is the mediator of the new testament, that by means of death, for the redemption of the transgressions that were under the first testament, they which are called might receive the promise of eternal inheritance. For where a testament is, there must also of necessity be the death of the testator. For a testament is of force after men are dead: otherwise it is of no strength at all while the testator liveth. (Heb. 9:15–17)

Paul used "testament," another word for "covenant," in the sense of a will. In other words, the testament, or covenant law, is not changeable after the death of the one who made it. If a change is to be made, it must be done while the testator is living so that he can approve of the agreement that will be executed upon his death.

We see here that Jesus made provision for those who died under the old covenant, the first testament, so that they might take part in the promises of the new covenant, though they were not alive when it went into effect. Hebrews goes on to describe the correlation between the pattern of the earthly sanctuary with the heavenly reality:

> It was therefore necessary that the patterns of things in the heavens should be purified with these; but the heavenly things themselves with better sacrifices than these. For Christ is not entered into the holy places made with hands, which are the figures of the true; but into heaven itself, now to appear in the presence of God for us. (Heb. 9:23, 24)

Paul is affirming the reality that there is a sanctuary in heaven and that it must be purified, just as we, the subjects needing redemption, are purified by the blood of Jesus.[9] Dear reader, please know, this purification, this cleansing is spiritual and unseen by us, but it is in practical reality a literal-physical cleansing from sin. Though the mortal eye cannot see it take place, it is nonetheless necessary. Scripture declares that Jesus is appearing face to face on your behalf in the actual presence of God the Father. His heavenly ministry is so that you can stand purified in the actual presence of God the Father after Jesus receives us in the clouds of glory so you can see the smile of God the Father face to face for yourself.

> And he shewed me a pure river of water of life, clear as crystal, proceeding out of the throne of God and of the Lamb. In the midst of the street of it, and on either side of the river, was there the tree of life, which bare twelve manner of fruits, and yielded her fruit every month: and the leaves of the tree were for the healing of the nations. And there shall be no more curse: but the throne of God and of the Lamb shall be in it; and his servants shall serve him: And they shall see his face; and his name shall be in their foreheads. (Rev. 22:1–4)

---

[9] The purification here described is the parallel to the purification of the sanctuary at its inauguration (compare Heb. 9:19, 21 with Exod. 24:6, 8).

CHAPTER 7

# A Shadow of Things to Come

> Just as I am, and waiting not
> To rid my soul of one dark blot,
> To Thee whose blood can cleanse each spot,
> O Lamb of God, I come.
> —Charlotte Elliot[10]

In this chapter, we will finish our study in Hebrews 10 regarding the reasons that the new covenant was needed to replace the old covenant. Chapter 10 of Hebrews begins with the crowning point of the epistle: explaining why the new covenant is necessary.

We will let the Bible itself tell us with its direct explicit words why God has given us a new covenant. With honest and thorough study of the Scriptures, a person cannot fail to see the truth, for the Bible states it quite plainly. God could not afford to leave matters of this importance ambiguous. Preachers of false doctrine often give what appears to be an honest Bible study. However, in reality, it is the superficial repetition of Bible verses explained by tradition. Error cannot endure the scrutiny of close examination. Superficial Bible study and false professions abound because the gospel is explained in a "I don't have to do anything," "cheap grace" false security. But those who desire victory will joyfully receive the grace given them, employing it to the

---

[10] Charlotte Elliot, "Just As I Am, Without One Plea," Hymnary, https://1ref.us/1kz (accessed February 17, 2021).

glory of God. Then and only then will the Almighty be seen in our lives as the God of love who is stronger than Satan.

The sad truth is that those who teach the false doctrine of grace declare that Satan is right, that he speaks the truth, and that he is stronger than the Creator. This false doctrine of grace implies that those who are saved by grace do not need to walk the strait and narrow path, nor can their sins be removed. Oh how awful will the results of that work be in the time of trouble!

Let us continue with Andreasen's introduction to Hebrews 10:

> Christ nowhere decreed the abolition of the sacrificial law. <u>Paul, on the other hand, is very emphatic that the ceremonial law is abrogated. It therefore becomes incumbent on the apostle to give weighty reasons for his position.</u> **If he can show that Christ brought in perfection, which the Levitical law could not and did not do, he has scored a decisive point; for cessation of sin would not only make sin offering unnecessary, but also the law which demanded them.** The vital point is to show that Christ came to do away with sin. If Paul can do this, he needs no more proof of the annulment of the law that required sin offerings. There would be no need of such a law.
>
> Admittedly the work in the first apartment of the earthly sanctuary was unsatisfactory, because it had to be repeated day by day. <u>The apostle shows that the work in the second apartment was</u> equally inadequate, in that while it did temporarily and pro-<u>visionally blot out sin, the service had to be repeated year after year,</u> **showing that it was not a permanent work**. (Andreasen, pp. 418, 419)

Hebrews 10 begins:

> For the law having a shadow of good things to come, and not the very image of the things, can never with those sacrifices which they offered year by year continually make the comers thereunto perfect. For then would they not have ceased to be offered? because that the worshippers once purged should have had no more conscience of sins. But in those sacrifices there is a remembrance again made of sins every year. For it is not possible that the blood of bulls and of goats should take away sins. (Heb. 10:1–4)

## Symbols of Salvation

The shadow "of good things to come" provides symbols of the plan of salvation and of Christ. Yet, the key point here is that the shadow found in the old covenant could "never with those sacrifices which they offered year by year continually make the comers thereunto perfect." The new covenant, on the other hand, can indeed make the believer "continually ... thereunto perfect." The transformation is real and literal, as we mentioned before, for the blood of Jesus actually cleanses us from sin. It will purge from us all abomination, transgression, idolatry, iniquity, and sin. In our conscience, thoughts, words, and actions, we will be perfect. God will have for Himself a redeemed people reflecting His holy law, the Ten Commandments, which is the emblem of His character. Paul's statement only confirms what the Old Testament prophets predicted.

Thus far, we have shown the reasons for the new covenant as given in Hebrews 7 to 9. In Hebrews 6, Paul had nailed down the purpose of the new covenant, emphasizing God's omnipotence. These reasons form a litmus test that shows the deficiency of other views of the gospel, a lack of belief in the omnipotence of God. Again, I ask: Haven't you ever wanted to be perfect? Isaiah tells you of the end product of the new covenant. "I will make a man more precious than fine gold; even a man than the golden wedge of Ophir" (Isa. 13:12). There are other indications of God's work in the perfecting of His people: "God is my strength and power: and he maketh my way perfect" (2 Sam. 22:33). "... and his love is perfected in us" (1 John 4:12). God's people are very precious to Him. He declares: "And they shall be mine, saith the LORD of hosts, in that day when I make up my jewels; and I will spare them, as a man spareth his own son that serveth him" (Mal. 3:17).

Hebrews 10:2 reiterates the reason for the new covenant, "For then would they *[the sacrifices]* not have ceased to be offered? because that the worshippers once purged should have had no more conscience of sins." We actually need God's purging, which is not some make believe cleansing. Daniel 8:14 is a true cleansing of the sanctuary in heaven. From October 22, 1844 forward, there has been a physical cleansing of believers through the health message, which calls for the use of fruits, vegetables, nuts, and grains instead of animal products, and the observance of all the eight laws of health, and it calls for the spiritual cleansing of the body, mind, and soul. In cleansing His people individually, the Lord will have effectively reached His objective in the redemption of mankind and in the production of a pure, victorious, triumphant church in the last and weakest generation. This concept may be hard to grasp, but it may be easier to understand in light of Wi-Fi or satellite signals. We may not be able see or hear beyond certain frequencies. Nonetheless, a document can be digitized, physically transmitted through Wi-Fi signals, and received and turned into a document, image, or video. Though invisible to the human senses, it is scientifically quantifiable in transmission and reception.

"And an highway shall be there, and a way, and it shall be called The way of holiness; the unclean shall not pass over it; but it shall be for those: the wayfaring men, though fools, shall not err therein" (Isa. 35:8). Therefore, "Awake, awake; put on thy strength, O Zion; put on thy beautiful garments, O Jerusalem, the holy city: for henceforth there shall no more come into thee the uncircumcised and the unclean" (Isa. 52:1) because, "In that day there shall be a fountain opened to the house of David and to the inhabitants of Jerusalem for sin and for uncleanness. And it shall come to pass in that day, saith the LORD of hosts, that I will cut off the names of the idols out of the land, and they shall no more be remembered: and also I will cause the prophets and the unclean spirit to pass out of the land" (Zech. 13:1, 2). Then, "In those days, and in that time, saith the LORD, the iniquity of Israel shall be sought for, and there shall be none; and the sins of Judah, and they shall not be found: for I will pardon them whom I reserve" (Jer. 50:20).

Andreasen comments on the reason for the covenant found in Hebrews 10:2:

> **Verse 2.** "Would they not have ceased to be offered?" The chief weakness of the sanctuary service, as has been noted before, was that it did not and could not "make the comers thereunto perfect." This was evident in the very plan itself, which provided for a yearly recurring service. If the sacrifices had accomplished their intended purpose, "would they not have ceased to be offered? because that the worshippers once purged should have had no more conscience of sins." But as soon as the yearly round of services ended, another round began that culminated in another Day of Atonement. No sooner were the expiatory services on the Day of Atonement concluded than the evening sacrifice began again, the lamb was killed, and the blood sprinkled—all showing that even the great atonement which had been made that day had not accomplished its purpose; it had not made the worshipers perfect. They still needed atonement, and a year from that day they would repeat the entire

service, thereby admitting its inefficiency to accomplish perfection or sanctification.

"Would they not have ceased to be offered?" is an interesting and far-reaching question, and the writer so puts it as to demand an affirmative answer: they *would have* ceased to be offered because the worshipers once purged would have had no more conscience of sin. (Andreasen, pp. 419, 420, emphasis in original)

Why would someone keep a feast or perform a ceremony or sacrifice that could not accomplish that which it symbolized? Once the antitype is in effect, it behooves a person to do that which God requires for his or her eternal salvation. The Lord had a purpose in having the children of Israel build a sanctuary and perform the services appropriate for the time. It was to point their minds to the one great Antitype in faith. Now that the "fountain" is opened for cleansing, let us "therefore come boldly unto the throne of grace *[in heaven]*, that we may obtain mercy, and find grace to help in time of need" (Heb. 4:16). The Bible is clear that there is now a way being ministered for you, that there is an opening into heaven itself through the services in the heavenly sanctuary. You can choose Jesus to be a literal representative for you before the throne of God. God considers you as virtually there, as Jesus speaks for you. Thus, you can come boldly unto the throne of grace.

In the very symbolism of the sanctuary service, the Lord in His wisdom indicated that, when the antitypical Lamb of God should die for the sins of the world, God's people were to no longer partake of the sanctuary services or offerings. To partake of an offering outside of the appropriate time is an abomination to God. It is a sin meriting being cut off—a death sentence in the eyes of God because it is an act of unbelief in the method of salvation given for the time. The Lord has done everything in His power to let the people know when to worship and how to receive His gifts and the conditions under which He gives them.

> And ye shall let nothing of it remain until the morning; and that which remaineth of it until the morning ye shall burn with fire. And thus shall ye eat it; with your loins girded, your shoes on your feet, and your staff in your hand; and ye shall eat it in haste: it is the LORD's passover. (Exod. 12:10, 11)
>
> And the flesh of the sacrifice of his peace offerings for thanksgiving shall be eaten the same day that it is offered; he shall not leave any of it until the morning. But if the sacrifice of his offering

> be a vow, or a voluntary offering, it shall be eaten the same day that he offereth his sacrifice: and on the morrow also the remainder of it shall be eaten: But the remainder of the flesh of the sacrifice on the third day shall be burnt with fire. And if any of the flesh of the sacrifice of his peace offerings be eaten at all on the third day, it shall not be accepted, neither shall it be imputed unto him that offereth it: it shall be an abomination, and the soul that eateth of it shall bear his iniquity. (Lev. 7:15–18)
>
> And if ye offer a sacrifice of peace offerings unto the LORD, ye shall offer it at your own will. It shall be eaten the same day ye offer it, and on the morrow: and if ought remain until the third day, it shall be burnt in the fire. And if it be eaten at all on the third day, it is abominable; it shall not be accepted. Therefore every one that eateth it shall bear his iniquity, because he hath profaned the hallowed thing of the LORD: and that soul shall be cut off from among his people. (Lev. 19:5–8)

From the beginning of time, the Lord has given His people times to observe—whether that be prophetic time or occasions for worship—and He clearly indicates what is appropriate and acceptable to Him. The ancient Israelites should have understood that there was to be a resurrection of the Messiah on the third day through this symbolism. But they forgot, and even some today are blind to this. At the beginning of time, mankind fell into sin and rebelled, as Cain later rebelled, when he chose not to worship in the appropriate manner. Please pray about these issues—issues that you may be dealing with in your life. Surrender your sacrifice, worship, life, and soul to the Lord in prayer that they may be acceptable to Him. Your redemption depends on it.

## Christ, the Sacrificial Lamb

I was taught that a lamb that is laid on its side will not move from that position. It is not like a cat or a dog, which will get up against the will of its master. A lamb will lie on its side in submission. Why is this significant? On the day of Passover, in the year the antitypical Lamb of God was sacrificed, there were two lambs offered. One was offered by the Lord God and Saviour Jesus Christ; the other was offered by the high priest of ancient Israel in the temple at Jerusalem. Would God accept both offerings? Were both needed? Who obtained the favor of the Lord on that day according to the feast kept at that time? You may answer: It was the eleven apostles. And you would be right, for there can be only one offering accepted, otherwise there would be more than one road to salvation. Let's take another look at the account of that day from the Testimony of Jesus:

> Amid the awful darkness, apparently forsaken of God, Christ had drained the last dregs in the cup of human woe. <u>In those dreadful hours **He had relied upon the evidence of His Father's acceptance heretofore given Him**</u>. He was acquainted with the **character** of His Father; He understood His **justice**, His **mercy**, and His great **love**. <u>By faith He rested in Him</u> whom it had ever been His joy to obey. And as in submission He committed Himself to God, the sense of the loss of His Father's favor was withdrawn. By faith, Christ was victor.
>
> Never before had the earth witnessed such a scene. The multitude stood paralyzed, and with bated breath gazed upon the Saviour. Again darkness settled upon the earth, and a hoarse rumbling, like heavy thunder, was heard. There was a violent earthquake. The people were shaken together in heaps. The wildest confusion and consternation ensued. In the surrounding mountains, rocks were rent asunder, and went crashing down into the plains. Sepulchers were broken open, and the dead were cast out of their tombs. Creation seemed to be shivering to atoms. Priests, rulers, soldiers, executioners, and people, mute with terror, lay prostrate upon the ground.
>
> When the loud cry, "It is finished," came from the lips of Christ, the priests were officiating in the temple. It was the hour of the evening sacrifice. The lamb representing Christ had been brought to be slain. Clothed in his significant and beautiful dress, the priest stood with lifted knife, as did Abraham when he was about to slay his son. With intense interest the people were looking on. <u>But the earth trembles and quakes; for the Lord Himself draws near</u>. **With a rending noise the inner veil of the temple is torn from top to bottom by an unseen hand, throwing open to the gaze of the multitude a place once filled with the presence of God.** In this place the Shekinah had dwelt. Here God had manifested His glory above the mercy seat. No one but the high priest ever lifted the veil separating this apartment from the rest of the temple. He entered in once a year to make an atonement for the sins of the people.

> But lo, this veil is rent in twain. **The most holy place of the earthly sanctuary is no longer sacred.**
>
> All is terror and confusion. The priest is about to slay the victim; but the knife drops from his nerveless hand, and the **lamb escapes**. Type has met antitype in the death of God's Son. The great sacrifice has been made. The way into the holiest is laid open. A new and living way is prepared for all. No longer need sinful, sorrowing humanity await the coming of the high priest. Henceforth the Saviour was to officiate as priest and advocate in the heaven of heavens. It was as if a living voice had spoken to the worshipers: **There is now an end to all sacrifices and offerings for sin**. The Son of God is come according to His word, "Lo, I come (in the volume of the Book it is written of Me,) to do Thy will, O God." "By His own blood" He entereth "in once into the holy place, having obtained eternal redemption for us." Heb. 10:7; 9:12. (*The Desire of Ages*, pp. 756, 757)

We see in Hebrews 9:8 and 10:19–23 that the death of Jesus, which had been prophesied 4,000 years before, was the event needed to end the ceremonial law, its sacrifices, and its services.

> The Holy Ghost this signifying, that the way into the holiest of all was not yet made manifest, while as the first tabernacle was yet standing: ... Having therefore, brethren, boldness to enter into the holiest by the blood of Jesus, By a new and living way, which he hath consecrated for us, through the veil, that is to say, his flesh; and having an high priest over the house of God; let us draw near with a true heart in full assurance of faith, having our hearts sprinkled from an evil conscience, and our bodies washed with pure water. Let us hold fast the profession of our faith without wavering; (for he is faithful that promised;) (Heb. 9:8; 10:19–23)

Dear reader, "hold fast" your faith, the Apostle says, "draw near with a true heart in full assurance of faith, having" your heart "sprinkled from an evil conscience," and your body "washed with pure water" "for He is faithful that promised" (Heb. 10:22, 23). Over and over the Bible implores us to have confidence in the acceptance we have in the Lord through Christ. With assurance and boldness, we can enter into the Most Holy Place in the heavenly sanctuary through the blood of Jesus who intercedes for us and speaks for us as we pray in His name to the Father as He taught us to do. We have without question a better covenant!

## The Limitations of the Shadows

In verse 4, Paul seals the point and the ultimate goal of the new covenant: "For it is not possible that the blood of bulls and of goats should take away sins" (Heb. 10:4). The blood of a bull or a goat has no righteousness connected with it, neither does it have a will like a higher being, and they did not choose to create man or die for him. Therefore, it is not possible for their blood to take away sins, but "the blood of Jesus Christ his Son" does cleanse "us from all sin" (1 John 1:7). Christ's sacrifice is the true sacrifice, and His blood is the blood that is needed for the redemption of mankind. Man could not be redeemed by an angel, much less an animal. Therefore, we now see that the ceremonial law was "a shadow of good things to come, and not the very image of the things, [which] can never with those sacrifices which they offered year by year continually make the comers thereunto perfect" (Heb. 10:1).

We then conclude that the reasons the old covenant, with its sacrificial system and ceremonies, ended at the cross were:

- It made nothing perfect.
- It was symbolic, a shadow.
- They were not the "very image," that is, the exact representation, of the represented item.
- It could not purge the conscience.
- A dead animal could not speak or mediate for us before God the Father.
- It could not make people continually perfect.
- It could not take away sin.

Conversely, the reasons the new covenant was needed are:

- Perfection of mankind is a necessity for salvation.
- Christ's priesthood is eternal.
- The law will be in the heart and minds of the people.
- Every man will know God personally.
- God will not remember our sins.
- Our conscience will be purged of guilt and remorse.
- We are cleansed by Christ's blood to serve the living God.

- Only one offering was needed to put away sin, and that was Christ's.
- It will make us continually perfect.
- It takes away sin.
- It is a real cleansing that is both spiritual and physical.

We simply extracted the points as stated in the Bible. Let us allow Paul to finish the context of the matter:

> In burnt offerings and sacrifices for sin thou hast had no pleasure. Then said I, Lo, I come (in the volume of the book it is written of me,) to do thy will, O God. Above when he said, Sacrifice and offering and burnt offerings and offering for sin thou wouldest not, neither hadst pleasure therein; which are offered by the law; then said he, Lo, I come to do thy will, O God. He taketh away the first, that he may establish the second. By the which will we are sanctified through the offering of the body of Jesus Christ once for all. And every priest standeth daily ministering and offering oftentimes the same sacrifices, which can never take away sins: But this man, after he had offered one sacrifice for sins for ever, sat down on the right hand of God; from henceforth expecting till his enemies be made his footstool. For by one offering he hath perfected for ever them that are sanctified. Whereof the Holy Ghost also is a witness to us: for after that he had said before, This is the covenant that I will make with them after those days, saith the Lord, I will put my laws into their hearts, and in their minds will I write them; and their sins and iniquities will I remember no more. Now where remission of these is, there is no more offering for sin. (Heb. 10:6–18)

The following quotations illustrate this crown jewel of the plan of salvation. Dear reader, the plan of salvation is not just to sin and repent. It is the actual removal of our poisoned memories of guilt and remorse. Only the true and full gospel has this component.

There is an important element in our salvation that no other denomination or religion has: sin is blotted out or removed from the sanctuary in heaven and from our mind; the consciousness of guilt is eliminated, our intimate relationship with God is fully restored, with the feeling of entire trust, confidence, and acceptance. The old covenant did not and could not provide all of this, for this component was significantly lacking.

Satan seeks to draw our minds away from the mighty Helper, to lead us to ponder over our degeneration of soul. But though Jesus sees the guilt of the past, He speaks pardon; and we should not dishonor Him by doubting His love. <u>The feeling of **guiltiness** must be laid at the foot of the cross, or it will **poison** the springs of life.</u> When Satan thrusts his threatenings upon you, turn from them, and comfort your soul with the promises of God. The cloud may be dark in itself, but when filled with the light of heaven, it turns to the brightness of gold; for the glory of God rests upon it. (*Testimonies to Ministers and Gospel Workers,* p. 518.3)

Had not Jacob previously repented of his sin in obtaining the birthright by fraud, God would not have heard his prayer and mercifully preserved his life. So, in the time of trouble, if the people of God had unconfessed sins to appear before them while tortured with fear and anguish, they would be overwhelmed; despair would cut off their faith, and they could not have confidence to plead with God for deliverance. <u>But while they have a deep sense of their unworthiness,</u> **they have no concealed wrongs to reveal**. <u>Their sins have gone beforehand to judgment and have been blotted out</u>, **and they cannot bring them to remembrance**. (*The Great Controversy*, p. 620.1)

## God's Absolute Will is Perfect Holiness

Many forget that the absolute will of God never was for sin to exist, yet God provided His covenant as a safety valve to restore order and vindicate His name and, ultimately, to put an end to sin forever. Even while sin reigns in this world, the will of God is that we never have to sacrifice to ask for forgiveness of sin. David remembered this and recorded it to remind us: "For thou desirest not sacrifice; else would I give it: thou delightest not in burnt offering. The sacrifices of God are a broken spirit: a broken and a contrite heart, O God, thou wilt not despise" (Ps. 51:16, 17). Paul clarifies what the Lord wants you to bring and what will be accepted: "I beseech you therefore, brethren, by the mercies of God, that ye present your bodies a living sacrifice, holy, acceptable unto God, which is your reasonable service" (Rom. 12:1).

The acceptable sacrifice we can offer the Lord, which He will receive, is a perfect, holy, and righteous life. Remember that Abraham's vow, which we take when we accept Christ as our God and Saviour, was "perpetual obedience." The vow of perpetual obedience is the covenant that God agreed to, and it is the only covenant that He will accept. If God were ever to change, He would no longer be holy. Yet, by allowing us to see the alternative path of Satan, He allows us to choose whether we want God's way or the way of the world and Satan. This choice allows us to see a distinct difference between the two ways of life. When, by faith, we live as the Lord has asked us to do, the purpose of our life becomes living out His absolute will. God's desire is that we live within His absolute will so that one day we will dwell in His direct presence as the angels now dwell with Him. He "that dwellest between the cherubims" calls you to come near. "Let us therefore come boldly unto the throne of grace, that we may obtain mercy, and find grace to help in time of need" (Heb. 4:16). "Herein is our love made perfect, that we may have boldness in the day of judgment: because as he is, so are we in this world" (1 John 4:17). Because we are accepted in the Beloved, we can boldly go today into the presence of God the Father in whose dwelling no sin can exist, and then we ourselves will also appear face to face and eye to eye before God in the New Jerusalem.

> Blessed is that man that maketh the LORD his trust, and respecteth not the proud, nor such as turn aside to lies. Many, O LORD my God, are thy wonderful works which thou hast done, and thy thoughts which are to us-ward: they cannot be reckoned up in order unto thee: if I would declare and speak of them, they are more than can be numbered. Sacrifice and offering thou didst not desire; mine ears hast thou opened: burnt offering and sin offering hast thou not required. Then said I, Lo, I come: in the volume of the book it is written of me, I delight to do thy will, O my God: yea, thy law is within my heart. (Ps. 40:4–8)

Marvel at these wonderful promises! We are blessed when we make the Lord our trust and do not favor the proud or the deceitful. David again makes clear here that the Lord does not want sacrifices. For modern Israel, continued sacrifices would mean the continual need of forgiveness. Yet, is confession of sins all the Lord desires? Scripture says that He wants our ears open and He wants us to delight to do His will and have His law within our heart (Ps. 40:8). To "delight to do" His will is not hard to understand. It means that we are to have delight in doing that which the Lord wrote for us to do. Consider how it is that human beings, given over to sin, love the acts of wickedness so much that they return again and again to do the same things, centering their life around these objects of pleasure. Would it not be wonderful, and even prudent, to be as devoted, as we are to pleasure, in matters of righteousness? When we consider a law written on the heart, we understand that a law is a rule to function by, principles to govern, to make a judgment, a decision. When we understand that in nature, gravity maintains its force by a law, we could also understand that the law written on the heart would be the rule by which the heart would actually function. In fact we say, "That's nature," or we simply call the functions of nature "the law of nature." Therefore, the law of God written on the heart is God's message to you that His law will be made part of your nature. Of course, unlike nature, your partaking of the divine nature is by choice (2 Peter 1:4). This law then is never deviated from just as gravity never fluctuates—not as a law for inanimate objects but acting by our own will.

## Choosing God's Way with Ears Open to Hear

I particularly want to look at and bring to your attention the phrase, "mine ears hast thou opened." In a good reference Bible, you will find in the marginal reading notation that the word "opened" could be translated "digged." The margin will also refer the reader to Exodus 21:6 for the scriptural understanding of this word. We will look at the context from verses 2 to 6:

> If thou buy an Hebrew servant, six years he shall serve: and in the seventh he shall go out free for nothing. If he came in by himself, he shall go out by himself: if he were married, then his wife shall go out with him. If his master have given him a wife, and she have born him sons or daughters; the wife and her children shall be her master's, and he shall go out by himself. And if the servant shall plainly say, I love my master, my wife, and my children; I will not go out free: Then his master shall bring him unto the judges; he shall also bring him to the door, or unto the door post; and his master shall bore his ear through with an aul; and he shall serve him for ever. (Exod. 21:2–6)

Are we not either servants of sin or servants of God? In this world, we have been given the opportunity to investigate both alternatives that we may choose whom we will serve. "Know ye not, that to whom ye yield yourselves servants to obey, his servants ye are to whom ye obey; whether of sin unto death, or of obedience unto righteousness?" (Rom. 6:16).

The Lord gave the ancient Israelites the spiritual object lesson of the slave who gave willing life-long service to his master as an explanation of the rendering of willing service to the Lord, the righteous Master. God desires that His people trust "every word that proceedeth out of the mouth of God." What a deep impression this lesson makes even to this day! Imagine a slave loving his master so much that he would willingly commit himself to remain under his master's rule, demands, and commands for the rest of his life. Why would he do that? It is because he has seen how good his master's decisions are and how prudent, wise, fair, caring, and loving has been his master's treatment to one who is a slave. In like manner, the God of heaven has given us the opportunity to see for ourselves that He is a good God. He has encouraged us to prove Him: "Taste and see that the Lord is good." Once we have experienced for ourselves that He is indeed good, then we must choose whether we will stay with Him or go free, following our own way. Understanding this brings more vivid meaning to the verses: "He that hath ears to hear, let him hear" (Matt. 11:15). "He that hath an ear, let him hear what the Spirit saith unto the churches" (Rev. 3:22). We have a calling to be good and faithful servants. Having found a good and faithful Master, it is sound judgment to allow His decisions to guide every component of our life.

## Lessons from the Stars

In our study of Genesis 15, you will remember verse 5: "And he brought him forth abroad, and said, Look now toward heaven, and tell the stars, if thou be able to number them: and he said unto him, So shall thy seed be." Ordinarily when we look at this verse, all that we think about is the multitude of stars and the vast number of descendants that God would provide Abraham. Yet is that the only lesson the infinite God wanted to share with us? As astute students of the Bible who have studied the tenor of God's instructions, we answer: No. Look what happens in the very next verse: "And he believed in the LORD; and he counted it to him for righteousness." Did Abraham believe God because of the numerous amounts of stars? I think not. He certainly drew many lessons from what he saw, one of which would have been regarding the perfect order of the universe. The preciseness of the position of the stars is such that we depend on them for time, seasons, and years. Isaiah wrote: "Lift up your eyes on high, and behold who hath created these things, that bringeth out their host by number: he calleth them all by names by the greatness of his might, for that he is strong in power; not one faileth" (Isa. 40:26). The vastness of the heavens and the power needed to create and sustain the celestial bodies, while recognizing that none of them has failed, would have to be one of the reasons why the faith of Abraham became what it was. The heavens most certainly spoke to the psalmist, who wrote: "For ever, O LORD, thy word is settled in heaven. Thy faithfulness is unto all generations: thou hast established the earth, and it abideth. They [the stars] continue this day according to thine ordinances: for all are thy servants" (Ps. 119:89–91). Look up into the heavens tonight and consider the stars in their courses. Then compare their immensity to your smallness. That God orders the celestial bodies lets you know that He can and will take care of you in all situations. Even more, the stars are an assurance that He will save us if we trust everything to Him and surrender our will to Him.

Many readers are familiar with the Canon of Ptolemy, which was used to pinpoint the date of 457 BC for Ezra 7 and the starting point for the 2300-day prophecy of Daniel 8; the 70-week prophecy of Daniel 9. Based on that precise date, we can locate the death of Christ in 31 AD and, more precisely, on March 25. These prophecies are so precise as to be unmovable by 24 hours or the entire Bible based on these truths would be destroyed. The Canon of Ptolemy has more than twenty eclipses in it that pinpoint the year as 457 BC. The moving of that one year would require that every historical date and book be re-dated. Simply stated, we have used the stars for thousands of years to precisely date events.

NASA, which launches satellites, rockets, space stations, telescopes, and space shuttles, has a computer that charts every object of sufficient size to damage a space vehicle. Every time they launch any spacecraft into space, they activate the computer with the craft's trajectory to avoid contact with any object of sufficient size to cause damage. Consider that spacecrafts typically travel at speeds of 15,000–25,000 miles per hour, and some even travel at 75,000+ miles per hour. NASA scientists must even keep track of the orbits of asteroids the size of a baseball or catastrophic damage could result. Because of the preciseness of the orbits of the objects of God's creation, mankind can safely send people and equipment into space without loss. Certainly if we can depend on God to keep immense high-speed objects in precise orbits, we can also trust Him to sustain us in the little struggles of our life, though each difficulty may seem enormous to you. Whenever you feel overwhelmed, look up at the stars and think about the Creator who made them. Then compare the size of your problem with the enormity of the cosmos and rest in the assurance that your Creator has everything under control as you surrender all things to Him. He will not allow you to fail in obtaining salvation when you exercise faith in Him.

## The Sins That God Can Forgive

Before we completely close on the topic of the ceremonial law and the old covenant, we need to consider another weakness of the ceremonial system, as pointed out by Andreasen:

> One of the chief weaknesses of the Levitical system was the fact that it provided only for the forgiveness of <u>unintentional sins</u>. In each case for which a sin offering was brought, it was specifically provided that it was only for sins done in ignorance. "If a soul shall sin through ignorance;" "if the whole congregation of Israel sin through ignorance;" "when a ruler hath sinned, and done somewhat through ignorance;" "if any one of the common people sin through ignorance." Lev. 4:2, 13, 22, 27. In each case, as noted, only sin done through ignorance was provided for. Thus, after a man had brought the required sin offering, he was still in uncertainty as to sins he had committed knowingly. For such there was no sacrifice. As he left the sanctuary, the burden of sin was not entirely lifted. Only minor sins, sins committed unwittingly, were forgiven; **but the sins that really held him down were those he *knew* were wrong**. In his heart he must have felt that though sins done in ignorance were deplorable, **they did not begin to compare with sins that he had deliberately planned and executed**. He could but feel that God would in some way cover his ignorant transgression. **What did concern him were the deliberate and willful sins**. For them there was no provision in the Mosaic system. But these were the very sins that counted. <u>These were the sins that touched the conscience</u>. And for them Moses had no forgiveness. (Andreasen, pp. 263, 264, italics in original)

Is assurance that your sins are forgiven not still an issue for us today? Every person that has come into the fellowship of the church has searched to one degree or another the Scriptures for this answer. By the grace of God through faith in the death of Jesus, sins committed in full knowledge can indeed be assuredly forgiven as our heavenly Mediator intercedes for us before God the Father, as Paul declared in Acts 13.

"Be it known unto you therefore, men and brethren, that through this man is preached unto you the forgiveness of sins: And by him all that believe are justified from all things, from which ye could not be justified by the law of Moses" (Acts 13:38, 39). Understandably, the death of Jesus and the provision for justification were widely discussed during the transition in dispensations. In Acts, the apostles preached the unquestionable benefits of the new covenant provided through the blood of Jesus. To those who accepted the death of Jesus, this must have brought great joy. Several books preserved in the biblical canon point to the new covenant, Hebrews being only the most direct of these. Paul's lengthy sermon in Acts 13 provides convincing evidence that his mission, as recorded in the epistles, was to herald God's new covenant and redirect the adherents of the ceremonial dispensation to the Christian dispensation with its heavenly Mediator, Jesus of Nazareth. Andreasen goes on to describe what types of sins could be forgiven under the old covenant:

> Lest any should think that only sins done unwittingly could be forgiven in Old Testament times, let us hasten to assert that there was a Saviour in the time of Moses as well as now. All that Paul contended was that there were many things from which they could not be justified *by the law of Moses*. He never for a moment meant to say that there was not full and free forgiveness for all kinds of sins—one excepted—then as well as now. His only contention was that there was no provision for willful sin *in the law of Moses*. And that is true.
>
> How, then, were willful sins forgiven at that time? **The same as now**. Though your sins were as scarlet, though they were red like crimson, forgiveness could be had. (Isa. 1:18.) But *forgiveness could not be had by offering a sacrifice*. If God had said, "If a man commit adultery with his neighbor's wife, and do that which is evil, let him bring to me a lamb without blemish," God would set a value on sin, and men would receive the idea that sin would be forgiven at a price. That would completely destroy moral values and do untold harm. It was such a conception that led Tetzel in the days of Luther to sell indulgences, which people perverted into liberty to commit sin at a price. In the Old Testament, adultery was punishable by death. (Lev. 20:10.) God could not afford to give man the idea that purposeful sin could be condoned or winked at in any way. David knew better. When he had sinned his grievous sin he stated, "Thou desires not sacrifice; else would I give it: thou delighted not in burnt offering. The sacrifices of God are a broken spirit: a broken

and a contrite heart, O God, thou wilt not despise." Ps. 51:16, 17. (Andreasen, pp. 265, 266, italics in original)

The absence of a sacrifice for willful sin provides an interesting lesson from the Lord to us. It prevented the ancient Israelites from following the pagan mindset (echoed today in the Catholic mindset) that sinning is not that important. What really matters is bringing the proper offering to make the sinner acceptable before God, for the sacrifice provides merit for the sinner to earn salvation. The reality is that no sin is small to God. Any sin would eventually require the death of the Son of God. An infinite gift.

## The Purpose of the Ceremonial System

In Galatians, Paul asks a searching question: "Wherefore then serveth the law?" Galatians 3:19. Other versions more graphically translate: "Why then the law?" As applied to the ceremonial law we may partially answer the question by saying that it did serve a very definite purpose. It taught men that sin meant death. It taught men that when they sinned, an innocent animal must die, and that they were the cause of its death, and hence had to slay the animal themselves. From this they would most certainly receive the idea that even sin done in ignorance was serious, and that when they sinned, an innocent victim must die in their stead. However, they would also be aware of the fact that after they had done all that the ceremonial law required, they were still not forgiven all their sins. Their conscience would call to mind many things for which no sacrifice could be brought. What were they to do about these sins? Here the prophetic message came to their aid. Isaiah—and the other prophets—directed their attention away from sacrifices of bulls and goats to the Lamb of God who "was wounded for our transgressions" and "bruised for our iniquities: the chastisement of our peace was upon him; and with his stripes we are healed. All we like sheep have gone astray; we have turned every one to his own way; and the Lord hath laid on him the iniquity of us all." Isa. 53:5, 6. The command of God was clear, "Thou shalt make his soul an offering for sin.... He shall bear their iniquities.... He bare the sin of many, and made intercession for the transgressor." Verses 10–12. (Andreasen, pp. 266, 267)

All along the way the Lord gave prophetic messages regarding the eventual changes that would nullify the old ceremonial covenant law and its services. I ask again: How did they miss this? They were no different from us. As sinners, we tend to think a certain way based on our preconceived ideas and prejudices. In seeking the truth, we must put these away and let the Word of God, in its simplicity, mold our mind and thoughts, accepting only that which the Bible states about doctrine and the plan of salvation. Using the Bible in a different way leads to perdition. We have on record the experience of the ancient Israelites that we might not make their same mistakes.

Let us return to the heart of our study on the definitions of a covenant where we left off in Andreasen's book:

> The person who is born a citizen does not formally subscribe to the constitution and the laws, but is under as solemn covenant to keep these as though he had sworn to do so. And he is under obligation to observe not only the laws in existence at the time he was born but all laws enacted thereafter. He may be living in a monarchy; he may have nothing whatever to do with the enactment of these laws, but he is under solemn obligation to keep them. His birth places him under the covenant rules, and in times of stress, as during war or rebellion, he may be asked to re-affirm his allegiance. But he was under obligation of obedience before he made the pledge as well as after. <u>His continued residence in a country is in itself a covenant pledge.</u>
>
> God made a covenant with His people when He took them out of Egypt. Said Moses, "The Lord spake unto you out of the midst of the fire: ye heard the voice of the words, but saw no similitude; only ye heard a voice. And he declared unto you his *covenant, which he commanded* you to perform, even ten commandments; and he wrote them upon two tables of stone." Deut. 4:12, 13. (Andreasen, p. 287, italics in original)

It is interesting that a person's continued residence in a country or membership in a church requires subscribing to specific laws and doctrines. Residency and church membership are in reality covenant pledges. Our profession of faith and baptism into the church are a much more serious matter than many believers take them to be. How foolish it is to go against the doctrines that we were baptized into, for, in so doing, we become more culpable than the person who has made no profession of faith but drinks, takes drugs, commits adultery, and engages in riotous pleasures. To make a pledge means agreeing to a certain course of action; it means giving support to a certain cause. But a pledge is just the first step. Once you have joined a church or become a citizen of a new country, you follow through with your pledge of support, making changes to bring yourself into line with your pledge. Why take a pledge in the first place if your plan was to change that which you agreed to? Would it not be better to find a church with laws or doctrines that you have no desire to change? When thoughtfully considering the laws and doctrines of a church, wanting to make changes in the church that one has joined is absolutely absurd. If people were thinking clearly, they would quickly realize that they have moved outside of being ready for salvation while desiring salvation, an explicit contradiction. Such a view has Satan's fingerprints all over it. Andreasen deals next with whom God made the covenant:

> The Ten Commandments are here called a covenant that God commanded, or a commanded covenant. Another such covenant God made with Israel in the land of Moab. (Deut. 29:1.) This was also a commanded covenant, and contained this provision: "Neither with you only do I make this covenant and this oath; but with him that standeth here with us this day before the Lord our God, and *also with him that is not here with us this day*." Verses 14, 15.
>
> This covenant was made with Israel, and also "with him that standeth here with us this day," that is, the stranger who perhaps had no intention of entering into a covenant. And not only with those who were present was the covenant made, but "also with him that is not here with us this day."
>
> A commanded covenant, in this sense, is merely an announcement of a law that imposes a universal duty of observance upon all, those who are present and those who are absent. In this sense the Ten Commandments are a commanded covenant of universal obligation. In another and more limited sense the commandments are the basis of the specific covenant made with Israel. Thus the law of God *is* the covenant, and is also the *basis* of the covenant. (Andreasen, pp. 287, 288, emphasis in original)

The thought of this last paragraph is important to keep in mind because many people do not understand that, while the whole Bible is the covenant, the Ten Commandments are the visible basis for the old covenant, with the two stone tablets of "the testimony" being placed inside the Ark of the Covenant (Exod. 25:21; 31:18) to represent the foundation of God's government.

The new covenant is described in Jeremiah 31:33: "But this shall be the covenant that I will make with the house of Israel; after those days, saith the LORD, I will put my law in their inward parts, and write it in their hearts; and will be their God, and they shall be my people." Thorough Bible students must ask: With which law will He do this? A thorough examination of the passage reveals no new law that was not already given in the Old Testament. This firmly implies that the Ten Commandments are the law that is used in the new covenant. These commandments are, therefore, the covenant and the basis of the covenant. Logically speaking, the dispensation before the cross and the dispensation after the cross require the same permanent law of God to be fair, though the ceremonial services were different for each. Clearly from the Bible we also saw that the covenant was made not for ancient Israel only but "also with him that is not here with us this day." That includes the whole world, not just the Jews. Thus you can see it has universal obligation. Andreasen goes on to introduce the conditions in a covenant:

> Even a promise is a covenant, according to Webster's definition quoted above, that in a theological sense a covenant is "the promise of God to man, usually carrying with it a condition to be fulfilled by man."[11] Conditions are attached to all God's promises. When God promises His people certain blessings and attaches to them certain conditions, the elements of a covenant are present.
>
> Thus God's promise to Adam, of life on condition of obedience, was in itself a covenant. The conditions laid down by God, decided upon in the councils of eternity, were "Obey and live; disobey and perish." These conditions could not be changed any more than God Himself could be changed, for they were the basis of life, and not arbitrary commandments. As man cannot live submerged in water, as a fish cannot live out of water, so man cannot violate the laws of his being and live. The laws of nature, the laws of life, forbid it, not as arbitrary rules, but as inviolable conditions of existence. (Andreasen, p. 288)

We have now completed our review of the technical definitions of the covenants. In our next chapter, we will look at the plan that God has for human redemption in the new covenant and why the covenant is structured the way that it is.

---

[11] "Webster defines a covenant in the theological sense as 'the promise of God to man, usually carrying with it a condition to be fulfilled by man'" (Andreasen, p. 286).

CHAPTER 8

# The Immense Cost in Securing Salvation

> Though He giveth or He taketh,
> God His children ne'er forsaketh;
> His the loving purpose solely,
> To preserve them pure and holy.
> —Carolina Sandell Berg[12]

Long before Adam and Eve sinned, God knew what it would take to redeem mankind, and He also knew what it would cost Him. Praise His name that He plans ahead and answers our prayers before we pray.

> God, being **infinite, eternal, immutable,** and **omniscient,** <u>must from eternity have formed a plan that would provide for **all foreseen emergencies**</u>. Knowing of the apostasy of Lucifer and the fall of man, with all the resulting consequences, He created the world with a view to redemption. **It is utterly unlike God,** <u>as well as unworthy of Him, to embark upon such an important enterprise as creation, fraught as it is with eternal consequences both to His creatures and to Himself,</u> **without having a plan which would provide a solution to all the problems that would arise, and would meet all challenges of His adversaries.** Furthermore, in the outworking of this plan, it would conform with God's nature so to

---

[12] Carolina Sandell Burg, "Children of the Heavenly Father," 1855, Hymnary, https://1ref.us/1l0 (accessed February 18, 2021).

conduct His work that the eventual outcome will not only reveal His wisdom, love, and justice, but also meet with the approval of His creatures, **even of such as should not care to take advantage of the life offered them**. This would **justify** God in creating. (Andreasen, pp. 288, 289)

Security! That's what we all want, and that is what God has provided through the new covenant. When we consider God's foresight it is simply amazing! In the statement above, Andreasen depicts God's thoroughness, love, and care in making the universe secure from sin, though for a time, human beings must battle sin and Satan. God is so just that even His enemies will acknowledge the fact, and the character of God will be vindicated in plain view of the entire universe. On two sides God will be acknowledged as just—by both the wicked and by the righteous. A unanimous verdict. In reality, God will have established that His judgment is fair by more than the minimum two or three witnesses. *Five* groups will vindicate His fairness and righteousness: (1) the holy angels, (2) Satan and his demons, (3) the unfallen worlds, (4) wicked human beings, and (5) redeemed human beings. Paul referred to the vindication of God's name and character before all humanity when he wrote: "Wherefore God also hath highly exalted him, and given him a name which is above every name: that at the name of Jesus every knee should bow, of things in heaven, and things in earth, and things under the earth; and that every tongue should confess that Jesus Christ is Lord, to the glory of God the Father" (Phil. 2:9–11).

By definition, for God to be God, He must be almighty, all-knowing, the provider of that which is always the best, and the doer of that which cannot be improved upon, with resources sufficient to provide for every situation. Our heavenly Father fulfills each of these requirements, and His ability will be made manifest in those who surrender their will to Him. It cannot be overstated that God will be vindicated as just—by every case that is examined. Each person—whether it be Lucifer down to his lowest demons, wicked men, or the redeemed—each person will look at his or her own case and the cases of others, and they will acknowledge that God has been fair with them personally and with every other person. This is not the case in the judicial systems of the world. On one side or the other, there is a cry of injustice. But the universe will be unanimous that God is just in having provided for everyone's needs, spiritually and physically, along with deliverance from every emergency.

As has been intimated, God's decision to create intelligent, thinking beings with freedom of will, involved **serious consequences** to His creatures, but **even more to God Himself**. In the decision to create lay imbedded **the incarnation, suffering, and death** of the Son of God. The deep reasons for creation may ever remain a mystery, but we believe them to be grounded in God's love, and in His desire to share with others the life that is His. "Because I live," said Christ, "ye shall live also." John 14:19.

God must have known—God did know—that creation would cost Him His Son. Under these conditions it is inconceivable that the decision to create was not the result of a council of the members of the Godhead, specifically between the Father and the Son.[13]

It is doubtless to such a council the prophet refers when he speaks of the "Branch" who shall "build the temple of the Lord; and he shall bear the glory, and shall sit and rule upon his throne; and he shall be priest upon his throne: and *the counsel of peace shall be between them both.*" Zech. 6:12, 13. While some see in this only a local fulfillment in the crowning of Joshua, it cannot be contended that this local fulfillment exhausts the prophecy. He that is here spoken of is king and priest; he rules upon his throne and is a priest upon the throne; he "shall bear the glory," and "the counsel of peace shall be between them both." This can find its complete fulfillment only in the council of eternity, where the plan was laid that eventuated in Christ's becoming a priest on His throne, and in the building of the temple of God reared without hands. (Andreasen, pp. 289, 290)

We little think of the expense and greatness of the undertaking in creating the universe and the great responsibility God has to His creatures in sustaining them and the universe, but our Lord gave careful attention to every detail in securing life for all who commit their life to Him. The effort He put forth is an indication of the value He places upon human beings:

> The Lord is disappointed when His people place a low estimate upon themselves. He desires His chosen heritage to value themselves according to the price He has placed upon them. God wanted them, else He would not have sent His Son on such an

---

[13] "The Godhead was stirred with pity for the race, and *the Father, the Son, and the Holy Spirit gave themselves to the working out of the plan of redemption*. In order to fully carry out this plan, it was decided that Christ, the only begotten Son of God, should give Himself an offering for sin. What line can measure the depth of this love?" (Ellen G. White, Lt. 12, 1901, emphasis added).

expensive errand to redeem them. He has a use for them, and He is well pleased when they make the very highest demands upon Him, that they may glorify His name. They may expect large things if they have faith in His promises. (*The Desire of Ages*, p. 668)

The value of your soul and of every other human being is without price. With our limited understanding, we should place a higher value upon ourselves, putting forth our energies to glorify God in our life and work, submitting completely to God and working to secure others for God's kingdom by encouraging our brothers and sisters in Christ to do the same. It is the least we can do since we do not have the ability to pay the debt we owe for the sins we have committed. David pondered: "What is man, that thou art mindful of him? and the son of man, that thou visitest him? What is man, that thou shouldest magnify him? and that thou shouldest set thine heart upon him?" (Ps. 8:4). And Job added: "What is man, that thou shouldest magnify him? and that thou shouldest set thine heart upon him? And that thou shouldest visit him every morning, and try him every moment?" (Job 7:17, 18).

In Gethsemane we get a small glimpse of the cost of creation and salvation. In His humanity, Christ shrunk from the weight of your sins being placed on Him and the suffering that lay ahead of Him: "Three times has He uttered that prayer. Three times has humanity shrunk from the last, crowning sacrifice" (*The Desire of Ages*, p. 690). Yes, three times in Gethsemane Christ asked the Father to remove the cup of suffering from Him as the weight of sin seemed almost unbearable for His human nature to bear, and He feared that He might fail. Yet, He submitted to His Father's will, who through rejecting His plea was gently reminding Him. He had given His word; He had made a covenant and considered the lost race (John 3:16). This verse shows that the Father loves us so much that He was unwilling to let humankind be lost without opening a door to the way of salvation.

But now the history of the human race comes up before the world's Redeemer. He sees that the transgressors of the law, if left to themselves, must perish. He sees the helplessness of man. He sees the power of sin. The woes and lamentations of a doomed world rise before Him. He beholds its impending fate, and His decision is made. **He will save man at any cost to Himself.** He accepts His baptism of blood, that through Him perishing millions may gain everlasting life. He has left the courts of heaven, where all is purity, happiness, and glory, to save the one lost sheep, the one world that has fallen by transgression. And He will not turn from His mission. He will become the

> propitiation of a race that has willed to sin. His prayer now breathes only submission: "If this cup may not pass away from Me, except I drink it, Thy will be done." (*The Desire of Ages*, pp. 690, 693)

Only the Father, the Holy Spirit, and the Son completely understand the value of a soul—your soul—that Christ would undertake this mission for the few people of the world who will accept the great offering of the love of God. Though few will be saved, He considers that it will be worth the great cost. Hebrews connects the psalm about man's status with Jesus' condescension to suffer death for mankind.

> But one in a certain place testified, saying, What is man, that thou art mindful of him? or the son of man, that thou visitest him? Thou madest him *a little while inferior to* the angels; thou crownedst him with glory and honour, and didst set him over the works of thy hands: ... But we see Jesus, who was made a little lower than the angels for the suffering of death, crowned with glory and honour; that he by the grace of God should taste death for every man. For it became him, for whom are all things, and by whom are all things, in bringing many sons unto glory, to make the captain of their salvation perfect through sufferings. (Heb. 2:6, 7, margin, 9, 10)

Because the redeemed will have gained the victory over Satan in the spiritual battle of life, they are to fill positions above even the unfallen angels because they have had an experience similar to that of Jesus. All who are victorious have, in reality, gained the victory over Lucifer, the highest created being, and have shown themselves stronger than the one who fell to sin without temptation and without inherent weakness, for they have taken hold of and utilized the power of God. This is indeed a mystery. Yet, "we know that all things work together for good to them that love God, to them who are the called according to his purpose" (Rom. 8:28).

## The Covenant between the Father and the Son

Andreasen below describes an eternal covenant that the Heavenly Father had with His Son:

> That a covenant has existed from eternity between the Father and the Son is evident both from Scripture and from reason. We present the following considerations:

> Christ considered His life and work on earth as the fulfillment of an agreed and prearranged plan. In Psalms 40:7 the preincarnate Christ announced His coming in response to the call of God: "Lo, I come: in the volume of the book it is written of me, I delight to do thy will, O my God: yea, thy law is within my heart." This coming was in perfect conformity to His own desires, as expressed in the words: "I delight to do thy will, O my God," and in the still stronger statement, "My meat is to do the will of him that sent me." Ps. 40:7; John 4:34....
>
> When Christ was about to leave this earth He declared, "I have finished the work which thou gavest me to do." John 17:4. The vital part of this work is that mentioned by John when he says that God "sent his Son to be the propitiation for our sins." 1 John 4:10. This included the suffering and death of the Son of God, and this also was according to God's plan. "This commandment have I received of my Father." John 10:18. (Andreasen, pp. 290, 291)

We see that Jesus had a commandment from the Father, making it imperative that He fulfill the commission or be found disobedient and, thus, a sinner, imperiling the universe and committing His soul and the world to the second death. God held Himself subject to the same requirements to which He holds man, with equal circumstances, that He might be an example and might be the unblemished sacrifice, the only acceptable substitute for man.

> Toward the close of His work Christ gave utterance to a most unique request. "Father," He said, "I will that they also, whom thou hast given me, be with me where I am." John 17:24. <u>This is not an ordinary prayer</u>. In fact, **it is a demand more than a prayer**. Christ prayed, and taught others to pray, "Thy will be done." But now He does not say, "Thy will be done," but simply announces, "I will." <u>He is not asking a favor</u>; **He is claiming a victor's reward**.
>
> In His high priestly prayer Christ repeatedly refers to those who have been given Him of God. (John 17:6, 9, 11, 12, 24) It is these He claims. "They have kept thy word," He says. Having fulfilled the conditions of making them "more precious than fine gold; even a man than the golden wedge of Ophir," **He demands that they be given Him and be with Him.** Isa. 13:12.
>
> <u>The foregoing texts suggest an agreement whereby Christ was to do a certain work, and in return be given those who should meet</u>

> the conditions set. As the salvation of men was the object of His coming to this earth; as He announced that He had finished the work given Him to do; and as **He claims as a reward those who have been given Him by the Father, we find the elements of a covenant present**: the very thing we have been led to believe from other scriptures. (Andreasen, pp. 291, 292)

What a wonderful God we have, that we have a Creator who wants us right where He is. Well may we say with the Psalmist, "What shall I render unto the LORD for all his benefits toward me? I will take the cup of salvation, and call upon the name of the LORD. I will pay my vows unto the LORD now in the presence of all his people" (Ps. 116:12–14). He reveals a small but important element of the science of prayer. When, like Christ, we have fulfilled that which the Father has commanded us, we can request—even demand—the proffered promise that God delightfully has obligated Himself to fulfill. One thing in Scripture is clear—God loves to answer our prayers.

> A covenant between the Father and the Son must in its very nature be eternal, as of necessity it must have been made before creation took place. For God to bring men and angels into existence—knowing that sin would result—without making provision for their restoration, and giving them the opportunity of a second trial should they wish to retrace their steps; for God to create beings, some of whom would reject the proffered mercy, without making provision for the eventual eradication of sin from the universe, **would show either shortsightedness on the part of God, or a lack of consideration commensurate with His power.** Either of these would be unworthy of God, and would call in question His right to the claim of being a kind and merciful Father.
> 
> Such considerations as these make it clear that creation must have included **every provision** for the safety of God and man, and that **the whole plan must have been completed before God ever began to create**. (Andreasen, p. 292)

Considering the heavy responsibility and issues listed above, we can better understand that, for God to be righteous or just, it is not simply a matter of forgiveness of sin. A person can forgive without being just. However, God had to consider all circumstances and all the events of life before creating the world, leaving nothing unconsidered or unprovided for that would benefit every created being and not just the one involved in a specific event. As we look at these issues, it is no wonder that, at the end of the review of all the events of this world of sin, it is said: "That at the name of Jesus every knee should bow, of things in heaven, and things in earth, and things under the earth; and that every tongue should confess that Jesus Christ is Lord, to the glory of God the Father" (Phil. 2:10, 11). Those bowing their knees includes Satan and all the angels and the deluded and rebellious humans that Satan has deceived, for they will recognize that there was no valid reason for their deception, delusion, or rebellion to have continued. They will see its fruitlessness, vanity, and destruction in the true light of each event and choice. They will also see that what they rejected was indeed good and that they would have enjoyed it had they considered things more thoughtfully. Andreasen calls attention to the promises of the Father and the Son on behalf of humanity:

> The plan of salvation, as revealed in the Scriptures, is best understood in the light of a covenant in which the contracting parties are the Father and Christ; the Father representing the Godhead in their unity, the Son representing those who should elect Him as their substitute and surety. On their behalf Christ promised and guaranteed the fulfillment of the conditions laid down for eternal life, and the Father promised to give the Son all those who should meet the requirements and for whom Christ should stand sponsor. <u>The administration of the covenant as regards men was left in Christ's hands, He becoming surety for the faithful performance of all conditions. When He had finished His work in and with the believers, and could certify that "they have kept thy word,"</u> **He would present them for acceptance**, <u>"faultless before the presence of his glory with exceeding joy."</u> John 17:6; Jude 22. (Andreasen, pp. 292, 293)

We are represented before God the Father in Jesus Christ, the Creator. The fact that we are represented not by the Heavenly Father nor by the Holy Spirit but by Jesus is significant. We understand from personal experience that no one likes to have their work destroyed, ignored, or be unfruitful. Therefore, we know that we have an Almighty Creator who is doing all in His power to assure our redemption in such a way that His actions will not be a mark against His own good name. Because we are Christ's creation and the work of His hands for which He sweated blood, we know that He will stand for us, by us, and behind us to assure our acceptance and redemption by the Father, the Holy Spirit, and the angels and unfallen worlds. As we have already mentioned, Christ guarantees our redemption from sin and our strengthening through His power for victory over the deceiver who charged God with having a law that could not be kept and with having made beings that were defective and therefore incapable of fulfilling God's commandments due to some fault of God.

> The working out of the covenant would be on this wise: <u>The moment Adam failed to live up to the requirement of God, thus forfeiting his right to life, Christ would take man's place and become his surety, thereby saving him from immediate death and ensuring him another trial.</u> As the second Adam, Christ would become the head of a new humanity, and God would deal with Him as man's representative. **This could be done, however, only on condition that Christ became truly man, and took man's place in every way, even to the point where He would take upon Himself the punishment justly due to man's sin.** As the second Adam He would have to stand test and trial as did the first Adam, and **by strict obedience demonstrate that it is possible for man to obey God**, and thus redeem Adam's disgraceful failure. In His obedience He **would justify God**, and **disprove Satan's claim** that God was requiring of man that which could not be done; and He would also **encourage man** to believe that by the help of God **he could reach the standard set by God for man**.
>
> The covenant between the Father and the Son in regard to the salvation of man may rightly be called the **covenant of redemption,** for its provisions made possible man's salvation. It was the substitution of the second Adam for the first, and the taking over by Christ of all the obligations incurred by man. On God's part, it was the acceptance by Him of Christ's assurance to bring man back to obedience, and present him at last before the throne of God, without spot or blemish, a fit candidate for immortality. **God promised to forbear awhile the execution of the penalty due to sin, give man time to recover himself;** <u>that is, grant him probationary time, not reckon unto him his trespasses, and turn the entire administration of the provisions of the covenant over to Christ, delegating to Him all powers in heaven and in earth.</u> As Christ is man's representative, **God deals only with Him; and as man deals only with Christ,**

> He becomes the go-between, the daysman, the mediator between God and man. Any request we may have is addressed to the Father through Christ; any communication from the Father comes to us through Christ. He is our mediator and surety. (Andreasen, pp. 293, 294)

David wrote:

> My flesh trembleth for fear of thee; and I am afraid of thy judgments. I have done judgment and justice: leave me not to mine oppressors. Be surety for thy servant for good: let not the proud oppress me. Mine eyes fail for thy salvation, and for the word of thy righteousness. Deal with thy servant according unto thy mercy, and teach me thy statutes. I am thy servant; give me understanding, that I may know thy testimonies. It is time for thee, LORD, to work: for they have made void thy law. Therefore I love thy commandments above gold; yea, above fine gold. Therefore I esteem all thy precepts concerning all things to be right; and I hate every false way. (Ps. 119:120–128)

For Jesus Christ, the Son of God, to represent both God and man requires that He be fair to both sides. To be declared just, He must give due consideration to both sides of the dispute and be an absolutely impartial judge to them both. He cannot give preference to the Father, nor to the human race. He must only act in accordance with that which is good for both sides.

It is not of small significance that Christ "would take upon Himself the punishment justly due to man's sin." In this, it is as if God held Himself accountable for the fall of man as far as possible without giving excuse for sin. For God to be willing to take responsibility as far as He can, speaks volumes of His character and love. He cannot excuse sin, yet He has provided deliverance from it for those who change their mind and want to live righteously though morally and physically weakened by their exposure to sin. The covenant agreement grants that any man with hereditary or cultivated tendencies to sin can overcome these tendencies and any other effects of sin. Scripture declares how much Christ loves the Father (John 14:31). Knowing that God is no respecter of persons means that Christ's love for us equals His love for the Father (Acts 10:34; cf. John 17:26).

Scripture contains many examples of Christ's love for the Father in neither sinning nor doing anything that would cause shame to God's name.

By the same token, we know that we have an Advocate who loves us equally and will do nothing that would endanger our salvation. It is significant that the covenant agreement between the Father and the Son includes an assurance from the Son that man would be able to obey. He will not leave us, when we choose Him, to the oppression of the devil, and He will give us wisdom to understand His law and its beauty and goodness that we may love it and keep it in joy.

## Jesus' Prayer of John 17

When we examine Jesus' prayer in John 17, we see overwhelmingly that it is a covenant-fulfilling prayer. As the longest prayer of Jesus recorded in Scripture, it is in reality the true "Lord's prayer," considering that the prayer that is called the "Lord's Prayer" is an outline lesson a model template for the structure on how His disciples are to pray. Jesus' prayer in John 17 is a prayer of reconciliation, a petition for power and equal blessings to man, the glorifying of God and the uplifting of mankind. Andreasen noted above that this prayer was a demand more than a petition, which was a fair demand in light of the Creator's great love and objectives for His creatures, His crowning work of creation, that He loves so that we might have the stated privileges of the covenant for which He suffered so much and died to assure us the right. Let us note the major elements of this greatest of prayers.

### John 17
1. These words spake Jesus, and lifted up his eyes to heaven, and said, Father, the hour is come; glorify thy Son, that thy Son also may glorify thee:
   *A request for the work of the Father and Son to be seen as worthy, valiant, and exalted as they are.*
2. As thou hast given him power over all flesh, that he should give eternal life to as many as thou hast given him.
   *Power for victory over thoughts, words, and actions to all who are surrendered to God, because lust, which is the beginning of temptation, starts in the brain, in our flesh; we need to know that Jesus came to give power over the thoughts and desires, which is where sin starts.*
3. And this is life eternal, that they might know thee the only true God, and Jesus Christ, whom thou hast sent.
   *A request for God's character to be revealed and known to man—particularly His immense love for mankind.*

4. I have glorified thee on the earth: I have finished the work which thou gavest me to do.
*Glory to the Father and the fulfilling of all covenant obligations, by revealing the character and image of the Father, making salvation available to all who through belief accept the proffered gift.*
5. And now, O Father, glorify thou me with thine own self with the glory which I had with thee before the world was.
*Jesus' request to return to His previous glory as the Commander in heaven on His throne.*
6. I have manifested thy name unto the men which thou gavest me out of the world: thine they were, and thou gavest them me; and they have kept thy word.
*Jesus represented the Father to man and claims mankind as His, based on His purchasing us anew through His blood. And how was the name of the Father manifested? By Jesus' keeping them victorious. John 14:21 points to the Father and Son being manifest through their experience.*
7. Now they have known that all things whatsoever thou hast given me are of thee.
*A clarification that the Father and Son are working together and cannot be separated in their work for mankind. The Father does not have different feelings for us than for Christ. He loves you and wants you to be redeemed. They work as One. This includes the third person of the Godhead, the Holy Spirit.*
8. For I have given unto them the words which thou gavest me; and they have received them, and have known surely that I came out from thee, and they have believed that thou didst send me.
*Through Christ, mankind has been given the word of the covenant, the promise.*
9. I pray for them: I pray not for the world, but for them which thou hast given me; for they are thine.
*Clarifying that mankind belongs to the Father also.*
10. And all mine are thine, and thine are mine; and I am glorified in them.
*Jesus seeks His glory through the redemption of man, the development of God's image in the life of fallen man.*
11. And now I am no more in the world, but these are in the world, and I come to thee. Holy Father, keep through thine own name those whom thou hast given me, that they may be one, as we are.
*The petition for our being kept obedient and God's name's being held sacred through mankind's victory that comes through dependence on God.*

*In addition, that we be sanctified/unified in our working for the kingdom of God.*

12. While I was with them in the world, I kept them in thy name: those that thou gavest me I have kept, and none of them is lost, but the son of perdition; that the scripture might be fulfilled.
*Christ's declaration of His faithfulness in keeping those who have surrendered to Him.*
13. And now come I to thee; and these things I speak in the world, that they might have my joy fulfilled in themselves.
*That we might be restored to full joy, the blessing of the covenant promises are available through the death, resurrection, and priestly ministration of Christ for us in the heavenly sanctuary.*
14. I have given them thy word; and the world hath hated them, because they are not of the world, even as I am not of the world.
*He has given us His word, which is the assurance of your redemption by faith. Therefore the world hates them because they have Our favor, blessing, redemption, and follow principles contrary to the world.*
15. I pray not that thou shouldest take them out of the world, but that thou shouldest keep them from the evil.
*This is a direct refutation of Satan's claim that God's law can't be kept—especially in light of mankind's overcoming in a world of sin and temptation. It is the vindication of God's name—that He is Almighty and never failing, able to keep us from falling into sin amidst continuous temptation, which is a situation that Satan did not have when he fell in the pure, holy, and perfect environment of heaven.*
16. They are not of the world, even as I am not of the world.
17. Sanctify them through thy truth: thy word is truth.
18. As thou hast sent me into the world, even so have I also sent them into the world.
19. And for their sakes I sanctify myself, that they also might be sanctified through the truth.
*Here is further mention of the work that Christ did and of the promise that those around us may also be redeemed when they see examples in other humans who live the sanctified life. By the example of a sanctified life, many will be sanctified and saved. Thus, this statement is a commission for you to accept to also accept the charge of being God's representative.*
20. Neither pray I for these alone, but for them also which shall believe on me through their word;

21. That they all may be one; as thou, Father, art in me, and I in thee, that they also may be one in us: that the world may believe that thou hast sent me.
*Through the church fulfilling its given mission, the wicked believe that God is God, and they will see living examples of victorious Christians. When the world sees this, they in like manner will believe and follow. This is the best testimony that God is all He has said He is.*
22. And the glory which thou gavest me I have given them; that they may be one, even as we are one:
*This promise is to extend Christ's glory, in verse 5, to human beings. To those who choose to live life, crucifying the flesh and following Christ, God gives the glory that Christ had before He made the world—glory that Satan coveted, causing His fall. But we cannot miss the point that to glorify God like Christ is to live a life carrying the cross of suffering without sin, whether tempted or afflicted.*
23. I in them, and thou in me, that they may be made perfect in one; and that the world may know that thou hast sent me, and hast loved them, as thou hast loved me.
*Fulfilling the promise for His followers to be perfect (see Gen. 17:1) and to manifest to the world that God is a keeper of His people and of His Word, Christ notes the amazing equal love of God the Father to us as He loves Christ. With this thought, all one needs to do is look at the four gospels and see how Christ related to the people, and we will also know how the Father will respond to us in our every need pertaining to life and redemption.*
24. Father, I will that they also, whom thou hast given me, be with me where I am; that they may behold my glory, which thou hast given me: for thou lovedst me before the foundation of the world.
*The demand of Christ for the redeemed, as covenanted for Christ's possession with full restoration into the heavenly kingdom, to behold the unveiled glory of God and to reveal the love that God has had for us even before creating us, though He knew that we would sin against Him. Amazing!*
25. O righteous Father, the world hath not known thee: but I have known thee, and these have known that thou hast sent me.
26. And I have declared unto them thy name, and will declare it: that the love wherewith thou hast loved me may be in them, and I in them.
*And, finally, the amazing love of God manifested in us—fallen, selfish, proud, and covetous mankind who have overcome. The final development of this prayer on earth will be the 144,000, who will become a sanctified church for the first time on earth. Amen!*

It should always be understood, emphasized, and remembered that God the Father and God the Son, the first and second persons of the Godhead, made a covenant—which is the Word— between Themselves to protect and keep Their name. This covenant effectively keeps them responsible to one another and to be eternally just, righteous, and holy toward the beings They created by providing for and sustaining them. "Thus speaketh the LORD of hosts, saying, Behold the man whose name is The BRANCH; and he shall grow up out of his place, and he shall build the temple of the LORD: Even he shall build the temple of the LORD; and he shall bear the glory, and shall sit and rule upon his throne; and he shall be a priest upon his throne: and the counsel of peace shall be between them both" (Zech. 6:12, 13). The playing out of this covenant of peace can be clearly seen in Jesus' prayer of John 17 in which Jesus calls upon the Father to glorify the Son but with the condition of the Son glorifying the Father. Then, in Gethsemane, we see the Father holding the Son to His commitment to be the sacrifice and surety for fallen man, as shown in Jesus' thrice-given prayer, "If it be Thy will take away this cup." The Father indicated that it was not His will to take away the cup when He required Christ to not turn back from His vow so that He would save fallen man at any cost to Himself. It emphasizes the equal desire of the Father and the Son to create, sustain, and redeem man when man chooses God. God has therefore obligated Himself to make you and me just, righteous, pure, perfect, and holy. Thus, in the significant words of the Abrahamic covenant of Genesis 15, God is effectively saying, "They can rightly demand of Us, the Godhead, that we fulfill any promise, word, or prophecy made with mankind and that, if We do not, Jesus should receive the second death, which is an execution symbolized by the dividing of these animals in the midst." The new covenant, then, is literally a blood covenant that is effective eternally backing up every prayer that claims any word, promise or prophecy in the Bible when it is rightly contextually asked. That is tremendous news beyond marvelous, just simply awesome. We have an Almighty God that has committed that much to our well-being. Rightly seen it can only inspire immense faith in the beholder for our God.

We will end this chapter with a statement from the Testimony of Jesus. Please take note of the comment on John 17:22.

> We are numbered with Israel. All the instruction given to the Israelites of old concerning the education and training of their children, <u>all the promises of blessing through obedience, are for us</u>.

God's word to us is, "I will bless thee, ... and thou shalt be a blessing." Genesis 12:2.

Of the first disciples and of all who should believe on Him through their word Christ said, "The glory which Thou gavest Me I have given them; that they may be one, even as We are one: I in them, and Thou in Me; that they may be made perfect in one; and that the world may know that Thou hast sent Me, and hast loved them, as Thou hast loved Me." John 17:22, 23.

**Wonderful, wonderful words, almost beyond the grasp of faith!** The Creator of all worlds loves those who give themselves to His service, even as He loves His Son. Even here and now His gracious favor is bestowed upon us to this marvelous extent. He has given us the Light and Majesty of heaven, and with Him He has bestowed all the heavenly treasure. Much as He has promised us for the life to come, He bestows princely gifts in this life. As subjects of His grace, He desires us to enjoy everything that will **ennoble, expand, and elevate our characters**. He is waiting to inspire the youth with power from above, that they may stand under the blood-stained banner of Christ, to work as He worked, to lead souls into safe paths, to plant the feet of many upon the Rock of Ages.

All who are seeking to work in harmony with God's plan of education will have His sustaining grace, His continual presence, His keeping power. To everyone He says:

"Be strong and of a good courage; be not afraid, neither be thou dismayed: for the Lord thy God is with thee." "I will not fail thee, nor forsake thee." Joshua 1:9, 5. (*The Ministry of Healing*, p. 405)

CHAPTER 9

# God's Justice in Our Redemption

> Fairest Lord Jesus, Ruler of all nature,
> O Thou of God and man the Son!
> Thee will I cherish, Thee will I honor,
> Thou art my glory, joy, and crown.
> —from the German[14]

"Now thanks be unto God, which always causeth us to triumph in Christ, and maketh manifest the savour of his knowledge by us in every place" (2 Cor. 2:14). Dear reader, I pray that God's plan of salvation has now become clear to you and that you realize that it will not fail any who allow it to be the governing principle of their life. We can thank God that we always "triumph in Christ"—not once in awhile, not sometimes, not most of the time but "always." In other words, we can begin today to thank God that we will be saved when we have purposed in our hearts and are committed to holiness. Our promised triumph does not eliminate the fact that the road is strait and narrow with many struggles and trials. Yet, we can move forward with confidence, knowing that God "always causeth us to triumph in Christ." We have not yet talked in detail about the application of the principles of the covenant. Nonetheless, based on the fact that the covenant's principles are sound, the application can be nothing less. Let us now consider the application of the covenant of grace.

---

[14] "Fairest Lord Jesus," 17th century German, Hymnary, https://1ref.us/1l1 (accessed February 18, 2021).

## The Covenant of Grace

Andreasen commented:

> The covenant of grace is by some considered the same as the covenant of redemption, but though they are closely related, for the sake of clarity it may be best to consider them separately. <u>The covenant of grace is in reality Christ's administration of the covenant of redemption as related to man</u>. In the covenant of redemption between the Father and the Son, Christ undertook to make man "more precious than fine gold; even a man than the golden wedge of Ophir." Isa. 13:12. The covenant of grace concerns itself with preparing man for his high destiny and getting him ready to stand the inspection of God. **It is merely an arrangement for bringing man back to the place where he can keep the commandments of God, where he can stand the test to which God will put him, and be worthy of the reward of the overcomer.** (Andreasen, p. 294)

Is it not good news that the purpose of the covenant of grace is to bring "man back to the place where he can keep the commandments of God," though living in a world of temptation, sin, suffering, and decided disadvantage in applying its principles? Satan was in heaven, a place that was pure and holy with an environment easy to develop and maintain holiness, yet he sinned. Beings that overcome in this world of sin will undoubtedly be able to stay holy in an environment free of the difficultly of temptation.

> This work embraces **two distinct phases**: <u>the forgiveness of sin, with the consequent and complete blotting out of the evil past; and the impartation of strength for the doing of the will of God.</u> **If** man could have all his sins blotted out; **if** by some means he could be born again, have his mind and whole attitude changed, and become an entirely new creation; **if** the old man could die and be buried, and a new man arise, with new hopes and aspirations; **if** all the old things should pass away, and all things become new; in other words, **if** he could simply die and be raised again, <u>he could start life over without any handicap of past sins</u>. This is the first of the two steps, and is provided for in <u>conversion and regeneration</u>, through which man has all the experiences here mentioned.

**This undoes all that the first birth brought him, and he stands where Adam stood, without a single sin charged to him.**

The **second step** is the acquisition of power adequate for the work that is required of the new man. **He will need more power than Adam did**; for even though he is a new creature, he is far below Adam in strength, and will need a special enduement of power from on high. Not only is he weaker than Adam, but the temptations are stronger. Of this condition God will have to take account. He will need to remember that "this man was born there," and so arrange matters that "where sin abounded, grace did much more abound." (Ps. 87:4, 6; Rom. 5:20.) If this is done, every man will have the same opportunity Adam had. No more can be asked. (Andreasen, pp. 294, 295)

Notice what the Spirit of Prophecy says:

"What greater promises could be given us than are found in these verses? A cunning and cruel foe attends our steps, and is working every moment, with all his strength and skill, to turn us from the right way. Ever since he succeeded in overcoming our first parents in their beautiful Eden home, he has been engaged in this work. **More than six thousand years of continual practice has greatly increased his skill to deceive and allure.** On the other hand, he who once yields to temptation becomes spiritually weak, and yields more readily the second time. Every repetition of sin blinds his eyes, stifles conviction, and weakens his power of resistance. **Thus while the power of the human race to resist temptation is continually decreasing, Satan's skill and power to tempt are continually increasing. This is one great reason why the temptations of the last days will be more severe than those of any other age.**" (*Signs of the Times*, Sept. 29, 1887)

Often when Christians talk about grace, they omit this second element entirely or simply reject the idea that there can be complete victory. Yet, the two elements together are what make the covenant so powerful in showing the wisdom, love, and mercy of God. We did not choose to be born the first time, but, with this plan, the circumstances of our birth are of no concern. We can choose to die and be born again and grow in grace, "perfecting holiness" (2 Cor. 7:1), and we can grow closer and closer each day to God, even though we need more power than Adam did. Not only is God vindicating His name from the charges brought by the first great apostate, but He is doing it through a generation that will have to battle more and under less favorable conditions, making the ultimate statement about the power of God more pronounced than any previous generation since the Fall. Though each successive generation has less innate strength, Christ was tested far above any man's need of spiritual strength in order to give us this strength and to succor anyone and everyone who has faith in His power. Thus, all mouths will be shut with all the excuses before God that circumstance and hereditary weakness made overcoming impossible.

"Therefore as by the offence of one judgment came upon all men to condemnation; even so by the righteousness of one the free gift came upon all men unto justification of life. For as by one man's disobedience many were made sinners, so by the obedience of one shall many be made righteous. Moreover the law entered, that the offence might abound. But where sin abounded, grace did much more abound:" "And he said unto me, My grace is sufficient for thee: for my strength is made perfect in weakness. Most gladly therefore will I rather glory in my infirmities, that the power of Christ may rest upon me" (Rom. 5:18–20; 2 Cor. 12:9).

> Strict justice demands that the one who breaks the rules of life shall perish. But **fairness** also **demands** that one who is born in sin, for which he is in no way responsible, shall have his disabilities removed, be placed on vantage ground, and **be given the same chance which the first man had**. This is not a matter of mercy but of **justice**. It is to this question of justice John refers when he says that God "is faithful and just *[literally "righteous"]* to forgive us our sins." 1 John 1:9. Whereas it is merciful of God to forgive us our trespasses, it is also true that there is justice in God's removing the sins for which we are not responsible—inherited weaknesses and sins—and not imputing them to us. Paul agrees with this when he states that it is God's righteousness, not merely His mercy, that is shown in the remission of sins. (Rom. 3:25, 26; Heb. 6:10). (Andreasen, pp. 295, 296)

In this statement, Andreasen defines justice as righteousness, or right doing. Going one step more, we can say that justice is "fairness." In light of this, not one person who goes to hell will have the right to claim—nor will they claim—that God is unjust, unrighteous, or unfair. If that were at all the case, God's name would not be vindicated, and the person would rightfully deserve another trial to prove himself. After all the evidence is presented, all the wicked—though unrepentant and lost—will of their own freewill confess that God is fair.

> God does not deviate one hair's breadth from justice in dealing with men, either good or bad, nor is His mercy confined to the righteous. "He maketh his sun to rise on the evil and on the good, and sendeth rain on the just and on the unjust." Matt. 5:45. Only when men, despite His pleadings, deliberately turn from Him to evil, does He reluctantly permit them to reap the fruit of their ill-doing.
>
> When man sinned, God did not change the sentence of death that He had pronounced upon the transgressor, but in view of Christ's mediation He **delayed its execution**. This delay granted Adam—and all men—is what we call probationary time. **This is a time of grace, granted in mercy to all alike, to give men opportunity to think things through. Unless, by repentance and a definite turning to God, man shows that he repudiates sin, the death sentence will at last be carried out.** But even in the case of the righteous, God's mercy does not conflict with His justice. Whether man be good or bad, he at last faces death; but in the case of the righteous there is a resurrection unto life. For such, death becomes a sleep from which he is raised again to life everlasting. (Andreasen, p. 296)

This is the point that distinguishes the covenant of grace: probationary time. The length of time may be different for each one, but I think that it can be clearly seen that the mind of the person is the significant factor in one's probation or life being shortened or extended.

> Probation is therefore God's solution to the problem of giving men continued existence though they have violated the law of life. **It is a day of grace granted all, during which time God does not impute to them their sins but does all that love can contrive to win them back to obedience.** It is a time of suspended sentence, a time of parole, but it is so only in a legal sense. It is a time of intense activity on the part of God to **woo men to repentance**, to show His love to them, to give them a glimpse of the joy that awaits the faithful,

and also to warn them of the loss that will be theirs should they reject God's invitation. (Andreasen, p. 296)

All that can be seen on thorough examination of the covenant is that God is *fair, fair,* and *fair*—or, if you prefer—that He is just, righteous, and merciful!

> Christ's work, under the covenant of grace, is to take sinners and make them into saints. <u>With unfailing kindness He will help those who are weak</u>, forgive them their sins, seventy times seven if need be, <u>forgive as long as there is any hope that man will at last turn to God</u>, take hold of His strength, and walk in newness of life. **He will suit the test to each man's strength, and not permit any to be tempted above that which he is able to bear.** <u>As soon as a man has passed one test, and gained a little strength as well as confidence, He will give him another test, carefully gauged to his peculiar need,</u> until he gradually grows in strength and grace, and **finally comes to the point where he will die rather than sin**. When he has reached this decision, **the work is done; he has completed his training; he is sanctified, ready for the kingdom**. Christ will then present him before the Presence with exceeding joy. <u>Satan is defeated, and God stands vindicated.</u> **A soul is saved**. (Andreasen, p. 297)

What an awesome God we serve! He provides all that we need to keep us from being lost. We can see this truth through the object lesson of the growth of a plant. The plant can be perfect at every stage, though not fully grown or bearing fruit. Would it not seem odd to see a blade of grass with a full ear of corn on it when it is not strong enough to support the load? From Andreasen's statement, we can see that God is working in such a way that one day His work can be considered finished when forgiven sinners have become overcomers under all circumstances—as firm to principle and unchangeable as God is and ready to fit right in and live in heaven with beings who have never sinned. It is a fantastic plan!

> <u>It should be emphasized beyond any possibility of misunderstanding, **that the aim of the covenant of grace is not merely the forgiveness of sin**, but it is **to bring men back** to the place **where they can**, by the grace of God, **keep** the commandments and **live**.</u> What God required of Adam in the garden, He requires of every man.

**God has not changed His requirements and cannot change them without laying Himself open to the charge of inconsistency and of being a respecter of persons**. For His own sake He must not change; for man's sake He must not change. **To require less now than He did of Adam would be disastrous. It was perfect obedience then. It is perfect obedience now**. (Andreasen, p. 297)

That God is not changeable on the standard of judgment is as much for our benefit as the law of gravity and as the orbits of the celestial bodies that never vary. These are things on which we can depend. Anyone from Adam to the last generation of the 144,000 will see that God was equally "fair," "just," and "righteous" with everyone and that He has been a respecter of none. Looking at holiness, perfection, and heaven, I can say without a doubt that I am glad that the Lord will never change His requirements, and I choose to be part of His kingdom. The Ten Commandments, which are a transcript of the character of the God who is love, are the foundation of the covenant. If the commandments are changeable, then love itself is variable, and that certainly would not be good. Since God never changes, His love for us remains constant, and we can always depend on that fact. If the Ten Commandments, or God's covenant, were like a fashion or a fad, they would benefit no one. As things go out of style, they are often criticized and considered worthless. God could never be "just" with such changeable standards. For Him to be just, the standards must be the same in the past, the present, and always. (The changeable nature of fashion is a good reason we should not allow ourselves to be guided by it. We should live by fixed righteous principles.)

We will now use Andreasen's summary to review all that we have discussed:

> *The Covenant of Life.* By this is meant the general rules of life, or the law of life, under which all things created have their being. Thus all forms of life—plants, flowers, trees, creeping things, animals, birds, or fish—must conform to their peculiar conditions of life, or perish. So, likewise, men and angels, and whatever other kinds of intellectual life God has created, must conform to the rules of life governing their existence. From the very nature of these rules they are inviolable, and continued existence depends upon strict adherence to them. "Obey and live; disobey and perish," is written upon every rule. <u>The consequences of disobedience are not penal in their nature; they are a *result* of transgression</u>, the

*wages* of sin rather than a punishment for sin. The man who drinks poison violates the rules of life and suffers the consequences. The punishment is inherent in the act itself.

This law of life is variously called a covenant of nature, or a natural covenant, a legal covenant, a covenant of works. As stated above, it is merely the rules of life by which all things consist, and with which all must comply. It is not a covenant entered into formally. All nature is subject to it, animate and inanimate. Thus God made a covenant with day and night, and also with fowl, cattle, and every beast, and set the rainbow in the heavens as a token of "the everlasting covenant between God and every living creature." (Jer. 33:20, 25; Gen. 9:9–17.)

We prefer to call this the covenant of life, as it is the general all-inclusive covenant embracing the whole creation, and by which life is promised on condition of obedience.

*The covenant of redemption* is that part of the everlasting covenant in which the Father and the Son enter into a solemn compact that they will save man at any cost to themselves. This covenant involves the **incarnation, suffering,** and **death** of the Son of God. Christ will take man's place, and as the second Adam **fulfill all man's obligations**; and God promises that He will accept not only this Son of *man* but also all those whom Christ can restore, and for whom He will become surety. Christ guarantees that He will make a man more precious than fine gold, restore the image of God in the soul, build him up to a holy temple of God, and **at last present him faultless before the throne of God**.

In this covenant Christ represents man, and the covenant is thus between God and man—the man Christ Jesus—**a covenant established upon promises that cannot be broken**. The administration of this covenant as regards man devolves upon Christ.

*The Covenant of Grace.* This covenant concerns the administration of the covenant of redemption, by which Christ is to redeem men and restore them to the favor of God. It is a covenant between Christ and fallen man, wherein, upon condition of turning *from sin* and turning *to Him*, Christ will forgive men their shortcomings, and help them become strong in their desire to do right. His work for man includes **two distinct**, yet closely connected, parts: **forgiveness of sin** and **sanctification**.

> When Christ's work in the human heart is done, He will present His work before the Father. **Each man must stand the test for himself.** Those who stand the test—and they include all for whom Christ is mediator and surety—will be saved.
>
> This covenant of grace was first made with man in the Garden of Eden after he fell. It is the covenant under which every redeemed man will be saved. There is no other way. It is the same covenant which God made with Abraham and all the saints of old. It is the covenant of salvation.
>
> It is to be noted that this covenant is not an end in itself but merely the administration of the covenant of redemption—God's way of preparing men to stand the test that will come to every man. It brings man back to the place where Adam stood before the fall, and **now he must stand the test of obedience before he can be admitted** to the benefits of the covenant of life and be accepted by the Father. This is the final test, and for this the covenant of grace prepares him. (Andreasen, pp. 297–300, italics in original)

The last paragraph is very significant. The covenant of grace gets us ready to stand the test of temptation as overcomers. Having prepared us to stand as Adam stood before his fall, we are tested again, and we demonstrate that "perpetual obedience" is the outcome of every type of experience we will have from that point forward. We will then have become as Adam was before the Fall, yet now we will be secure from returning to a fallen state. Having experienced the bitter results of sin, we will be purposed mentally—of our own free will—to only seek after holiness.

As our Mediator, Christ is more significantly also our surety, which means that He is the guarantor that the human race will be perpetually obedient. In His wisdom, God allows us to suffer the consequences of sin so that He may reap from us, without force, a harvest of obedience, which He has desired from the very beginning. To allow His children to develop lives of willing obedience is why, in His love, God allows so many bad things to take place in our world of sin. By difficult circumstances, we come to know, as God already knew, "that all things work together for good to them that love God, to them who are the called according to his purpose" (Rom. 8:28). When we understand this truth the blessing of the experience that was so painful and so sad is clearly discerned, and it eliminates the need to ask God why He has allowed such things to take place. Then we can ask with the prophet, "What do ye imagine against the LORD? he will make an utter end: affliction shall not rise up the second time" (Nahum 1:9). Though this world has gone to the lowest of depths, the experience has priceless value because sin, rebellion, and deceit will never again arise in the universe. Thus, the world will be completely restored, and the universe will be eternally secure through depending on Him.

> The old covenant was formed between God and Israel at Sinai. Men have never ceased to believe that they are able to establish their own righteousness. When Jesus asked the two disciples who desired a high place, if they were able to pay the price that such position would cost, they promptly answered, "We are able." Matt. 20:22. There was not the slightest doubt in their minds as to their ability to do what was required. When Christ asked the young man to keep the commandments, he immediately replied, "All these things have I kept from my youth up: what lack I yet?" Matt. 19:20. There was no question in his mind that he not only kept the commandments but had always done so. That he took for granted. "What lack I yet?" is a most revealing statement. When God at Sinai asked Israel to keep the law as a condition of His favor, they unhesitatingly answered, "All that the Lord hath spoken we will do." Ex. 19:8.
>
> When Israel thus answered, God had little choice as to what to do. He had miraculously delivered Israel at the Red Sea, when they were utterly helpless against the army of Pharaoh. He hoped they had learned their lesson of dependence upon Him. But they had not. He was still ready to help them, and hoped they might realize their utter helplessness and their need of divine aid. But they felt no such need. They felt fully able to keep the law. (Andreasen, p. 300)

Once fallen and with a sinful nature, mankind wants to be independent, and this has produced so many problems in the world, including pride and self-righteousness so that they believe they can be righteous separate of God. Comparing these last two paragraphs with the cry of the majority today, it might appear that man has come to the realization that they need the help of God, yet, in reality, they are even further away. Ancient Israel proclaimed, "All that the Lord hath spoken we will do." Conversely, modern Israel cries, "The law of God cannot be kept." On the surface, these seem to be opposites but not when we look at them more closely.

Ancient Israel attempted to keep the law of God on their own without God. Modern "Israel" says that they accept the grace, mercy, and forgiveness of God, yet God is absent in how they live. They say: "Forgiveness and grace is all we can expect from God. Spiritual power to live a godly life is not needed. He will save us just as we are. Our characters are what they are. We cannot change that we are sinners, and neither can God in this world, so there is no use bothering to ask Him to help us to be perfect when we can be saved without obedience but only by faith." Those with this belief are living apart from God just as truly as did ancient Israel. Like ancient Israel, they have not learned to depend on God for everything in life—especially righteousness, commandment keeping, and developing the character of Christ. In a backwards sort of way, they are seeking salvation through the standard of their own works and righteousness. Almost all false doctrines and theology are a form of paganism. In other words, they rely on a method of salvation developed by human beings who do not believe that God can rescue them *from* sin in the circumstances they live in and in the manner specified. Thus, they must come up with a means of sanctification that does not require God's help. Self-confidence and pride are the most disastrous character traits in the life of any Christian; they are readily developed in these false paths, which are based on the only two things needed to feel saved in any false religion. They render the possessors of such traits incapable of seeing that they have a great spiritual need, though their spiritual lack is constantly staring them in the face. Let's take a short walk through inspiration and see what it says about the two types of humans and their response to the means of salvation that God requires.

## Two Responses to God's Means of Salvation

The Spirit of Prophecy gives us a wonderful study on the two types of individuals through Cain and Abel. Let us closely consider them. To save space, I will let the added emphasis serve as my commentary:

> **These brothers were tested**, as Adam had been tested before them, **to prove** whether they would **believe** and **obey** the word of God. They were acquainted with the provision made for the salvation of man, and understood the system of offerings which God had ordained.
>
> **They knew** that in these offerings they **were to express faith** in the Saviour whom the offerings typified, and at the same time to

**acknowledge** their **total dependence** on Him for pardon; and **they knew** that by thus conforming to the divine plan for their redemption, they were giving proof of their obedience to the will of God. Without the shedding of blood there could be no remission of sin; **and they were to show their faith in the blood of Christ** as the promised atonement by offering the firstlings of the flock in sacrifice. Besides this, the first fruits of the earth were to be presented before the Lord as a thank offering....

Cain came before God with **murmuring** and **infidelity** in his heart in regard to the promised sacrifice and the necessity of the sacrificial offerings. **His gift expressed no penitence for sin.** He felt, as many now feel, that it would be an acknowledgment of weakness to follow **the exact plan** marked out by God, **of trusting his salvation wholly to the atonement of the promised Saviour.** He chose the course of **self-dependence.** He would come **in his own merits**. He would not bring the lamb, and mingle its blood with his offering, but would present *his* fruits, the products of *his* labor. He presented his offering as **a favor done to God**, through which **he expected to secure the divine approval**. Cain obeyed in building an altar, obeyed in bringing a sacrifice; **but he rendered only a partial obedience**. The essential part, the recognition of the need of a Redeemer, **was left out**.

So far as birth and religious instruction were concerned, these brothers were equal. Both were sinners, and both acknowledged the claims of God to reverence and worship. To outward appearance their religion was the same up to a certain point, **but beyond this the difference between the two was great**.

"**By faith** Abel offered unto God a more excellent sacrifice than Cain." Hebrews 11:4. Abel grasped the great principles of redemption. **He saw himself a sinner**, and he saw sin and its penalty, death, standing between his soul and communion with God. He brought the slain victim, the sacrificed life, thus acknowledging the claims of the law that had been transgressed. Through the shed blood he looked to the future sacrifice, Christ dying on the cross of Calvary; and **trusting in the atonement** that was there to be made, he had the witness that he was righteous, and **his offering accepted**.

Cain had the same opportunity of learning and accepting these truths as had Abel. He was not the victim of an arbitrary purpose. One brother was not elected to be accepted of God, and the other to be rejected. **Abel chose faith and obedience**; Cain, unbelief and rebellion. **Here the whole matter rested**.

Cain and Abel represent **two classes** that will exist in the world till the close of time. **One class avail themselves** of the appointed sacrifice for sin; **the other venture to depend upon their own merits**; theirs is a sacrifice without the virtue of divine mediation, **and thus it is not able to bring man into favor with God**. It is **only** through the merits of Jesus that our transgressions can be pardoned. Those who feel no need of the blood of Christ, who feel that without divine grace they can by their **own** works **secure** the **approval** of God, are making the same mistake as did Cain. If they do not accept the **cleansing** blood, they are under condemnation. **There is no other provision made whereby they can be released from the thralldom of sin**.

The class of worshipers who follow the example of Cain includes by far the greater portion of the world; **for nearly every false religion** has been based on the same principle—that man can depend upon his own efforts for salvation. It is claimed by some that the human race is in need, not of redemption, but of development—that it can refine, elevate, and regenerate itself. As Cain thought to secure the divine favor by an offering that lacked the blood of a sacrifice, so do these expect to exalt humanity to the divine standard, **independent** of the atonement. The history of Cain shows what must be the results. It shows what man will become apart from Christ. **Humanity** has **no power to regenerate itself**. It does not tend upward, toward the divine, but downward, toward the **satanic**. Christ is our only hope. "There is none other name under heaven given among men, whereby we must be saved." "Neither is there salvation in any other" Acts 4:12.

**True faith, which relies wholly upon Christ**, will be **manifested** by obedience to **all the requirements of God**. From Adam's day to the present time the great controversy has been concerning obedience to God's law. In all ages there have been those who claimed a right to the favor of God **even while they were disregarding some of His commands**. But the Scriptures declare that by works is "faith made perfect;" and that, without the works of obedience, faith "is dead." James 2:22, 17. He that professes to know God, "and keepeth not His commandments, is a liar, and the truth is not in him." 1 John 2:4. (*Patriarchs and Prophets*, pp. 71–73)

## The Jews During the Time of Christ

Turning to the Jews at the time of Christ, we see the same thinking as that of Cain, though manifest in a different form. Ultimately, it is the same works-righteousness, which has only partial obedience based on self-dependence. It is attempting to gain God's approval through human means without accepting the true sacrifice of "divine atonement" and divine mediation. Therefore, the Jews were left without divine mediation as a nation.

> As the Jews departed from God, and **failed to make the righteousness of Christ their own by faith**, the Sabbath lost its significance to them. Satan was seeking to exalt himself and to draw men away from Christ, and he worked to pervert the **Sabbath**, because it is the sign of the power of Christ. The Jewish leaders accomplished the will of Satan by surrounding God's rest day with burdensome requirements. In the days of Christ the Sabbath had become so perverted that its observance reflected the character of selfish and arbitrary men rather than the character of the loving heavenly Father. **The rabbis virtually represented God as giving laws which it was impossible for men to obey**. They led the people to look upon **God as a tyrant**, and to think that the observance of the Sabbath, as He required it, made men hard-hearted and cruel. It was the work of Christ to clear away these misconceptions. Although the rabbis followed Him with merciless hostility, He did not even appear to conform to their requirements, but went straight forward, keeping the Sabbath according to the law of God. (*The Desire of Ages*, pp. 283, 284)
>
> **Through heathenism**, Satan had for ages turned men away from God; but he won his **great triumph** in perverting the faith of Israel. By contemplating and worshiping their own conceptions, the heathen had lost a knowledge of God, and had become more and more corrupt. So it was with Israel. **The principle that man can save himself by his own works lay at the foundation of every heathen religion**; it had now become the principle of the Jewish religion. **Satan** had implanted this principle. **Wherever it is held, men have no barrier against sin**. (*The Desire of Ages*, pp. 35, 36)

Is it not the same today as it was before the Flood and during the time of Christ? Mankind does not want to acknowledge their weakness. They do not want to render complete dependence on God through penitence. Rather, they prefer to rely on their own abilities and to come to God in their own merits, presenting the fruits of their own labor as *a favor* to God, expecting to receive divine approval while rendering only partial obedience—the obedience that they are comfortable giving. To the superficial glance, this false religion can appear to be the same religion as God's path, and yet the two are vastly different. The whole matter of the foundation of true worship rests on faith. The false professors of righteousness by faith actually have no faith, and they are seeking to gain God's approval through a system of works-righteousness disguised as faith. To prove that they are saved by faith and are not Pharisees, they may purposely try not to obey some of God's requirements. "It is claimed by some that the human race is in need, not of redemption, but of development—that it can refine, elevate, and regenerate itself" (*Patriarchs and Prophets*, p. 73). Of course, they seek to bring about this self-development without God's help because they believe that human nature can never be overcome and that it can never be brought under sanctified control. "As Cain thought to secure the divine favor by an offering that lacked the blood of a sacrifice, so do these expect to exalt humanity to the divine standard, independent of the atonement" (*Patriarchs and Prophets*, p. 73). The lack of blood with the offering is saying, in effect, "I don't deserve death. I didn't break the law—in fact, there is no law. What I offer to you is a favor. Accept me 'just as I am.' I won't change because I cannot change, and neither do I want to change." Little do such people realize that they cannot break free from the thralldom of sin without coming to God in His appointed manner. They unknowingly submit themselves to the control of demons. *True faith in God leads people to obey all the requirements of God*. These false professors present a false picture of God, giving Him the attributes of the devil, who is a tyrant, and they do their utmost to push those who are truehearted away from keeping all of God's commandments. The devil, the thief that he is, steals the attributes of God to clothe himself in apparent righteousness as an "angel of light" (2 Cor. 11:14). Do not be deceived. Under this false religion, mankind has no barrier against sin and Satan, and Satan has them trapped in a system without deliverance.

As Andreasen stated, "God had little choice as to what to do." To be fair, He first had to allow Satan the opportunity to try to serve Him and keep His commandments without His help. Then He had to give the same opportunity to mankind. His willingness to do so makes quite a statement about how God works in using the freewill of His creatures to keep them sanctified, pure, and holy.

Satan is the epitome of power and extraordinary intelligence, yet he is completely hopeless and helpless in keeping the law of God. Only God can make us holy, and Satan's best attempts at holiness apart from God have failed, and they always will. Before the Prince of heaven expelled Satan from heaven, Satan's only option to keep on living, when the paycheck for sin is death, was to rebel and promote the claim that the law of God cannot be kept. His course of action will only delay the execution of his sentence against a God whose grace is sufficient to empower mankind to keep his law through faith. If he could prove his point, God, in justice, would have to grant him continued life, for God did not create His creatures with a desire to die, even though they might be miserable sinners.

Mankind has the opportunity while living to change their mind about sin after tasting its misery. This choice is what the covenant provides for, which, in itself, is a revealing statement about the justice of God. Once this world of sin has come to an end and all the created beings of God stand before Him, this multitude of beings will include holy angels, unfallen beings, fallen angels, holy and redeemed human beings, and unrepentant lost human beings. Each category will make a statement about the wisdom, justice, mercy, love, and sustaining and redeeming power of God.

Turning to the Word of God, I encourage you to consider the words, "faileth not," in the following verses. Dear reader, the Lord continues to ask you, "Do you believe in Me? Have faith and live!"

> If then God so clothe the grass, which is to day in the field, and to morrow is cast into the oven; how much more will he clothe you, O ye of little faith? And seek not ye what ye shall eat, or what ye shall drink, neither be ye of doubtful mind. For all these things do the nations of the world seek after: and your Father knoweth that ye have need of these things. But rather seek ye the kingdom of God; and all these things shall be added unto you. Fear not, little flock; for it is your Father's good pleasure to give you the kingdom. Sell that ye have, and give alms; provide yourselves bags which wax not old, a treasure in the heavens that <u>faileth not</u>, where no thief approacheth, neither moth corrupteth. (Luke 12:28–33)
>
> The just LORD is in the midst thereof; he will not do iniquity: every morning doth he bring his judgment to light, he <u>faileth not</u>; but the unjust knoweth no shame. I have cut off the nations: their towers are desolate; I made their streets waste, that none passeth by: their cities are destroyed, so that there is no man, that

there is none inhabitant. I said, Surely thou wilt fear me, thou wilt receive instruction; so their dwelling should not be cut off, howsoever I punished them: but they rose early, and corrupted all their doings. Therefore wait ye upon me, saith the LORD, until the day that I rise up to the prey: for my determination is to gather the nations, that I may assemble the kingdoms, to pour upon them mine indignation, even all my fierce anger: for all the earth shall be devoured with the fire of my jealousy. For then will I turn to the people a pure language, that they may all call upon the name of the LORD, to serve him with one consent. (Zeph. 3:5–9)

Lift up your eyes on high, and behold who hath created these things, that bringeth out their host by number: he calleth them all by names by the greatness of his might, for that he is strong in power; not one faileth. Why sayest thou, O Jacob, and speakest, O Israel, My way is hid from the LORD, and my judgment is passed over from my God? Hast thou not known? hast thou not heard, that the everlasting God, the LORD, the Creator of the ends of the earth, fainteth not, neither is weary? there is no searching of his understanding. He giveth power to the faint; and to them that have no might he increaseth strength. (Isa. 40:26–29)

Charity never faileth. (1 Cor. 13:8)

## Again the Lord asks, "Do you believe in Me? Have faith and live!"

<u>When we study the divine character in the light of the cross we see **mercy**, **tenderness**, and **forgiveness** blended with **equity** and **justice**</u>. We see in the midst of the throne One bearing in hands and feet and side the marks of the suffering endured to reconcile man to God. <u>We see a Father, infinite, dwelling in light unapproachable, **yet receiving us to Himself through the merits of His Son**</u>. The cloud of vengeance that threatened only misery and despair, in the light reflected from the cross reveals the writing of God: **Live, sinner, live! ye penitent, believing souls, live! I have paid a ransom.**

In the contemplation of Christ we linger on the shore of a love that is measureless. We endeavor to tell of this love, and language fails us. We consider His life on earth, His sacrifice for us, His work in heaven as our advocate, and the mansions He is preparing for those who love Him, and we can only exclaim, O the height and

> depth of the love of Christ! "Herein is love, not that we loved God, but that He loved us, and sent His Son to be the propitiation for our sins." "Behold, what manner of love the Father hath bestowed upon us, that we should be called the sons of God." 1 John 4:10; 3:1. (*The Acts of the Apostles*, pp. 333, 334)

As we close this chapter, please take special note that the biblical, contextual definition of a "son of God" is someone without sin, someone who is perfect, pure, holy, and sanctified. This is a tremendous thought, underlining the restorative grace and love of God to fallen man. Yes, we have sinned. Yes, we were deceived. Yes, we even rebelled. But God does not want you to forget that He is still unwilling to just let you be lost. It is true that believing in the truth path of salvation takes a tremendous amount of faith grown from a mustard seed. Why is this? It is because, in the principles of Satan, which the world follows, there is a remembrance of your past sins and an unwillingness to forgive. The devil does this on purpose to make it that much harder for you to accept the real gift of salvation, the gift of the atoning sacrifice of Christ by faith without your own merits. Praise God for His marvelous plan and covenant!

CHAPTER 10

# Security through Dependence

> When He shall come with trumpet sound,
> O may I then in Him be found;
> Clad in His righteousness alone,
> Faultless to stand before the throne.
> —Edward Mote[15]

From the experience of ancient Israel, we learn that only when they surrendered to His will, in complete dependence on what God did for and through them, then were they spiritually successful. Paul summarized these experiences in First Corinthians and Hebrews:

> Now all these things happened unto them for ensamples: and they are written for our admonition, upon whom the ends of the world are come. Wherefore let him that thinketh he standeth take heed lest he fall. (1 Cor. 10:11, 12)
>
> Therefore we ought to give the more earnest heed to the things which we have heard, lest at any time we should let them slip. (Heb. 2:1)
>
> Wherefore (as the Holy Ghost saith, To day if ye will hear his voice, Harden not your hearts, as in the provocation, in the day of temptation in the wilderness: When your fathers tempted me,

---

[15] Edward Mote, "My Hope Is Built on Nothing Less," 1834, Hymnary, https://1ref.us/1kx (accessed February 17, 2021).

proved me, and saw my works forty years. Wherefore I was grieved with that generation, and said, They do alway err in their heart; and they have not known my ways. So I sware in my wrath, They shall not enter into my rest.) Take heed, brethren, lest there be in any of you an evil heart of unbelief, in departing from the living God. But exhort one another daily, while it is called To day; lest any of you be hardened through the deceitfulness of sin. For we are made partakers of Christ, if we hold the beginning of our confidence stedfast unto the end; while it is said, To day if ye will hear his voice, harden not your hearts, as in the provocation.... So we see that they could not enter in because of unbelief. Let us therefore fear, lest, a promise being left us of entering into his rest, any of you should seem to come short of it. For unto us was the gospel preached, as well as unto them: but the word preached did not profit them, not being mixed with faith in them that heard it. For we which have believed do enter into rest, as he said, As I have sworn in my wrath, if they shall enter into my rest: although the works were finished from the foundation of the world. (Heb. 3:7–15, 19; 4:1–3)

As we have previously discussed, the plan for making the universe secure, should sin arise, was not an afterthought, hastily conceived when Adam and Eve sinned. Rather, it was a "revelation of the mystery, which was kept secret since the world began" (Rom. 16:25), and God put it into effect after sin entered the world. Notice how the Spirit of Prophecy puts it:

> The plan for our redemption was not an afterthought, a plan formulated after the fall of Adam. It was a revelation of "the mystery which hath been kept in silence through times eternal." Romans 16:25, R. V. **It was an unfolding of the principles that from eternal ages have been the foundation of God's throne.** From the beginning, God and Christ knew of the apostasy of Satan, and of the fall of man through the deceptive power of the apostate. God did not ordain that sin should exist, but He foresaw its existence, and made provision to meet the terrible emergency. <u>So great was His love for the world, that He **covenanted** to give His only-begotten Son</u>, "that whosoever believeth in Him should not perish, but have everlasting life." John 3:16. (*The Desire of Ages*, p. 22)

The great immediate lesson we can learn from Israel's example is dependence on the Almighty. Though we have a part to act, we must do so in dependence upon the One who has asked us to believe in Him and keep His commandments. Remember, justice requires that He not leave us to ourselves to work out our own salvation but, rather, to look to Him who is "faithful and just." Ancient Israel did not have a risen Saviour as we do now. That we have one puts us at an increased obligation to trust in His blood and powerful hand to deliver us from this world of sin.

## An Opportunity for Faith and Faithfulness

Ancient Israel had forty years to prove God and respond to His faithfulness. Only two of their number learned the lesson. In our time, the number of people learning the lesson of faith need not be so small. In fact, Scripture is clear—at least 144,000 will be saved out of the last generation. The question is: Will you be one of them? God created you for this purpose. Believe Him and accept His calling and watch the glory of the Lord in the experience of your life. The Lord has given us thousands of promises to carry us through life as we trust in His power to save and to produce the ultimate miracle of redemption, unseen until it is experienced. Yet, we must believe first, or we will be lost. God's promises are not only for others; they are for you as well. "Hold fast the profession of [your] faith without wavering" (Heb. 10:23).

> To make very sure that the people knew the contents of the covenant they were entering into, God publicly proclaimed to them the law, the Ten Commandments. To make doubly sure that there would be no misunderstanding as to the extent of their obligation, He made a detailed application of the principles of the Ten Commandments to their situation, so that they would know exactly what was demanded of them. (Ex. 20:22 to 23:33.) In the course of these explanatory judgments and statutes, He warned them of what they were facing. "Behold," said God, "I send an Angel before thee.... Beware of him, and obey his voice, provoke him not; for *he will not pardon your transgressions:* for my name is in him." Exod. 23:20, 21.
>
> These significant words should have made them pause. Did they still feel that there was no cause for alarm? Did they still feel that they were able to keep the law? They did. They had learned nothing. They felt no need of pardon. They did not ask for any. They were willing to enter into covenant with God.
>
> God, of course, knew that they would fall. But He had no choice. Had He refused them the opportunity of trying, had He said that it was no use, and that He would not even give them the

privilege of showing what they could do, <u>Israel could justly have claimed that they had not had a fair chance, that they *could* have kept the law, but that God would not give them a chance to prove it</u>. **God had no choice but to let them try it**. The result was failure, as God foreknew. (Andreasen, pp. 300, 301, boldfacing and underlining added, italics in the original)

This same story has been repeated in the life of every single man and woman on earth except Jesus Christ. The human nature is bent on pleasing self. It indulges selfishness, self-confidence, and self-exaltation. When we learn dependence on our Almighty God, through partaking of the divine nature that He offers to us, we have victory. In fact, in this manner, we cannot fail when we "have obtained like precious faith … through the righteousness of God and our Saviour Jesus Christ: Grace and peace be multiplied unto you through the knowledge of God, and of Jesus our Lord, according as his divine power hath given unto us all things that pertain unto life and godliness, through the knowledge of him that hath called us to glory and virtue: Whereby are given unto us exceeding great and precious promises: that by these ye might be <u>partakers of the divine nature</u>, having escaped the corruption that is in the world through lust" (2 Peter 1:1–4).

See what the Word is saying to us here: Everything we need for "life and godliness"—even a "divine nature" that does not commit sin—is provided. We need not look to any other source, for there is no other source. "Assemble yourselves and come; draw near together, ye that are escaped of the nations: they have no knowledge that set up the wood of their graven image, and pray unto a god that cannot save. Tell ye, and bring them near; yea, let them take counsel together: who hath declared this from ancient time? who hath told it from that time? have not I the LORD? and there is no God else beside me; a just God and a Saviour; there is none beside me. Look unto me, and be ye saved, all the ends of the earth: for I am God, and there is none else" (Isa. 45:20–22).

Thus, you have the promise, "Whosoever is born of God doth not commit sin; for his seed remaineth in him: and he cannot sin, because he is born of God" (1 John 3:9). So many people question this verse. However, either God is Almighty, or He is not; either He can save, or He cannot; either He can keep us from sinning, or He cannot. Trust Him; trust His Word, which was written for you, and see the salvation of the Lord in your life. We will study the application of the covenant promises in a later chapter. Andreasen continues with the lessons we can learn from ancient Israel:

> God, however, did not intend to leave Israel to their own devices and to discouragement at their failure. Even while they were dancing around the golden calf, God was instructing Moses to build Him a tabernacle that He might dwell among them and teach them His ways more perfectly. They needed to understand the heinousness of sin, and that even the least transgression meant death. They needed to know more of the holiness of God and the need of forgiveness. They needed to have a more vivid conception of the need of a heavenly mediator, prefigured in the earthly priesthood. They needed to know that without an intercessor there was no way for them to approach God. All this God meant to teach them in the sanctuary service. (Andreasen, p. 301)

The same lessons are for us today, for we little recognize the heinousness of sin or our need of forgiveness. Without this recognition, we will not feel the need of a Saviour or seek His salvation. That is why God allows us to suffer, from time to time, the consequences of our actions. Until we realize how low we have gone, we do not ask for redemption or look to God in faith for deliverance. Until we have a desire for righteousness and experience our lack of strength to attain it, we do not have a complete understanding of our need to depend on God's power. Yes, even "the least transgression meant death." Too often we only think about our own death, to which this statement does refer. However, when you choose to sin, you are saying in reality that I want to kill God and would do so if given the opportunity. It is that serious! Do we not have the cross as the demonstration of this truth? It was because of our sin that Jesus suffered and died. Men sought Jesus' life and succeeded in killing Him. Do not think lightly of this, for these men are the representatives of all sinners. That includes you and me. Jesus is a king, and He is seated in rulership with His Father in heaven. However, our heart is also to be His throne. Yet, self cannot share our heart's throne with Jesus. For self to reign, the rightful King, who is our Creator and the living God, must be dethroned. The only way a new empire can come into power is through the death of the reigning king. In reality, when we sin, we are saying, "I will not have you, God, interfering with the desires of my human nature. My wisdom is superior to yours, and I know best what I need. I am the god of my life, and I can function without your interference." The "man of sin" is appropriately named for his character traits—he "opposeth and exalteth himself above all that is called God, or that is worshipped; so that he as God sitteth in the temple of God, shewing himself that he is God" (2 Thess. 2:4).

Everyone that is lost is categorized under this king because each subject of that kingdom has the same ideology as that king. God does not label things just to give them a nice name. There is significance to all He says.

The cross is the fullest manifestation of the smallest act of sin. Stealing a paper clip is a minor offense and may appear harmless. Yet, it is still a sin, and the full manifestation of any sin leads to the death of King Jesus. The utter insanity of getting rid of Jesus so that we can do our own thing is that, in killing the living God, there is no one to sustain our life, the world, and the universe. Thus, the heinousness of sin saw its fullest demonstration in Satan's deceiving of humans into killing the Son of God—the Creator and Sustainer of life—by crucifixion. The instrument that was used to accomplish this task was unforeseen by Lucifer, his angels, the unfallen worlds, the holy angels, and mankind. Yet, therein is the immensity of the love of God revealed, for in knowing full well what the result would be, He nonetheless allowed the events to transpire. What an ingenious plan of the divine mind—to use our heinous crime to save us!

## A Witness to God's Goodness

Returning to Andreasen's comments, we read:

> Israel had broken the covenant which they had solemnly made with God. "They continued not in my covenant," said God, "and I regarded them not." Heb. 8:9. God proposed to Moses that He reject the people, and make of Moses a great nation. But Moses interceded for the people, asking God to spare them, and he was successful. (Ex. 32:11–14.) But when he asked the Lord to forgive their sin, God rather curtly responded, "Whosoever hath sinned against me, him will I blot out of my book." Verse 33.
>
> God then commanded Moses to lead the people to the place which He had chosen, stating that He would not go with them Himself, but would send His angel instead. Then He repeated His warning of punishment to come: "Nevertheless in the day when I visit I will visit their sin upon them." Verse 34.
>
> As a sign of God's displeasure, the tabernacle was pitched "without the camp, afar off from the camp." Ex. 33:7. As a result of this "every one which sought the Lord went out unto the tabernacle of the congregation, which was without the camp." Verse 7.

Moses then appeared as the mediator of his people. God had rejected Israel; they had broken the covenant, and He regarded them not. They were no longer His people. He did not own them as His, but spoke of them to Moses as *"thy* people, which *thou* brought out of the land of Egypt." Ex. 32:7. Moses, however, came back with the rejoinder that they were God's people, not his. "Lord," he said, "why does thy wrath wax hot against *thy* people, which *thou* hast brought forth out of the land of Egypt?" Verse 11.

Moses was not satisfied with having an angel go with them on the journey. He wanted the Lord Himself to go up with them. He had found favor with God, and made the most of it. "If I have found grace in thy sight," he said, "show me now thy way, that I may know thee, ... consider that this nation is *thy* people." Ex. 33:13. God relented and said, "My presence shall go with thee." Verse 14. Moses felt encouraged by this, but was not yet satisfied. He boldly asked not only that God's presence go with them, but "that *thou* goest with us." Verse 16. God graciously answered, "I will do this thing also that thou hast spoken." Verse 17.

But Moses was not yet satisfied. He pressed the point: "Shew me now thy way, that I may know thee." He urged, "Shew me thy glory." Verse 18. God's glory is His character. Justice is part of God's glory, but so is mercy. Thus far God had shown mostly the justice side of His character, but Moses now asked to be shown God's *ways*, that he might know *Him*. He well knew that if he could get God to reveal Himself, such a revelation would stress God's mercy and loving kindness, and that this would give him an opportunity to call upon God to be gracious to His people.

And Moses was not mistaken. He was given a revelation of "The Lord, The Lord God, merciful and gracious, longsuffering, and abundant in goodness and truth, keeping mercy for thousands, forgiving iniquity and transgression and sin, and that will by no means clear the guilty; visiting the iniquity of the fathers upon the children, and upon the children's children, unto the third and to the fourth generation." Ex. 34:6, 7.

The Lord having revealed Himself as a merciful and gracious God, Moses made his final request. God had already promised that instead of sending an angel, He Himself would go with the people. Moses asked two things. First: "O Lord, let the Lord, I pray thee, go in the *midst* of us." Verse 9, R.V. God had been dwelling without

> the camp, "afar off." Ex. 33:7. Moses now asked that He go up "in the midst of us." This request had been once denied when God said, "I will not go up in the midst of thee." Verse 3. The other request was this: "Pardon our iniquity and our sin, and take us for thine inheritance." Ex. 34:9.
>
> To both of these requests God answered, "Behold, I make a covenant." Verse 10. This was as much as to say, "**My dwelling in your midst** and forgiving your sins **depends upon your attitude.** I make a covenant. Upon the faithful adherence to this covenant will hang My decision." (Andreasen, pp. 302–304, emphasis in original)

Something that is little considered is that God has to destroy sin. If it ever appeared in His universe, justice would require that He remove it. Knowing this ahead of time, He prepared for a plan of redemption. Then, in the experience of ancient Israel, we see the need of justice, salvation, forgiveness, and empowering for the recovery of fallen humanity.

Moses knew that all that had been accomplished thus far in his experience with God was through God's power. In the incident in which he killed the Egyptian, Moses failed in his attempt to bring about positive results for Israel. When he returned to the people after forty years in the wilderness, he was not readily received, and he knew that only by the demonstration of the Lord's power and through their seeing God's providential leading would the people accept him as their human leader. Moses was not about to try, even for a little bit, to lead a rebellious, murmuring, and easily idolatrous people without the power of the Lord with him. He had the example of his brother Aaron, who only succeeded in calming the people through compromise, showing the futility and disastrous results of trying to lead carnal people without the Spirit of God. Moses' eighty years of experience and training by the Lord were now bearing abundant fruit. The Lord, who is no respecter of persons, surely would have destroyed the people were it not for finding in Moses an intercessor with whom he was able to commune as with no one since. Moses so perfectly reflected the image of God after this experience that his face shone brighter than the sun, and the people could not bear to look upon him without a veil. The Lord needed an especially strong and humble leader like Moses to help Him reform a nation of former slaves, who had been exposed to idolatry for centuries. Through Moses, the people were able to see the character of Christ—through one who was dependent upon the Lord in the smallest of issues, who was unselfish and not self-confident, and who did not take credit for the work that the hand of the Lord had accomplished. Moses always loved God's people, even when they did not particularly manifest love to him. Realizing their lack of love, he knew that they needed to be cared for patiently. This caring man authored the first five books of the Bible, known as the Torah, or "the Law." It is the Law that gives the foundational history for the battle against sin as well as the principles of salvation. Moses' question, "Why doth thy wrath wax hot against thy people?" appears almost as if it were spoken in a sense of bewilderment. It is clear that Moses understood the character of God, and that is why he was puzzled why the Lord would not be merciful. On the other hand, Moses' experience of victory over sin taught him that God required obedience. Thus, he appealed to God not to mar His name before the nations, even though he knew he was interceding for an erring, stubborn, and stiff-necked people. Moses understood the covenant that God made with Abraham, and he thought first to protect God's name.

> God's **covenant** with His people had been **disannulled**, and He declared to Moses, "Let Me alone, that My wrath may wax hot against them, and that I may consume them: and I will make of thee a great nation." The people of Israel, especially the mixed multitude, would be constantly disposed to rebel against God. **They would also murmur against their leader, and would grieve him by their unbelief and stubbornness, and it would be a laborious and soul-trying work to lead them through to the Promised Land.** Their sins had already forfeited the favor of God, and **justice** called for their **destruction**. The Lord therefore proposed to destroy them, and make of Moses a mighty nation.
>
> "Let Me alone, ... that I may consume them," were the words of God. If God had purposed to destroy Israel, who could plead for them? How few but would have left the sinners to their fate! How few but would have gladly exchanged a lot of toil and burden and sacrifice, repaid with ingratitude and murmuring, for a position of ease and honor, **when it was God Himself that offered the release**.
>
> But Moses discerned ground for hope where there appeared only discouragement and wrath. The words of God, "Let Me alone," **he understood not to forbid but to encourage intercession, implying that nothing but the prayers of Moses could save Israel, but that if thus entreated, God would spare His people.** He "besought the Lord his God, and said, Lord, why doth Thy wrath

wax hot against Thy people, which Thou hast brought forth out of the land of Egypt with great power, and with a mighty hand?"

God had signified that He disowned His people. He had spoken of them to Moses as *"thy* people, which *thou* broughtest out of Egypt." But Moses humbly disclaimed the leadership of Israel. They were not his, but God's—*"Thy* people, which *Thou* has brought forth ... with great power, and with a mighty hand. Wherefore," he urged, "should the Egyptians speak, and say, For mischief did He bring them out, to slay them in the mountains, and to consume them from the face of the earth?"

During the few months since Israel left Egypt, the report of their wonderful deliverance had spread to all the surrounding nations. Fear and terrible foreboding rested upon the heathen. All were watching to see what the God of Israel would do for His people. Should they now be destroyed, their enemies would triumph, and God would be dishonored. The Egyptians would claim that their accusations were true—instead of leading His people into the wilderness to sacrifice, He had caused them to be sacrificed. They would not consider the sins of Israel; the destruction of the people whom He had so signally honored, would bring reproach upon His name. **How great the responsibility resting upon those whom God has highly honored, to make His name a praise in the earth!** With what care should they guard against committing sin, to call down His judgments and cause His name to be reproached by the ungodly!

As Moses interceded for Israel, his timidity was lost in his deep interest and love for those for whom he had, in the hands of God, been the means of doing so much. The Lord listened to his pleadings, and granted his unselfish prayer. God had proved His servant; He had tested his faithfulness and his love for that erring, ungrateful people, and nobly had Moses endured the trial. His interest in Israel sprang from no selfish motive. **The prosperity of God's chosen people was dearer to him than personal honor, dearer than the privilege of becoming the father of a mighty nation.** God was pleased with his faithfulness, his simplicity of heart, and his integrity, and He committed to him, as a faithful shepherd, the great charge of leading Israel to the Promised Land. (*Patriarchs and Prophets*, pp. 318, 319)

The promise of the Lord is sure, and He will have a last generation who will be translated. Will you help? Will you sanctify yourself today that you may intercede for the erring, ungrateful, stubborn, stiff-necked, murmuring, and rebellious people around you? Help glorify the name of the Lord by allowing Him to reflect His image fully through you. Take hold of the covenant promises and see the salvation of the Lord in your life that you may be a vessel of honor, filled with the Holy Spirit. Let us follow and walk as our Creator and Redeemer has said, "And for their sakes I sanctify myself, that they also might be sanctified through the truth" (John 17:19). Too many times we throw up our hands in discouragement and frustration when working for the Lord among His people in the church, and this should not be. We must know that every promise of the covenant is sure, and, when it comes to sin and redemption, the Lord is especially willing to work. As you sanctify yourself, the Lord can put His seal of approval on your work to enable you to affect positively those around you as you lead them to salvation.

Intercessory prayer is the highest order of prayer, and the Lord wants to have an intercessor whose prayers He can hear to the utmost that is possible without forcing anyone to accept the gift of salvation. Let us stop blaming and criticizing the people around us for their spiritual wretchedness when, if we sanctify ourselves and surrender ourselves for this purpose, God will have an instrument that He can use for the salvation of those He so dearly loves. What a sober statement inspiration gives, "Their sins had already forfeited the favor of God, and justice called for their destruction," would this not be true for the church today, which is 178+ years outside of Canaan and unprepared to enter the promised land? As you depend on the Lord no matter which side of the equation you are on, He will be faithful and save to the uttermost that His name may be glorified. Take hope, take courage, "Fear not, little flock; for it is your Father's good pleasure to give you the kingdom" (Luke 12:32).

> But thanks be to God, which giveth us the victory through our Lord Jesus Christ. Therefore, my beloved brethren, be ye stedfast, unmoveable, always abounding in the work of the Lord, forasmuch as ye know that your labour is not in vain in the Lord. (1 Cor. 15:57, 58)

Though we as a people have erred in like manner, know that the Lord will be strong for those who turn with contrition of heart and have a resolved mind to serve Him. This battle is not ours but the Lord's, and He will fight for His name and glory. Praise the Lord that, though we have been foolish, He has not cast us off. Thus, when you turn to Him, His loving kindness, compassion, and tender mercy are ready for expression. Don't forget that you should pray, "For thy name sake," or "according to thy word," or "be it done unto us." These are keys to answered prayer. God is simply fulfilling what He has promised that He would do under the stated conditions. Notice how the Lord answered Moses in a later experience when Moses had petitioned Him. In like manner, dear reader, you can depend on God to keep His word to you.

> And now, I beseech thee, let the power of my Lord be great, **according as thou hast spoken**, saying, The Lord is longsuffering, and of great mercy, forgiving iniquity and transgression, and by no means clearing the guilty, visiting the iniquity of the fathers upon the children unto the third and fourth generation. Pardon, I beseech thee, the iniquity of this people according unto the greatness of thy mercy, and as thou hast forgiven this people, from Egypt even until now. And the Lord said, I have pardoned according to thy word: But as truly as I live, all the earth shall be filled with the glory of the Lord. (Num. 14:17–21)

This last phrase, dear reader, is talking about you and me, and about all the redeemed who will eventually fill the entire earth with the glory of the Lord. This is what those who have depended on God's name for deliverance, in any and every circumstance of life, have had to experience, but, through it, they will glorify God by not sinning.

## The New Covenant in Old Testament Types

Many times we talk in our church discussions about the Israelites being under the old covenant and especially about their response to the commandments of God. At some point, we have to ask: How would they know about or understand that the new covenant was to go into effect at the death of the prophesied Messiah? They had to have some understanding of the new covenant to realize where their actual salvation comes from so that they would not trust in the symbolic offerings and sacrifices of lambs, rams, goats, and bulls. Recognizing the coming Messiah would give them a clearer understanding of the signs and symbols of the sanctuary services. Ancient Israel accepted the Ten Commandments, their covenant with God, and they had the lesson of the old covenant and of the new covenant through the parallel of their rejection of God as a nation and their reinstatement through subsequent events. They were not fully reinstated until just before they entered Canaan.

> At that time the LORD said unto Joshua, Make thee sharp knives, and circumcise again the children of Israel the second time. And Joshua made him sharp knives, and circumcised the children of Israel at the hill of the foreskins. And this is the cause why Joshua did circumcise: All the people that came out of Egypt, that were males, even all the men of war, died in the wilderness by the way, after they came out of Egypt. Now all the people that came out were circumcised: but all the people that were born in the wilderness by the way as they came forth out of Egypt, them they had not circumcised. For the children of Israel walked forty years in the wilderness, till all the people that were men of war, which came out of Egypt, were consumed, because they obeyed not the voice of the LORD: unto whom the LORD sware that he would not shew them the land, which the LORD sware unto their fathers that he would give us, a land that floweth with milk and honey. And their children, whom he raised up in their stead, them Joshua circumcised: for they were uncircumcised, because they had not circumcised them by the way. And it came to pass, when they had done circumcising all the people, that they abode in their places in the camp, till they were whole. And the LORD said unto Joshua, This day have I rolled away the reproach of Egypt from off you. Wherefore the name of the place is called Gilgal unto this day. And the children of Israel encamped in Gilgal, and kept the passover on the fourteenth day of the month at even in the plains of Jericho. (Joshua 5:2–10)

You may be wondering: What does circumcision represent with reference to their entering the Promised Land of Canaan? It is that Canaan represents the New Jerusalem in the New Earth and circumcision is a symbol of the removal of sin.

> Speak not thou in thine heart, after that the LORD thy God hath cast them out from before thee, saying, For my righteousness the

> LORD hath brought me in to possess this land: but for the wickedness of these nations the LORD doth drive them out from before thee. Not for thy righteousness, or for the uprightness of thine heart, dost thou go to possess their land: but for the wickedness of these nations the LORD thy God doth drive them out from before thee, and that he may perform the word which the LORD sware unto thy fathers, Abraham, Isaac, and Jacob. Understand therefore, that the LORD thy God giveth thee not this good land to possess it for thy righteousness; for thou art a stiffnecked people. Remember, and forget not, how thou provokedst the LORD thy God to wrath in the wilderness: from the day that thou didst depart out of the land of Egypt, until ye came unto this place, ye have been rebellious against the LORD. Also in Horeb ye provoked the LORD to wrath, so that the LORD was angry with you to have destroyed you.... And the LORD said unto me, Arise, get thee down quickly from hence; for thy people which thou hast brought forth out of Egypt have corrupted themselves; they are quickly turned aside out of the way which I commanded them; they have made them a molten image. Furthermore the LORD spake unto me, saying, I have seen this people, and, behold, it is a stiffnecked people: Let me alone, that I may destroy them, and blot out their name from under heaven: and I will make thee a nation mightier and greater than they. (Deut. 9:4–8, 12–14)

Moses told the people: "Circumcise therefore the foreskin of your heart, and be no more stiffnecked" (Deut. 10:16). In the act of circumcising the younger ones who had not been circumcised before, we see a practical application of the new covenant to ancient Israel in their inheritance of Canaan. The redeemed of mankind are not redeemed because of their righteousness but because of the name of the Lord by His mercy and name's sake. We are accepted because we have repented and have accepted the blood of Jesus to speak on our behalf. Therefore, God, who keeps His word, looks favorably upon us.

When we reach the kingdom and view the grand panorama of world history, we will gladly throw our crowns at Jesus' feet, realizing that we were just as guilty as the unrepentant and lost with whom we were once companions and even instigators or leaders in sin. When we see the many lost ones with whom we participated in sin, it will make the reality of our salvation all the more overwhelming and momentous, reminding us that we are not saved because we are worthy. All our appreciation for redemption will be directed to God for His great love and mercy. Let us bow our knees today and confess with our tongues and lives that Jesus is the Lord, the Saviour, the Redeemer, and the Almighty. When we understand that confession is by definition an actual statement of truth, our lives will be an example of His power to redeem amidst a world of sin and manifold temptations.

"Whosoever shall confess that Jesus is the Son of God, God dwelleth in him, and he in God" (1 John 4:15). Looking at the contextual definition of "confess" in the above verse, it can only make sense to apply it while a person lives, having victory over sin and temptation. To confess Jesus to be the Son of God is not a one-time verbal statement. Rather, it is an action, a demonstration of the power of the Almighty Redeemer. The context, found in chapter 5, states this explicitly: "Whosoever believeth that Jesus is the Christ is born of God: and every one that loveth him that begat loveth him also that is begotten of him. By this we know that we love the children of God, when we love God, and keep his commandments. For this is the love of God, that we keep his commandments: and his commandments are not grievous. For whatsoever is born of God overcometh the world: and this is the victory that overcometh the world, even our faith. Who is he that overcometh the world, but he that believeth that Jesus is the Son of God?" (1 John 5:1–5). Those who confess Christ will live out their confession. In this way they demonstrate that they believe that Jesus is the Christ, the Messiah, and the Son of God and that they love God. The overriding theme of First John is love and victory over sin in human flesh though it has a sinful nature.

Let us pick up from the last section of Andreasen's commentary in which he describes Moses' return the second time to the mountain to receive the second set of Ten Commandments from God. If you are paying attention to types and anti-types, you may recognize that the first giving of the Commandments to the children of Israel was, in type, the old covenant acted out. You may also recognize that the re-issuance of the Ten Commandments is the acting out, during Old Testament times, of the description of the new covenant in Jeremiah 31:33, 34. This was done to show the people, in symbolic form, what the new covenant would be, when, centuries later, it would be ratified by the blood of Jesus, though it is based on the same law as the old covenant.

> When Moses was called up into the mount at this time, he was told to appear there alone. Six weeks before, Aaron, Nadab, Abihu, and seventy of the elders were also called up. (Ex. 24:9.)

There "they saw the God of Israel.... They saw God, and did eat and drink." Verses 10, 11.

But not so this time. Now Moses only appeared. It is with him God speaks. It is with him, primarily, that the covenant was made. The usual formula, "Speak unto the children of Israel and say unto them," did not appear. Moses represented Israel. When the covenant was finally made, God said, "I have made a covenant with *thee* and with Israel." Ex. 34:27. No representative of the people was called up into the mount; they were not called upon to ratify or agree to the covenant; Moses was the only one with whom God dealt. Israel indeed had a part in it, for the covenant was made with them as well as with Moses, though in a secondary sense. "I have made a covenant with thee *and* with Israel."

This covenant is different from the one recorded in Exodus, chapters 19–24. *There* it was said of the angel, "Take ye heed before him, and hearken unto his voice; provoke him not; for *he will not pardon your transgression:* for my name is in him." Ex. 23:21, A.R.V. *Here* God reveals Himself as the merciful and gracious God, who forgives iniquity, transgression, and sin. In the first covenant there was no mediator. In the covenant of Exodus 34, Moses pleads for the people, and at last gains God's good will and forgiveness, based upon obedience to the commandments. In this covenant <u>mercy is the outstanding feature</u>. God reveals Himself in a special manifestation as the merciful God who forgives, and He graciously accepts Moses as the mediator for the people. <u>This covenant has all the marks of the new covenant, established under Old Testament conditions.</u> God moves back into the midst of the camp; the sanctuary service is established, all the ceremonies of which point to forgiveness; a mediator—in the person of the high priest—is established, and in him Israel appears before the Lord and obtains forgiveness for all their uncleanness, transgression, and sins. <u>True, it is all in type, but it is prophetic of that better covenant of which Christ Himself is the mediator, and through whose merits sins are in verity forgiven and blotted out</u>. (Andreasen, pp. 304, 305, underline added but italics in original)

It is significant that Moses appeared alone this time before God. When Adam fell into sin, the effect rippled to all generations. Yet, salvation occurs individually. We see individual salvation on this occasion as each of the children of Israel were to receive the Lord for themselves as a personal Saviour. We who have received and accepted all that God offers can, like Moses, only go back and offer God's gift to our brethren in the hopes of their receiving it in the joy of the Lord as have we. The new covenant is a document that faithfully expresses one of the outstanding character traits of God—mercy. However, we must not let God's mercy get in the way of committing ourselves to the keeping of the covenant as stipulated, which we agreed to do when we accepted the blood of Jesus.

CHAPTER 11

# The Spirit of Prophecy on the Covenant

> Love divine, all loves excelling,
> Joy of heaven, to earth come down;
> Fix in us Thy humble dwelling,
> All Thy faithful mercies crown!
> —Charles Wesley[16]

In this brief chapter I have compiled several precious gems of thought that reveal the new covenant throughout sacred history. I will allow the added emphasis to speak along with the context of each statement.

## The Covenant First Revealed at the Fall

The angels related to them the grief that was felt in Heaven, as it was announced that they had transgressed the law of God, which had made it expedient for Christ to make the great sacrifice of his own precious life.

When Adam and Eve realized how exalted and sacred was the law of God, the transgression of which made so costly a sacrifice necessary to save them and their posterity from utter ruin, they plead to die themselves, or to let them and their posterity endure the penalty of their transgression, rather than that the beloved Son of God should make this great sacrifice. The anguish of Adam was increased. He saw that his sins were of so great

---

[16] Charles Wesley, "Love Divine, All Loves Excelling," 1747, Hymnary, https://1ref.us/1l2 (accessed February 18, 2021).

magnitude as to involve fearful consequences. And must it be that Heaven's honored Commander, who had walked with him, and talked with him, while in his holy innocence, whom angels honored and worshiped, must be brought down from his exalted position to die because of his transgression. Adam was informed that an angel's life could not pay the debt. <u>The law of Jehovah, the foundation of his government in Heaven and upon earth, was as sacred as God himself</u>; and for this reason the life of an angel could not be accepted of God as a sacrifice for its transgression. <u>His law was of more importance in his sight than the holy angels around his throne</u>. The Father could not abolish nor change one precept of his law to meet man in his fallen condition. But the Son of God, who had in unison with the Father created man, could make an atonement for man acceptable to God, by giving his life a sacrifice, and bearing the wrath of his Father. Angels informed Adam that, as his transgression had brought death and wretchedness, life and immortality would be brought to light through the sacrifice of Jesus Christ.

To Adam were revealed future, important events, from his expulsion from Eden to the flood, and onward to the first advent of Christ upon the earth. His love for Adam and his posterity would lead the Son of God to condescend <u>to take human nature, and thus elevate, through his own humiliation, all who would believe on him</u>. Such a sacrifice was of sufficient value to save the whole world; but only a few would avail themselves of the salvation brought to them through such a wonderful sacrifice. The **many** <u>would not comply with the conditions required of them</u> **that they might be partakers of his great salvation**. They would prefer sin and transgression of the law of God, rather than repentance and obedience, relying by faith upon the merits of the sacrifice offered. <u>This sacrifice was of such **infinite value** as to make a man who should avail himself of it, **more precious** than fine gold, even a man than the golden wedge of Ophir.</u>

Adam was carried down through successive generations, and saw the increase of crime, of guilt and defilement, because man would yield to his naturally strong inclinations to transgress the holy law of God. He was shown the curse of God resting more and more heavily upon the human race, upon the cattle, and upon the earth, because of man's continued transgression. He was shown that iniquity and violence would steadily increase; yet amid all the tide of human misery and woe, there would ever be a few who would preserve the knowledge of God, and would remain unsullied amid the prevailing moral degeneracy. Adam was made to comprehend what sin is—the transgression of the law. He was shown that moral, mental, and physical degeneracy would result to the race, from transgression, until the world would be filled with human misery of every type.

The days of man were shortened by his own course of sin in transgressing the righteous law of God. The race was finally so greatly depreciated that they appeared **inferior**, and **almost valueless**. They were generally incompetent to appreciate the mystery of Calvary, the grand and elevated facts of the atonement and the plan of salvation, because of the indulgence of the carnal mind. Yet, notwithstanding the weakness, and enfeebled mental, moral and physical, powers of the human race, Christ, true to the purpose for which he left Heaven, continues his interest in the feeble, depreciated, degenerate specimens of humanity, and invites them to hide their weakness and great deficiencies in him. **If they will come unto him, he will supply all their needs.**

When Adam, according to God's special directions, made an offering for sin, it was to him a **most painful ceremony**. His hand must be raised to take life, which God alone could give, and make an offering for sin. It was the first time he had witnessed death. As he looked upon the bleeding victim, writhing in the agonies of death, he was to look forward by faith to the Son of God, whom the victim prefigured, who was to die man's sacrifice.

This ceremonial offering, ordained of God, was to be a perpetual reminder to Adam of his guilt, and also a penitential acknowledgment of his sin. This **act of taking** life gave Adam **a deeper** and **more perfect** sense of his transgression, which **nothing less than the death of God's dear Son could expiate**. He marveled at the infinite goodness and matchless love which would give such a ransom to save the guilty. As Adam was slaying the innocent victim, **it seemed to him that he was shedding the blood** of the Son of God **by his own hand**. He knew that if he had remained steadfast to God, and true to his holy law, there would have been no death of beast nor of man. Yet in the sacrificial offerings, pointing to the great and perfect offering of God's dear Son, there appeared a star of hope to illuminate the dark and terrible future, and relieve it of its utter hopelessness and ruin. (*The Spirit of Prophecy*, vol. 1, pp. 50–53)

> **The salvation of human beings is a vast enterprise**, that calls into action **every** attribute of the divine nature. The **Father, the Son, and the Holy Spirit have pledged themselves to make God's children more than conquerors** through him that has loved them. The Lord is gracious and long-suffering, not willing that any should perish. He has provided power to enable us to be overcomers. (*Review and Herald*, Jan. 27, 1903, Art. A, par. 9)

## The Guarantee of the Power of Transforming Grace

> Let those who are oppressed under a sense of sin remember that there is hope for them. The salvation of the human race has **ever been** the object of the councils of heaven. **The covenant of mercy was made before the foundation of the world.** It has existed from all eternity, and is called **the everlasting covenant**. So surely as there never was a time when God was not, so surely there never was a moment when it was not the delight of the eternal mind to manifest His grace to humanity. He is ever calling, "Let the wicked forsake his way, and the unrighteous man his thoughts; and let him return unto the Lord, and He will have mercy upon him; and to our God, for He will abundantly pardon." "Behold, the Lord's hand is not shortened, that it can not save, neither His ear heavy, that it can not hear."
>
> Christians, is Christ revealed in us? **Are we doing all in our power** to gain a body that is not easily enfeebled, a mind that looks beyond self to the cause and effect of every movement, that can wrestle with hard problems and conquer them, a will that is firm to resist evil and defend the right? **Are we crucifying self?** Are we growing up unto the full stature of men and women in Christ, preparing to endure hardness as good soldiers of the cross? (*Signs of the Times*, June 12, 1901, pars. 7, 8)

All Heaven mourned on account of the disobedience and fall of Adam and Eve, which brought the wrath of God upon the whole human race. They were cut off from communing with God, and were plunged in hopeless misery. The law of God could not be changed to meet man's necessity, for in God's arrangement it was never to lose its force, or give up the smallest part of its claims.

The Son of God pities fallen man. He knows that the law of his Father is as unchanging as himself. He can only see one way of escape for the transgressor. He offers himself to his Father as a sacrifice for man, to take their guilt and punishment upon himself, and redeem them from death by dying in their place, and thus pay the ransom. The Father consents to give his dearly beloved Son to save the fallen race; and through his merits and intercession promises to receive man again into his favor, and to restore holiness to as many as should be willing to accept the atonement thus mercifully offered, and obey his law. **For the sake of his dear Son the Father forbears awhile**

**the execution of death**, and to Christ He commits the fallen race. (*Spiritual Gifts*, vol. 3, pp. 46, 47)

> <u>In the intercessory prayer of Jesus with his Father, he claimed that he had fulfilled the conditions which made it obligatory upon the Father to fulfill his part of the contract made in Heaven, with regard to fallen man</u>. (*The Spirit of Prophecy*, vol. 3, p. 260; 5BC 1146.1)

Jesus refused to receive the homage of his people until he knew that his sacrifice had been accepted by the Father, and until he had received the assurance from God himself that his atonement for the sins of his people had been full and ample, that through his blood they might gain eternal life. Jesus immediately ascended to Heaven and presented himself before the throne of God, showing the marks of shame and cruelty upon his brow, his hands, and feet. <u>But he refused to receive the coronet of glory, and the royal robe, and he also refused the adoration of the angels as he had refused the homage of Mary, until the Father signified that his offering was accepted.</u>

He also had a request to prefer concerning his chosen ones upon earth. He wished to have the relation clearly defined that his redeemed should hereafter sustain to Heaven, and to his Father. <u>His church must be justified and accepted before he could accept heavenly honor.</u> **He declared it to be his will that where he was, there his church should be; if he was to have glory, his people must share it with him.** They who suffer with him on earth must finally reign with him in his kingdom. <u>In the most explicit manner Christ pleaded for his church, identifying his interest with theirs, and advocating, with a love and constancy stronger than death, their rights and titles gained through him.</u>

God's answer to this appeal goes forth in the proclamation: "Let all the angels of God worship him." Every angelic commander obeys the royal mandate, and Worthy, worthy is the Lamb that was slain; and that lives again a triumphant conqueror! echoes and re-echoes through all Heaven. The innumerable company of angels prostrate themselves before the Redeemer. The request of Christ is granted; the church is justified through him, its representative and head. <u>Here the Father ratifies the contract with his Son, that he will be reconciled to repentant and obedient men, and take them into divine favor through the merits of Christ.</u> **Christ guarantees** that he will make a man "more precious than fine gold, even a man than the golden wedge of Ophir." All power in Heaven and on earth is now given to the Prince of life; yet he does not for a moment forget his poor disciples in a sinful world, but prepares to return to them, that he may impart to them his power and glory. Thus did the Redeemer of mankind, by the sacrifice of himself, connect earth with Heaven, and finite man with the infinite God. (*The Spirit of Prophecy*, vol. 3, pp. 202, 203)

**As the Bible presents two laws, one changeless and eternal, the other provisional and temporary, so there are two covenants**. The covenant of grace was first made with man in Eden, when after the Fall there was given a divine promise that the seed of the woman should bruise the serpent's head. To all men this covenant **offered pardon** and the **assisting grace** of God **for future obedience** through faith in Christ. **It also promised them eternal life on condition of fidelity to God's law**. Thus the patriarchs received the hope of salvation.

This same covenant was renewed to Abraham in the promise, "In thy seed shall all the nations of the earth be blessed." Genesis 22:18. This promise pointed to Christ. So Abraham understood it (see Galatians 3:8, 16), and **he trusted in Christ for the forgiveness of sins**. It was **this faith** that was accounted unto him for righteousness. The covenant with Abraham also maintained the authority of God's law. The Lord appeared unto Abraham, and said, "I am the Almighty God; walk before Me, and be thou perfect." Genesis 17:1. The testimony of God concerning His faithful servant was, "Abraham **obeyed My voice**, and **kept My charge**, **My commandments**, **My statutes**, and **My laws**." Genesis 26:5. And the Lord declared to him, "I will establish My covenant between Me and thee and thy seed after thee in their generations, for an *everlasting covenant*, to be a God unto thee and to thy seed after thee." Genesis 17:7.

**Though this covenant was made with Adam and renewed to Abraham, it could not be ratified until the death of Christ.** It had existed by the promise of God since the first intimation of redemption had been given; it had been accepted by faith; **yet when ratified by Christ, it is called a *new* covenant**. The law of God was the basis of this covenant, which was simply an arrangement for bringing men again into harmony with the divine will, **placing them where they could obey God's law**.

**Another compact**—called in Scripture the **"old" covenant**—was formed between God and Israel at Sinai, and was then ratified by the blood of a sacrifice. **The Abrahamic covenant was ratified by the blood of Christ**, and it is called the **"second," or "new," covenant**, because the blood by which it was sealed was shed after the blood of the first covenant. That the new covenant was **valid in the days of Abraham** is evident from the fact that it was then confirmed both by the promise and by the oath of God—the "**two immutable things**, in which it was impossible for God to lie." Hebrews 6:18.

But if the Abrahamic covenant contained the promise of redemption, why was another covenant formed at Sinai? **In their bondage the people had to a great extent lost the knowledge of God and of the principles of the Abrahamic covenant.** In delivering them from Egypt, God sought to reveal to them His power and His mercy, that they might be led to love and trust Him. He brought them down to the Red Sea—where, pursued by the Egyptians, escape seemed impossible—that they might realize their utter helplessness, their need of divine aid; and then He wrought deliverance for them. Thus they were **filled** with **love** and **gratitude** to God and with **confidence** in His power to help them. He had **bound them to Himself** as their deliverer from temporal bondage.

But there was **a still greater truth to be impressed upon their minds**. Living in the midst of idolatry and corruption, they had no true conception of the **holiness of God**, of the **exceeding sinfulness** of their own hearts, **their utter inability**, in themselves, to render obedience to God's law, and their need of a Saviour. **All this they must be taught**.

God brought them to Sinai; He manifested His glory; He gave them His law, with the promise of great blessings on condition of obedience: "If ye will obey My voice indeed, and keep My covenant, then ... ye shall be unto Me a kingdom of priests, and an holy nation." Exodus 19:5, 6. The people did not realize the sinfulness of their own hearts, and that without Christ it was impossible for them to keep God's law; and they readily entered into covenant with God. Feeling that they were able to establish their own righteousness, they declared, "All that the Lord hath said will we do, and be obedient." Exodus 24:7. They had witnessed the proclamation of the law in awful majesty, and had trembled with terror before the mount; and yet only a few weeks passed before they broke their covenant with God, and bowed down to worship a graven image. They could not hope for the favor of God through a covenant which they had broken; and now, seeing their sinfulness and their need of pardon, they were brought to feel their need of the **Saviour revealed in the Abrahamic covenant** and shadowed forth in the sacrificial offerings. Now by faith and love they were bound to God as their deliverer from the bondage of sin. **Now they were prepared to appreciate the blessings of the new covenant.**

The terms of the "old covenant" were, Obey and live: "If a man do, he shall even live in them" (Ezekiel 20:11; Leviticus 18:5); but "cursed be he that confirmeth not all the words of this law to do them." Deuteronomy

27:26. The **"new covenant"** was established upon **"better promises"**—the promise of forgiveness of sins and of the grace of God to renew the heart and bring it into harmony with the principles of God's law. "This shall be the covenant that I will make with the house of Israel; after those days, saith the Lord, *I will put my law* in their inward parts, *and write it in their hearts....* I will *forgive* their iniquity, and will remember their sin no more." Jeremiah 31:33, 34.

The same law that was engraved upon the tables of stone is written by the Holy Spirit upon the tables of the heart. **Instead of going about to establish our own righteousness we accept the righteousness of Christ.** His blood atones for our sins. His obedience is accepted for us. **Then the heart renewed by the Holy Spirit will bring forth "the fruits of the Spirit."** Through the grace of Christ we shall live in obedience to the law of God written upon our hearts. Having the Spirit of Christ, we shall walk even as He walked. Through the prophet He declared of Himself, "I delight to do Thy will, O My God: yea, Thy law is within My heart." Psalm 40:8. And when among men He said, "The Father hath not left Me alone; for I do always those things that please Him." John 8:29.

The apostle Paul clearly presents the relation between faith and the law under the new covenant. He says: "Being *justified by faith*, we have peace with God through our Lord Jesus Christ." "Do we then make void the law through faith? God forbid: yea, we establish the law." "For what the law could not do, in that it was weak through the flesh"—it could not justify man, because in his sinful nature he could not keep the law—"God sending His own Son in the likeness of sinful flesh, and for sin, condemned sin in the flesh: that *the righteousness of the law* might be fulfilled in us, who walk not after the flesh, but after the Spirit." Romans 5:1, 3:31, 8:3, 4.

God's work is the same in all time, although there are **different degrees of development and different manifestations of His power**, to meet the wants of men in the different ages. Beginning with the first gospel promise, and coming down through the patriarchal and Jewish ages, and even to the present time, there has been a gradual unfolding of the purposes of God in the plan of redemption. The Saviour typified in the rites and ceremonies of the Jewish law is the very same that is revealed in the gospel. The clouds that enveloped His divine form have rolled back; the mists and shades have disappeared; and Jesus, the world's Redeemer, stands revealed. He who proclaimed the law from Sinai, and delivered to Moses the precepts of the ritual law, is the same that spoke the Sermon on the Mount. The great principles of love to God, which He set forth as the foundation of the law and the prophets, are only a reiteration of what He had spoken through Moses to the Hebrew people: "Hear, O Israel: The Lord our God is one Lord: and thou shalt love the Lord thy God with all thine heart, and with all thy soul, and with all thy might." Deuteronomy 6:4, 5. "Thou shalt love thy neighbor as thyself." Leviticus 19:18. The **teacher** is the **same** in both dispensations. God's **claims are the same**. The **principles** of His government are the **same**. For all proceed from Him "with whom is no variableness, neither shadow of turning." James 1:17. (*Patriarchs and Prophets*, pp. 370–373)

## Victory Through Christ

Will man take hold of divine power, and with **determination** and **perseverance** resist Satan, as Christ has given him example in His conflict with the foe in the wilderness of temptation? God cannot save man against his will from the power of Satan's artifices. Man must work with his human power, aided by the divine power of Christ, to resist and to **conquer at any cost to himself**. In short, man must overcome as Christ overcame. And then, through the victory that it is his privilege to gain by the all-powerful name of Jesus, he may become an heir of God, and joint heir with Jesus Christ. This could not be the case if Christ alone did all the overcoming. **Man must do his part; he must be victor on his own account, through the strength and grace that Christ gives him. Man must be a co-worker with Christ in the labor of overcoming, and then he will be partaker with Christ of His glory.** (*Testimonies for the Church*, vol. 4, pp. 32, 33)

## Christ Provides the Complete Package

**Entire justice** was done in the atonement. In the place of the sinner, **the spotless Son of God received the penalty**, and the sinner goes free as long as he receives and holds Christ as his personal Saviour. Though guilty, he is looked upon as innocent. **Christ fulfilled every requirement demanded by justice.** God's character as a God of holiness, a God of goodness, compassion, and love combined, was revealed in his Son. In the cross of Christ, God gave the world a mighty pledge of his justice and love. "For if the blood of bulls and of goats, and the ashes of an heifer sprinkling the unclean, sanctifieth to the purifying of the flesh: how much more shall the blood of Christ, who through the eternal Spirit offered himself without spot to God, **purge your conscience** from dead works to serve the living God?"

When Christ bowed his head and died, **he bore the pillars of Satan's kingdom with him to the earth.** He vanquished Satan in the **same nature** over which in Eden Satan obtained the victory. **The enemy was overcome by Christ in his human nature**. The power of the Saviour's Godhead was hidden. **He overcame in human nature,** *relying upon God for power*. This is the privilege of all. **In proportion to our faith will be our victory.** (*The Youth's Instructor*, April 25, 1901, par. 10)

## The Key to Our Personal Victory

The **good resolutions** made in one's own strength avail nothing. Not all the pledges in the world will break the power of evil habit. Never will men practice temperance in all things until their hearts are renewed **by divine grace**. We cannot keep ourselves from sin for one moment. **Every moment we are dependent upon God.**

**True reformation** begins with soul cleansing. Our work for the fallen **will achieve real success only** as the grace of Christ reshapes the character and the soul is brought into living connection with God.

Christ lived a life of perfect obedience to God's law, and in this He set an example for every human being. **The life that He lived in this world we are to live through His power and under His instruction.**

In our work for the fallen the claims of the law of God and the need of loyalty to Him are to be impressed on mind and heart. **Never fail to show that there is a marked difference between the one who serves God and the one who serves Him not**. God is love, but **He cannot excuse willful disregard for His commands**. The enactments of His government are such that men do not escape the consequences of disloyalty. Only those who honor Him can He honor. Man's conduct in this world decides his eternal destiny. As he has sown, so he must reap. Cause will be followed by effect.

Nothing less than perfect obedience can meet the standard of God's requirement. He has not left His requirements indefinite. He has enjoined nothing that is not necessary in order to bring man into harmony with Him. We are to point sinners to His ideal of character and to lead them to Christ, by whose grace only can this ideal be reached.

The Saviour took upon Himself the infirmities of humanity and lived a sinless life, that men might have no fear that because of the weakness of human nature they could not overcome. Christ came to make us "partakers of the divine nature," and His life declares that *humanity, combined with divinity, does not commit sin*. (*The Ministry of Healing*, pp. 179, 180).

## The Existence of the Law of God before Creation

The law of God existed before man was created. It was adapted to the condition of holy beings; **even angels were governed by it**. After the fall, the principles of righteousness were unchanged. Nothing was taken from the law; not one of its holy precepts could be improved. And as it has existed from the beginning, **so will it continue to exist throughout the ceaseless ages of eternity**. "Concerning Thy testimonies," says the psalmist, "I have known of old that Thou has founded them forever." (*Signs of the Times*, April 15, 1886, par. 14)

> When the Jews rejected Christ they rejected the foundation of their faith. And, on the other hand, **the Christian world of today who claim faith in Christ, but reject the law of God** are making a mistake similar to that of the deceived Jews. Those who profess to cling to Christ, centering their hopes on him, while they pour contempt upon the moral law, and the prophecies, **are in no safer position than were the unbelieving Jews**. They cannot understandingly call sinners to repentance, **for they are unable to properly explain what they are to repent of**. The sinner, upon being exhorted to forsake his sins, has a right to ask, **What is sin?** Those who respect the law of God can answer, Sin is the transgression of the law [1 John 3:4]. In confirmation of this the apostle Paul says, I had not known sin but by the law [Rom. 7:7].
>
> **Those only** who acknowledge the binding claim of the moral law **can explain the nature of the atonement**. Christ came to mediate between God and man, to make man one with God by bringing him into allegiance to his law. **There was no power in the law to pardon its transgressor.** Jesus alone could pay the sinner's debt. **But the fact that Jesus has paid the indebtedness of the repentant sinner does not give him license to continue in transgression of the law of God; but he must henceforth live in obedience to that law.**
>
> The law of God existed before the creation of man **or else Adam could not have sinned**. After the transgression of Adam the principles of the law were not changed, but were **definitely arranged and expressed to meet man in his fallen condition**. Christ, in counsel with his Father, instituted the system of sacrificial offerings: that death, **instead of being immediately visited**

> **upon the transgressor,** should be transferred to a victim which should prefigure the great and perfect offering of the Son of God. (*Signs of the Times*, March 14, 1878, pars. 1–3)

The law of Jehovah, dating back to creation, was comprised in the two great principles, "Thou shalt love the Lord thy God with all thy heart, and with all thy soul, and with all thy mind, and with all thy strength. This is the first commandment. And the second is like, namely this: Thou shalt love thy neighbor as thyself. There is none other commandment greater than these." These two great principles embrace the first four commandments, showing the duty of man to God, and the last six, showing the duty of man to his fellow-man. The principles were more explicitly stated to man after the fall, and worded to meet the case of fallen intelligences. **This was necessary in consequence of the minds of men being blinded by transgression.** (*Review and Herald*, May 6, 1875, par. 13)

> But it was part of the covenant made in heaven, **that Christ, having taken humanity, was not to work miracles in his own behalf, but was to stand as a man among men.** And therefore he answered Satan with these words, "It is written, Man shall not live by bread alone, but by every word that proceedeth out of the mouth of God."
>
> Have you had light upon the Scriptures? **Have you advanced from light to greater light?** With the light of the Holy Spirit shining upon the word, **have we any reason for becoming uncertain in regard to what is truth?** any reason to go back to an uncertain faith?—No, no! The foundation of God standeth sure. **Sentiments, theories, and doctrines will not of themselves save any one.** Doctrine, however true, is powerless to save without **a living faith in God.** (*The Southern Watchman*, March 1, 1904, Art. B, par. 32, 10)

## Elements Essential for Success

Christ has warned us against the danger of departing from the faith. There is need of constant, intimate communion with God. Only as we hold this communion with him shall we be kept from making shipwreck of faith. I am instructed to warn our people that everything that can be shaken will be shaken, that those things that can not be shaken may remain. Temptations will come to every soul. Every one will be tried and tested. Those who

**strive to hold fast** to the faith will find that they must indeed pray and watch unto prayer.

The record of Christ's contest with Satan was chronicled **for the help and encouragement of the people of God today**. In this contest <u>Christ worked</u> **no miracle** and gave **no sign.** <u>His only dependence was</u> **God** and **his word.** In the future, Satan is to come down with great power, to work signs and wonders. **He will bring down fire from heaven in the presence of his devotees**, and, to those who have allowed themselves to be led away from the only true foundation,—**the word of God,**—will give proof of his authority. He will deceive if possible the very elect. <u>Those who are standing firm upon the word of the everlasting God will meet Satan with the weapon with which Christ met him,—</u>**"It is written."** <u>This will be of more power than the working of miracles.</u> The people of God **will conquer through** the Holy Spirit's working, which is **stronger** than miracles or aught else. It is from the Lord that we are to obtain power. (*The Southern Watchman*, March 1, 1904, article B, par. 29, 39)

Key Points from above:

√ The covenant's complete blessing of fulfillment are conditional.
√ The new covenant is from everlasting but called new because it was ratified at the cross many years after the old covenant was given.
√ The unfolding of the plan of salvation has been gradual through the progression of the ages.
√ The old covenant was needed to show through symbolism and their experience their utter dependence of God. Their inability to keep His law on their own, to demonstrate the holiness of God and His power to forgive and bring their/our natures back into harmony with His law.
√ Man must overcome on his own account using the strength God has given him.
√ Man must believe he is forgiven and empowered and then exercise his will to receive those benefits.
√ Satan is overcome in human nature, the same nature that had fallen into sin. Not unfallen nature or divine nature.
√ **"In their bondage the people had to a great extent lost the knowledge of God and of the principles of the Abrahamic covenant. ...** <u>they had no true conception of the</u> **holiness of God,** of the **exceeding sinfulness** <u>of their own hearts,</u> **their utter inability,** <u>in themselves, to render obedience to God's law, and their need of a Saviour.</u> **All this they must be taught.** ... The "new covenant" was established upon "better promises"—<u>the</u> **promise**

of **forgiveness of sins** and of the **grace of God** to **renew the heart** and bring it into harmony with the principles of God's law."

Dear reader, the Spirit of Prophecy has spoken—take heed. "It is written" is the key to spiritual victory in your personal battles with temptation. Unless you are using these encouragements and the very words of Scripture, you will not have the power that God intended to give you in overcoming temptation. God gave the Bible, which is the new covenant in its entirety, to guide your life. When followed in its explicit and implied meaning, you are guaranteed victory. The words you are to claim in prayer are what God has covenanted: "to keep you from falling, and to present you faultless before the presence of his glory with exceeding joy" (Jude 24).

In our last two chapters, we will study in detail how to have victory. As Jesus said, "Arise, let us go hence"—overcoming the enemy and glorifying God by revealing His character and power to the world, as Jesus Himself did.

CHAPTER 12

# Utilizing the Covenant for Victory

> The temple has been yielded,
> And purified of sin;
> Let Thy Shekinah glory
> Now shine forth from within,
> And all the earth keep silence,
> The body henceforth be
> Thy silent, gentle servant,
> Moved only as by Thee.
> —Frances Ridley Havergal[17]

Dear reader, you have come to a level of knowledge about the covenant and plan of salvation. Though this is an important achievement, without application in your practical life, such knowledge becomes a curse. I pray now that your heart is open to utilizing this information to obtain the victory that God desires for you to have. If you are feeling blessed and encouraged thus far, which is one of my goals, you will receive a tenfold blessing when you re-read this book after having begun to apply the following principles in your life. Keep in mind why the following promises are guaranteed: If God does not answer your prayers according to the conditions covenanted, He is worthy of death, which would be a second death without a resurrection. As the Father stood by His promises in Gethsemane for Christ, so will He

---

[17] Frances R. Havergal, "Live Out Thy Life within Me," Hymnary, https://1ref.us/1lb (accessed February 18, 2021).

do for you, to give you personal victory over temptation and sin. Ultimately, you, as a part of the church of the last generation, can fulfill the promise of the 144,000—a people without spot, wrinkle, or blemish, and faultless to stand before the throne of God and fit for translation. This is the fulfillment of the "more sure word of prophecy." It is guaranteed by blood.

> The days of man were shortened by his own course of sin in transgressing the righteous law of God. The race was finally so greatly depreciated that they <u>appeared inferior, and almost valueless.</u> **They were generally incompetent to appreciate the mystery of Calvary, the grand and elevated facts of the atonement and the plan of salvation, because of the indulgence of the carnal mind.** Yet, notwithstanding the weakness, and enfeebled mental, moral and physical, powers of the human race, Christ, true to the purpose for which he left Heaven, continues his interest in the <u>feeble, depreciated, degenerate specimens of humanity,</u> and **invites them to hide their weakness and great deficiencies in him**. <u>If</u> **they will come unto him,** <u>he will supply</u> **all their needs**. (*The Spirit of Prophecy*, vol. 1, pp. 52, 53)

Without controversy, attaining to the biblical standard of righteousness is something not easily accomplished. Because many recognize that Christ is the standard after whom we are to pattern our life, many embrace a theology that lowers the standard to a level they feel they can reach. Their new theology is, in reality, a type of works-righteousness. Then, attaining the lower standard and professing to be saved by grace, these people can rest in the delusion of carnal security that is fatal to their salvation. However, their mind, soul, and spirit are resting in a false security, a false hope, and a deceptive peace. Their security, hope, and peace rest in the false belief that their salvation is accomplished through their reaching a standard that is easily attainable within the moral degradation of the world. In reality, they have accepted a form of paganism, a method of appeasing a god in their own strength. When we think about false systems of salvation, why would we even need God if we could follow a method of salvation that we can accomplish by ourselves? Even worse is that this false method of salvation is called "Christianity," which, by its nature, sets forth a singular path as the only truth. Truth, by absolute definition, is singular; it cannot be many things at the same time. Alarmingly, if there can be no salvation found within

"Christianity," and it is true that there is only one way of truth, then there is no possibility of salvation at all, an absolute disaster. It should also be said that, if man himself prescribes the method of salvation, he should, in no way, expect to be saved. On closer observation, we see many giving up in despair, bringing Satan joy in having led another soul into atheism. The real method of salvation can only be the method that an omnipotent God gave, hence the importance of the New Covenant and of a proper understanding of it.

> **The sanctification now gaining prominence** in the religious world carries with it <u>a spirit of self-exaltation and a disregard for the law of God</u> that mark it as foreign to the religion of the Bible. **Its advocates teach** that sanctification is **an instantaneous work, by which, through faith alone,** they attain to perfect holiness. "Only believe," say they, "and the blessing is yours." **No further effort on the part of the receiver is supposed to be required.** <u>At the same time they deny the authority of the law of God, urging that they are released from obligation to keep the commandments.</u> **But is it possible for men to be holy, in accord with the will and character of God, without coming into harmony with the principles which are an expression of His nature and will, and which show what is well pleasing to Him?**
>
> <u>The desire for an easy religion that requires no striving, no self-denial, no divorce from the follies of the world, has made the doctrine of faith, and faith only,</u> **a popular doctrine**; but what saith the word of God? Says the apostle James: "What doth it profit, my brethren, though a man say he hath faith, and have not works? can faith save him? ... Wilt thou know, O vain man, that faith without works is dead? Was not Abraham our father justified by works, when he had offered Isaac his son upon the altar? Seest thou how faith wrought with his works, and by works was faith made perfect? ... Ye see then how that by works a man is justified, and not by faith only." James 2:14–24.
>
> The testimony of the word of God is against this ensnaring doctrine of faith without works. <u>It is **not** faith that claims the favor of Heaven without complying with the conditions upon which mercy is to be granted</u>, **it is presumption;** for **genuine faith** has its foundation in the **promises** and provisions of the Scriptures. (*The Great Controversy*, pp. 471, 472)

The Bible declares: "Beloved, now are we the sons of God, and it doth not yet appear what we shall be: but we know that, when he shall appear, <u>we shall be like him</u>; for we shall see him as he is. **And every man that hath this hope in him purifieth himself, even as he is pure**. Whosoever committeth sin transgresseth also the law: for <u>sin is the transgression of the law</u>" (1 John 3:2–4). "For even hereunto were ye called: because <u>Christ also suffered for us, leaving us an example, that ye should follow his steps</u>: **Who did no sin ....**" (1 Peter 2:21, 22). Christ is our example. Only by following in the footsteps of the Sinless One will we be saved. It would be fair to ask, since His life is the standard: How do we accomplish such a life of holiness, sanctification, righteousness, and victory over all temptations and sin? We cannot overemphasize that the beauty of God's covenant with mankind is that it includes as a condition that God will help us in any area of need in attaining His holiness, righteousness, and character, recovering us entirely from sin while we still live in a world of "manifold temptations." In other words, using the understanding that we have already gained, we recognize that God has given us His word that, on pain of death—the second death, from which there is no resurrection—He will keep us sanctified once we have accepted His offer of being forgiven, or being justified. God justifies us through our belief and acceptance of the sacrifice of Christ and also provides power to maintain a sanctified life, provided we follow the conditions set forth in the covenant that we are also obligated to comply with. Rightly understood, the covenant in the Old and New Testaments is the document that God gave mankind to utilize in recovering from sin and sinning. If a person follows every particular, the result will be victory over sin and, ultimately, redemption. It is just like following a recipe to make bread. Here's my classic reliable recipe:

**WHOLE-WHEAT BREAD**
3¾ cups organic whole-wheat flour
¾ cup organic cornmeal
2 cups water
2 tsp yeast
2 tsp sea salt
2 T raw unfiltered honey

When these ingredients are properly mixed and baked for the right amount of time, they make bread—not pizza, not ice cream, not cheesecake, not beef stew, and not soup. Bread will be the result—not just once or twice, nor only one hundred times, nor only 999,999 times, but every time.

It is the same way in our Christian walk. If we follow the recipe exactly, without deviating according to our own wisdom, we shall have victory. Herein lies the key.

From my experience, the only reasons people fail at being a good cook are laziness, not paying attention to small details and unwillingness to follow the directions exactly as given. Such people may be inattentive to God's details because they want to do things their way or they are not applying the instructions properly or they have not learned to read properly or they do not accept the words in the instructions according to their intended meaning or they are unwilling to follow the method as described. These same defects may keep us from attaining victory over every temptation. Dear reader, examine yourself and be honest in judging yourself that, when God pronounces the final sentence, you will have His character and will be declared holy.

> The terms of the "old covenant" were, Obey and live: "If a man do, he shall even live in them" (Ezekiel 20:11; Leviticus 18:5); but "cursed be he that confirmeth not all the words of this law to do them." Deuteronomy 27:26. The **"new covenant"** was established upon **"better promises"**—the **promise of forgiveness of sins** and of the **grace of God** to **renew the heart** and bring it into harmony with the principles of God's law. "This shall be the covenant that I will make with the house of Israel; After those days, saith the Lord, *I will put my law* in their inward parts, *and write it in their hearts* …. I will *forgive* their iniquity, and will remember their sin no more." Jeremiah 31:33, 34. (*Patriarchs and Prophets*, p. 372)

"And God said unto Abraham, Thou shalt keep my covenant therefore, thou, and thy seed after thee in their generations" (Gen. 17:9). These words, "Thou shalt keep my covenant" can be taken as a personal prophecy to us or as commonly known, a promise that we will be commandment keepers when we follow the covenant as stipulated. God will not force us; we must give Him our will, as the Testimony of Jesus declares:

> Will man take hold of divine power, and with **determination** and **perseverance** resist Satan, as Christ has given him example in His conflict with the foe in the wilderness of temptation? God cannot save man against his will from the power of Satan's artifices. Man must work with his human power, aided by the divine power of

Christ, to resist and to **conquer at any cost to himself**. In short, <u>man must overcome as Christ overcame</u>. And then, through the victory that it is his privilege to gain by the all-powerful name of Jesus, he may become an heir of God and joint-heir with Jesus Christ. <u>This could not be the case if Christ alone did all the overcoming.</u> **Man must do *his* part; he must be victor <u>on his own account</u>, through the strength and grace that Christ gives him. Man must be a co-worker with Christ in the labor of overcoming, and then he will be partaker with Christ of his glory**. (*Testimonies for the Church*, vol. 4, pp. 32, 33)

We have a part to play. We must cooperate with God in our salvation. He can only accept willing obedience. He will force no one to keep His law, giving us an opportunity, through our experience, to see the blessing of keeping the law as well as the curse in breaking it. With this knowledge, we can intelligently decide to follow God or to rebel against Him.

When we do our part, God has obligated Himself to do His part. And what is His part? It is to give us the Holy Spirit to impart knowledge, wisdom, and understanding in how to follow the prescribed method and to give us His holy angels to protect us and strengthen us for victory. As God told Paul: "My grace is sufficient for thee: for my strength is made perfect in weakness" (2 Cor. 12:9). When we rely wholly on the grace of God, then we will attain perfection of character and perpetual obedience. God has given us this mighty encouragement:

> **None need fail of attaining, in his sphere, to perfection of Christian character.** By the sacrifice of Christ, <u>provision has been made for the believer to receive all things that pertain to life and godliness</u>. God calls upon us to reach the standard of perfection and places before us the example of Christ's character. In His humanity, perfected by **a life of constant resistance of evil**, the Saviour showed that through co-operation with Divinity, human beings may in this life attain to perfection of character. This is **God's assurance** to us that we, too, may obtain **complete victory**.
>
> Before the believer is held out the wonderful possibility of being like Christ, obedient to all the principles of the law. But of himself man is utterly unable to reach this condition. <u>The holiness that God's word declares he must have before he can be saved is the result of the working of divine grace as he bows **in submission**</u>

**to the discipline and restraining influences** of the Spirit of truth. Man's obedience can be made perfect only by the incense of Christ's righteousness, which fills with divine fragrance every act of obedience. **The part of the Christian** is to persevere in overcoming every fault. **Constantly** he is to **pray** to the Saviour to heal the disorders of his sin-sick soul. He has not the **wisdom** or the **strength** to overcome; these belong to the Lord, and He bestows them on those who in humiliation and contrition seek Him for help.

The work of transformation from unholiness to holiness is a **continuous one**. Day by day God labors for man's sanctification, and man is to co-operate with Him, **putting forth persevering efforts in the cultivation of right habits**. He is to add grace to grace; and as he thus works on the plan of addition, God works for him on the plan of **multiplication**. Our Saviour is always ready to hear and answer the prayer of the contrite heart, and grace and peace are multiplied to His faithful ones. **Gladly** He grants them the blessings they need in their struggle against the evils that beset them. (*The Acts of the Apostles*, pp. 531, 532)

We must ask God for wisdom that we may know how to overcome. Salvation is a science, not just something that happens by chance. Oh, dear reader, look to Jesus and allow Him to lead you in everything! Doing so is the key to your success. Bring every detail to the Lord and, with a willing heart, be ready to follow Him in the method He brings to your attention through the study of His Word and the Spirit of Prophecy. "If any of you lack wisdom, let him ask of God, that giveth to all men liberally, and upbraideth not; and it shall be given him" (James 1:5). God gave us this promise for the express purpose of gaining the victory over sin. Many have used it for wisdom in every area except in victory over temptation. Yet, the Lord's primary purpose for this verse is wisdom against all the wiles of Satan that we may gain the victory over "the lust of the flesh, and the lust of the eyes, and the pride of life" (1 John 2:16). Notice the context of the promise of wisdom:

> My brethren, count it all joy when ye fall into divers temptations; knowing this, that the trying of your faith worketh patience. But let patience have her perfect work, that ye may be perfect and entire, wanting nothing.
>
> Blessed is the man that endureth temptation: for when he is tried, he shall receive the crown of life, which the Lord hath

promised to them that love him. Let no man say when he is tempted, I am tempted of God: for God cannot be tempted with evil, neither tempteth he any man: But every man is tempted, when he is drawn away of his own lust, and enticed. Then when lust hath conceived, it bringeth forth sin: and sin, when it is finished, bringeth forth death. Do not err, my beloved brethren. Every good gift and every perfect gift is from above, and cometh down from the Father of lights, with whom is no variableness, neither shadow of turning. (James 1:2–4, 12–17)

There is no variableness with God, therefore, we can depend on Him to do that which He has promised in His Word. We can depend on God, His covenant, and His law as much as we can depend on the law of gravity. It is a constant, just as the Word of God is a constant. Victory is assured when we follow the prescribed plan in Scripture. Many may have overlooked the simplicity of asking for wisdom from God to teach them how to overcome, which we cannot come up with on our own. I cannot overstate the importance of the Word of God as a treasure house of tools to utilize for obtaining victory or the importance of availing ourselves of these resources by scouring every area of God's Word to grasp and maintain a firm hold on its principles. Thoroughly studied and understood, the Bible provides every tool necessary to defeat the devil and his angels, regardless of the artifice they use against us. "Make haste, O God, to deliver me; make haste to help me, O LORD. Let them be ashamed and confounded that seek after my soul: let them be turned backward, and put to confusion, that desire my hurt. Let them be turned back for a reward of their shame that say, Aha, aha" (Ps. 70:1–3).

> **Nothing less than perfect obedience can meet the standard of God's requirement. He has not left His requirements indefinite.** He has enjoined nothing that is not necessary in order to bring man into harmony with Him. We are to point sinners to His ideal of character and to lead them to Christ, by whose grace only can this ideal be reached.
>
> <u>The Saviour took upon Himself</u> **the infirmities of humanity** and **lived a sinless life**, that men might have **no fear** that because of the **weakness of human nature they could not overcome**. Christ came to make us "partakers of the divine nature," and His life declares that *__humanity, combined with divinity, does not commit sin__*. (*The Ministry of Healing*, p. 180)

Remember that it was God in human flesh—as a baby, a child, a teenager, and a young adult—with the liabilities that humanity carries who did not sin. His accomplishment is a statement of omnipotence, a statement that gives us immense faith when we accept it, magnifying, in our comprehension, the sufficiency of the power of God to overcome all that the devil can throw at us, no matter our age or condition. Why some will not accept this fact is a mystery, for failure to believe it is only to their detriment. This most assuring element—that we can have victory in our own body—should be grasped for all it is worth. God, in human flesh, overcame sin for us. His victory is like Samson's victory when he toppled the temple of Dagon in his death:

> When Christ bowed his head and died, **he bore the pillars of Satan's kingdom with him to the earth**. He vanquished Satan in the same nature over which in Eden Satan obtained the victory. **The enemy was overcome by Christ in his human nature**. The power of the Saviour's Godhead was hidden. **He overcame in human nature, relying upon God for power**. This is the privilege of all. **In proportion to our faith will be our victory**. (*The Youth's Instructor,* April 25, 1901, par. 11)

Christ overcame in His human nature, not as God in His divine nature. Additionally, every demon that fell from heaven with Satan had a stake in the conflict. If they could overcome Christ, they would secure for themselves eternal life—yes, eternal life—even though they are depraved, sinful beings. Thus, in Gethsemane and at Calvary, with such high stakes, Satan used every weapon he could imagine to overcome Christ. The adversary directed every demon within his forces to apply his best artifice against Christ to gain the victory and to secure life for themselves and all their host of evil. Yet, not one of Satan's demons—not even Lucifer himself—could overcome Christ. Not one! What does this mean? The demons that have had so much success in your life—the very demons with whom you are struggling right now, who are on your track, constantly tempting, harassing, and oppressing you, that you must overcome—were defeated by Christ personally and individually. They could not achieve victory in the slightest with Christ. Therefore, those demons are defeated. They are losers when confronted by the resurrected Christ who is authorized to bestow "all power" upon you. Now that He has the full capacity to function as God on your behalf, He cannot be overcome. He is the all-knowing God who understands by experience how to avoid falling into any and all of their tricks.

Therefore, rest in certainty in the knowledge of the immense love that He has for you as one of His creations. He will do everything to secure you victorious as He was, for He was not overcome in His human body. We see this by the gift of His costly sweat and blood. Therefore, you are guaranteed everything that you need to overcome, using His strength on your behalf to His glory. Jesus told His disciples just before Gethsemane: "Hereafter I will not talk much with you: for the prince of this world cometh, and hath nothing in me" (John 14:30). There was nothing in Jesus that responded to the temptations of Satan and his demons, and if you allow Christ to live in you, you will have the same experience in your life. Do not forget that your individual, personal sins were placed on Christ in Gethsemane and Calvary. Therefore, Jesus is not caught off-guard. He knows the power and the awfulness of your sins, and He took their full weight, which you could never bear yourself. Complete victory is yours by faith. Absolute rejection of all that is in the world, of any impression or temptation of Satan, is the ultimate objective of the Godhead. And it will come to fruition in the time of Jacob's trouble. If we allow the Lord to take us through the fire, He will bring the purification process to completion. Before this can be accomplished, we must learn to utilize the resources He has made available to us, which are nothing short of all things necessary for victory over Satan and sin. "He that spared not his own Son, but delivered him up for us all, how shall he not with him also freely give us all things?" (Rom. 8:32). "These things I have spoken unto you, that in me ye might have peace. In the world ye shall have tribulation: but be of good cheer; I have overcome the world" (John 16:33). Be of good cheer—Jesus has overcome, in human nature, a whole world full of demons.

I cannot overstate the importance of the Bible's being your sword. It is the only offensive weapon in your spiritual armor. God gave it for victory in this combat "that ye may be able to stand against the wiles of the devil" (Eph. 6:11). The entire Bible is the covenant. The covenant is God's promise that He will do everything that He has promised. It is your privilege and obligation to utilize this wonderful resource given us. On judgment day, all will see who took advantage of God's infinite source of power. All will see that God obligated Himself to keep every word of His covenant to the human family, whether we were faithful or not, He has kept them. "If we believe not, yet he abideth faithful: he cannot deny himself" (2 Tim. 2:13). Know also that you will not get victory, nor can you ever attain to the character of Christ without praying the promises that He has given us. It is through these that we fight by faith. Let us look to Christ, our example, and learn from His victory the specifics of obtaining victory over all temptation and sin:

> Then was Jesus led up of the Spirit into the wilderness to be tempted of the devil. And when he had fasted forty days and forty nights, he was afterward an hungred. And when the tempter came to him, he said, If thou be the Son of God, command that these stones be made bread. But he answered and said, <u>It is written</u>, Man shall not live by bread alone, but by every word that proceedeth out of the mouth of God. Then the devil taketh him up into the holy city, and setteth him on a pinnacle of the temple, And saith unto him, If thou be the Son of God, cast thyself down: for <u>it is written</u>, He shall give his angels charge concerning thee: and in their hands they shall bear thee up, lest at any time thou dash thy foot against a stone. Jesus said unto him, It is written again, Thou shalt not tempt the Lord thy God. Again, the devil taketh him up into an exceeding high mountain, and sheweth him all the kingdoms of the world, and the glory of them; and saith unto him, All these things will I give thee, if thou wilt fall down and worship me. Then saith Jesus unto him, Get thee hence, Satan: for <u>it is written</u>, Thou shalt worship the Lord thy God, and him only shalt thou serve. Then the devil leaveth him, and, behold, angels came and ministered unto him. (Matt. 4:1–11)

What are the elements from His example that are connected with victory?

- ✓ Allowing the Spirit to lead you into a place of solitude for communion with the Father
- ✓ Fasting
- ✓ Praying
- ✓ Quoting Scripture against every temptation, as Jesus replied, "It is written"
- ✓ Commanding the devil by the authority of Scripture in the name and blood of Jesus.

Dear reader, has the Holy Spirit not convicted you to spend time alone with the Lord? Doing so is critical to your success because, within the hectic pace of modern life, it is far too easy for the devil to crowd our time with temporal things that we need to do to sustain ordinary life but that, ultimately, will undermine our spiritual life and render us inadequately prepared for eternal life. Obtaining eternal life and strength for victory over temptation only comes through communion with the Lord. Prayer and study of the Bible to learn the promises of God are necessary to rescue us from all the trials of life. I cannot tell you how many professed Christians I have talked with—even gospel workers, literature evangelists, Bible workers, church officers, and missionaries—who have said, "I am struggling spiritually."

Then I have asked them, "How are your morning prayer and Bible study going?"

They have answered, "I have very little time"; "It is inconsistent"; "It's random; I just choose a book or chapter and read, but I don't understand much"; "I have so many things to do that I don't have time in the morning to pray or study the Bible like I should."

How can a person expect to be victorious under such circumstances? I guess the answer would be that they thought they were strong enough to go about life without the Lord's help. Amazing! Of course, this is self-righteousness or works-righteousness, though they would never consciously say so. Yet, sub-consciously, it is what we do when we attempt to work in the flesh.

My dear friend, please take time out every day, even three times a day, as did Daniel, to secure yourself in the arms of the Lord and call upon Him to send His angels to lift up a standard around you against Satan that he will not be able to overcome you.

> So shall they fear the name of the LORD from the west, and his glory from the rising of the sun. When the enemy shall come in like a flood, <u>the Spirit of the LORD shall lift up a standard against him</u>.[18] And the Redeemer shall come to Zion, and unto them that turn from transgression in Jacob, saith the LORD. As for me, this is my covenant with them, saith the LORD; my spirit that is upon thee, and my words which I have put in thy mouth, shall not depart out of thy mouth, nor out of the mouth of thy seed, nor out of the mouth of thy seed's seed, saith the LORD, from henceforth and for ever. Arise, shine; for thy light is come, and the glory of the LORD is risen upon thee. For, behold, the darkness shall cover the earth, and gross darkness the people: but the LORD shall arise upon thee, and his glory shall be seen upon thee. (Isa. 59:19–60:2)

---

[18] Ellen White comments that this is a wall of fire in the form of angels.

The Lord has admonished us to call upon Him every morning, and He will lift up a standard of holy angels against the enemy's artifices and will put His words in your mouth—the verses you have studied will come to mind—to defeat the devil in every attack. Then the glory of the Lord will be seen in your life—a glory that can only be seen in its fullness when we are not sinning.

The Lord has obligated Himself to protect us when we call upon Him at the rising of the sun. Every morning we can choose to have His protection throughout the day to help us overcome all the snares of Satan. Calling upon Him from the start is the key to victory. In no other way can victory be achieved. Of Jesus' practice, Mark wrote: "And in the morning, rising up a great while before day, he went out, and departed into a solitary place, and there prayed" (Mark 1:35). Rain or shine, sleet or snow, hail or high water, at home or traveling—never ever varying—your morning prayer and study will give you the strength of God wherever you go.[19]

As we have noted, the Bible is your sword, and you must use it to gain the victory. With practice and continual application of the promises that it contains, you will not fail. The difficulty in our struggle is to remain persevering and diligent in using the Word of God against Satan's temptations. Indolence in this matter is fatal.

Let us now look at some of the Scriptures that the Lord has provided for you to use to gain the victory. As you become acquainted with these valuable promises in spiritual warfare, your eyes will become keen to recognize other promises. The Lord has included in Scripture a promise that you can claim for victory in every possible type of temptation, trial, affliction, or difficulty that you may experience. It behooves us to study continually to find these promises and, in using them, to experience the hand of the Lord leading us to victory. It is our privilege to claim every promise in the Word of God. As you continue in the experience of life, you will see more acutely the need for warfare prayer in gaining the victory under all of Satan's attacks. Christ Himself gave us, through His Word, the authority to command Satan and his host. Therefore, we will gain the victory when we use Scripture as a weapon against Satan. Let us begin our study at how we can equip ourselves with scripture and utilize its power. Here are some important promises in Psalm 119:

---

[19] For a consistent systemic method of spiritual nourishment, download "EFFECTIVE BIBLE STUDY AND SPIRITUAL GROWTH," available online at https://1ref.us/1kr (accessed February 17, 2021).

"Wherewithal shall a young man cleanse his way? by taking heed thereto according to thy word. With my whole heart have I sought thee: O let me not wander from thy commandments. Thy word have I hid in mine heart, that I might not sin against thee" (Ps. 119:9–11).

"Remember the word unto thy servant, upon which thou hast caused me to hope" (Ps. 119:49).

"My soul fainteth for thy salvation: but I hope in thy word" (Ps. 119:81).

"Plead my cause, and deliver me: quicken me according to thy word" (Ps. 119:154).

In one form or another, the whole of Psalm 119 is about the word of God, and it is a tremendous prayer of help in combating the enemy. Most have not taken this psalm as a weapon given for victory, and yet they mourn because of the wretchedness of their soul. Dear reader, become acquainted with these words of power and accept the Lord's invitation that you may honor and glorify Him, "According as his divine power hath given unto us all things that pertain unto life and godliness" (2 Peter 1:3). Accept it as God's promise that you will lack nothing for a permanent "born again" spiritual life, to live "godly, in this present world." As Psalm 119:154 says, life-giving deliverance is according to the Word of God, not according to our preconceived ideas about victory. "Arise, O LORD, disappoint him [Satan], cast him down: deliver my soul from the wicked, which is by thy sword [the Word of God]" (Ps. 17:13, margin).

What is your normal response to temptation? Do you sweat it out? Do you grit your teeth and tough it out? Do you run and hide your head like the proverbial ostrich? Such questions may sound strange, but if you are not using the Word of God to meet temptation, then you will inevitably be using a method that is as ineffective as the ones I have just mentioned, and you will also get the expected results of trying to hide your head in the sand. You will not achieve real victory; it will only be self-deception. Let's take a moment to note some of Satan's most effective weapons. One of these is to instill doubt—especially when we are despondent. Remember that faith—faith that God has strengthened us for victory—is not a feeling, and it is not based on the circumstances or conditions that you encounter.

> The words from heaven, "This is My beloved Son, in whom I am well pleased" (Matt. 3:17), were still sounding in the ears of Satan. But **he was determined to make Christ disbelieve this testimony**. The word of God was Christ's assurance of His divine mission.

He had come to live as a man among men, and <u>it was the word that declared His connection with heaven</u>. **It was Satan's purpose to cause Him to doubt that word**. <u>If Christ's confidence in God could be shaken, Satan knew that the victory in the whole controversy would be his</u>. He could overcome Jesus. He hoped that under the force of **despondency** and **extreme hunger**, Christ would lose faith in His Father, and work a miracle in His own behalf. Had He done this, the plan of salvation would have been broken.

… Though Jesus recognized Satan from the beginning, He was not provoked to enter into controversy with him. Strengthened with **the memory** of the voice from heaven, He rested in His Father's love. He would not parley with temptation. (*The Desire of Ages*, pp. 119, 120)

Satan's studied purpose is to get us to doubt that which we already know from the Word of God and from the Testimony of Jesus, which is to be our dependence. God asked Adam after his fall, "Hast thou eaten of the tree, whereof I commanded thee that thou shouldest not eat?" (Gen. 3:11). It matters not what someone else has said or done; it matters not what the circumstances may be. The only thing that matters is God's word—"whereof I commanded thee." Again and again, Satan seeks to destroy your confidence in what the Lord has told you. He attacks reality, trying to cause doubt—even in the living experience someone has had. Imagine that! This cannot be overstated. Many people have been truly converted and baptized and, because they have doubted their past experience, they have given in to the deception of the father of lies.

Notice in the paragraph below how Satan attacks us at the time of our greatest weakness, causing us to doubt the love of God when perplexed, afflicted, distressed, or attacked for your character weaknesses. Parlaying with Satan about this is fatal to your success.

> <u>It was in the time of **greatest weakness** that Christ was assailed by the **fiercest temptations**</u>. Thus Satan thought to prevail. By this policy he had gained the victory over men. When strength failed, and the will power weakened, and faith ceased to repose in God, then those who had stood long and valiantly for the right were overcome. Moses was wearied with the forty years' wandering of Israel, when for the moment his faith let go its hold upon infinite power. He failed just upon the borders of the Promised Land.

> So with Elijah, who had stood undaunted before King Ahab, who had faced the whole nation of Israel, with the four hundred and fifty prophets of Baal at their head. After that terrible day upon Carmel, when the false prophets had been slain, and the people had declared their allegiance to God, Elijah fled for his life before the threats of the idolatrous Jezebel. Thus Satan has taken advantage of the weakness of humanity. **And he will still work in the same way.** <u>Whenever one is encompassed with clouds, perplexed by circumstances, or afflicted by poverty or distress, Satan is at hand to tempt and annoy.</u> He attacks our weak points of character. **He seeks to shake our confidence in God, who suffers such a condition of things to exist.** We are tempted to distrust God, to question His love. Often the tempter comes to us as he came to Christ, **arraying before us our weakness and infirmities.** <u>He hopes to discourage the soul, and to break our hold on God.</u> Then he is sure of his prey. **If we would meet him as Jesus did, we should escape many a defeat.** By parleying with the enemy, we give him an advantage. (*The Desire of Ages*, pp. 120, 121)

We cannot contemplate too frequently the example that Christ gave us in the wilderness, battling with Satan. Look to Jesus, my dear friend. Though you are trembling, weary, tired, sick, afflicted, oppressed, or even perplexed, remember that, by covenant promise, the Lord will not and cannot give you more than you can bear. Paul wrote: "There hath no temptation taken you but such as is common to man: but God is faithful, who will not suffer you to be tempted above that ye are able; but will with the temptation also make a way to escape, that ye may be able to bear it" (1 Cor. 10:13). Confront Satan, as Jesus did, with the Word of God. "It is written"—this is the door of escape. It is unvarying and always available. Remember, there is no need to discuss your circumstances, feelings, or past. Simple trust in what God has declared this will lead you into victory. Here is more encouragement:

> Jesus rested upon the wisdom and strength of His heavenly Father. He declares, "The Lord God will help Me; therefore shall I not be confounded: ... and I know that I shall not be ashamed. ... Behold, the Lord God will help Me." Pointing to His own example, He says to us, "Who is among you that feareth the Lord, ... that walketh in darkness, and hath no light? **let him trust in the name of the Lord, and stay upon his God.**" Isa. 50:7–10.

"The prince of this world cometh," said Jesus, "and hath nothing in Me." John 14:30. There was in Him nothing that responded to Satan's sophistry. He did not consent to sin. Not even by a thought did He yield to temptation. **So it may be with us**. Christ's humanity was united with divinity; He was fitted for the conflict by the indwelling of the Holy Spirit. And He came to make us partakers of the divine nature. So long as we are united to Him by faith, sin has no more dominion over us. **God reaches for the hand of faith in us to direct it to lay fast hold upon the divinity of Christ, that we may attain to perfection of character.**

And how this is accomplished, Christ has shown us. By what means did He overcome in the conflict with Satan? **By the word of God. Only by the word could He resist temptation**. "It is written," He said. And unto us are given "exceeding great and precious promises: that by these ye might be partakers of the divine nature, having escaped the corruption that is in the world through lust." 2 Peter 1:4. **Every promise in God's word is ours**. "By every word that proceedeth out of the mouth of God" are we to live. When assailed by temptation, look not to circumstances or to the weakness of self, but to the power of the word. All its strength is yours. "Thy word," says the psalmist, "have I hid in mine heart, that I might not sin against Thee." "By the word of Thy lips I have kept me from the paths of the destroyer." Ps. 119:11; 17:4. (*The Desire of Ages*, p. 123)

The scriptures that I will include below are not for holding a conversation with Satan but for issuing commands under the authority of Jesus Christ Himself to gain the victory. In no other way can we achieve victory but by following the example of our Redeemer, trusting in the Father's Word and using the Word of God in conflict with Satan. This will guarantee that you get the victory.

Jesus met Satan with the words of Scripture. "It is written," He said. In every temptation the weapon of His warfare was the word of God. Satan demanded of Christ a miracle as a sign of His divinity. **But that which is greater than all miracles, a firm reliance upon a** "Thus saith the Lord," was a sign that could not be controverted. **So long as Christ held to this position, the tempter could gain no advantage.** (*The Desire of Ages*, p. 120)

Have you wanted to experience great miracles in your life comparable to the experience of the people in the Bible? Often we look at the experiences of Moses, Joshua, Samson, David, Elijah, and Elisha as events that would bolster our faith. However, the Testimony of Jesus is clear that firm reliance upon a "Thus saith the Lord" is greater than any miracle, and it is incontrovertible. When we have this experience and appreciate it, we will become grounded in our dependence, trust, confidence, and faith in the Word of God. God Himself calls upon you to prove Him and see the results for yourself. "If any man will do his will, he shall know of the doctrine, whether it be of God, or whether I speak of myself" (John 7:17). When I encourage you to keep Jesus' testimony inside you and see for yourself the working of the grace of God in your life, I am not just writing my opinion, which would serve you no purpose. "He that believeth on the Son of God hath the witness in himself: he that believeth not God hath made him a liar; because he believeth not the record that God gave of his Son" (1 John 5:10). Satan wants you to believe that God is a liar. Yet, as we have seen, it is "impossible for God to lie," because His Word has creative power in it, and when we allow it in our life, we will see the marvelous results in the transformation of our character. The more that we are living testimonies of God, the more conversions of others there will be. This transformation of individual church members is the missing ingredient in the power of the church, leading to conversions of those outside in the world. "But the manifestation of the Spirit is given to every man to profit withal" (1 Cor. 12:7). "For the earnest expectation of the creature waiteth for the manifestation of the sons of God" (Rom. 8:19). "And this gospel of the kingdom shall be preached in all the world for a witness unto all nations; and then shall the end come" (Matt. 24:14).

## Personal Discoveries about the Biblical Way to Victory

Now let us consider some other Scriptures that can be used in the battle. The verses that I will share below were spiritually lifechanging to me as the discovery of flight was technologically lifechanging to man. Victories that seemed intangible became possible by trusting in the Word of God.

When we are under temptation, Psalm 119:113–117 is exceptionally valuable. It is, in fact, where I first began to understand this method of obtaining victory. It is basically the same method of victory that Christ taught us: praying and quoting Scripture directly and specifically to make a request of God or to command Satan when under his spiritual assault. It may even be to command him to "get thee hence," in the name and blood of Jesus.

When you are tempted, use these verses. The key for me was to repeat verse 115 audibly, commanding Satan to depart.

**Psalm 119**
113. I hate vain thoughts: but thy law do I love.
114. Thou art my hiding place and my shield: I hope in thy word.
115. Depart from me, ye evildoers: for I will keep the commandments of my God.
116. Uphold me according unto thy word, that I may live: and let me not be ashamed of my hope.
117. Hold thou me up, and I shall be safe: and I will have respect unto thy statutes continually.

I came across this promise almost by accident one day as I was *praying* Psalm 119 in my mind while lying on my sofa. Yet, it seemed strange to say in my mind, when talking to the Lord, "Depart from me, ye evildoers: for I will keep the commandments of my God," so I decided to audibly speak the words. What I did not realize was that, at that particular moment, Satan was touching my body, giving me a feeling that was not holy but sinful, which I now realize that he was giving me so I would make that feeling my own and choose to sin. God is good, and He keeps His word whether we know it or not and whether we understand it completely or not. I really had no idea what was going on and what I was about to be shown by the Holy Spirit. Yet, immediately after repeating the words of that verse, that sinful feeling instantly began to go away. I was amazed and even shocked! I had not considered that it might be Satan acting upon my body. The feeling came back some hours later, but I prayed the words again and immediately gained the victory over it. It became clear to me that those feelings were really only Satan causing me to feel a certain way to lead me into sin if I accepted the feelings he impressed upon me as my own and acted upon them.

This realization became to my spiritual life what the technological advance of the airplane was to travel. It became clear to me that victory over every sin was possible. Dependence on the Word of God was the key. I also saw that perseverance, diligence, and willingness to continue in prayer is an absolute necessity for me. It was, in fact, a requirement that the Lord wants to instill in us because victory is not always instantaneous but must be fought for with perseverance. Through perseverance we develop spiritual strength and fortitude. It became obvious that Satan, though defeated every time I would use Scripture, would come back time and time again, tempting me.

If I delayed in responding to the feelings, the fight would take longer than I would have liked. However, I would still obtain the victory so long as I would continue with the Lord in prayer. It is true that, if I did not persevere, I would fall into sin, and it made looking in the mirror quite difficult because I now knew the key to victory and that failure was always my fault, not God's. At this point it was clear the reason for failure; simply a lack of perseverance in prayer, no matter how long a time was necessary.

Paul was serious when he said, "Pray without ceasing." It is God's command that we walk continually with Him. In praying without ceasing, I have discovered that we can choose for the Lord to be with us, putting Him in a position that allows Him to send forth His angels to fight for us and defeat the enemy of our souls. The reality of the matter is that, when we know where our strength is, we also realize that our defeats are because we wanted to sin, and we chose to lay down the armor of God and eat of the tree of knowledge of good and evil like Adam and Eve.

After I saw the power in Psalm 119, it was not too long afterward that I saw another direct weapon to access the power found in Psalm 35. For some reason, as surprised as I was about my sinful feelings going away when I prayed Psalm 119:115, I was flabbergasted by the words of Psalm 35—even utterly overjoyed. I was smiling and laughing and absolutely overjoyed to see that the following verses applied directly to Satan and his angels: "Let them be confounded and put to shame that seek after my soul: let them be turned back and brought to confusion that devise my hurt. Let them be as chaff before the wind: and let the angel of the LORD chase them. Let their way be dark and slippery: and let the angel of the LORD persecute them" (Ps. 35:4–6). I had studied spiritual warfare as well as the statements of the Testimony of Jesus that described the strength and size of Satan and his angels. I was thinking to myself, *What a wonderful series of verses!* Who can chase a twenty-foot-tall demon and match his strength? We certainly can't. But what a wonderful God we serve that He would send an army of holy angels down from heaven to help us in the battle, fighting for us when we give our consent. Thus, after finding these two series of verses, I began to see many other direct spiritual warfare prayer verses throughout the Bible, given especially by God that we might obtain victory over our adversaries when we are presented with temptation. Notice below what happens when holy angels arrive at a location where demons have congregated to hold a person captive:

> The disciples rested on the Sabbath, sorrowing for the death of their Lord, while Jesus, the King of glory, lay in the tomb. As night

Chapter 12: Utilizing the Covenant for Victory  237

drew on, soldiers were stationed to guard the Saviour's resting place, while angels, unseen, hovered above the sacred spot. The night wore slowly away, and while it was yet dark, the watching angels knew that the time for the release of God's dear Son, their loved Commander, had nearly come. As they were waiting with the deepest emotion the hour of His triumph, <u>a mighty angel came flying swiftly from heaven</u>. His face was like the lightning, and his garments white as snow. **His light dispersed the darkness from his track and caused the evil angels**, <u>who had triumphantly claimed the body of Jesus</u> *[because He had died for your sin]*, **to flee in terror from his brightness and glory**. One of the angelic host who had witnessed the scene of Christ's humiliation, and was watching His resting place, joined the angel from heaven, and together they came down to the sepulcher. The earth trembled and shook as they approached, and there was a great earthquake.

Terror seized the Roman guard. Where was now their power to keep the body of Jesus? They did not think of their duty or of the disciples' stealing Him away. As the light of the angels shone around, brighter than the sun, that Roman guard fell as dead men to the ground. One of the angels laid hold of the great stone and rolled it away from the door of the sepulcher and seated himself upon it. The other entered the tomb and unbound the napkin from the head of Jesus. Then the angel from heaven, with a voice that caused the earth to quake, cried out, "**Thou Son of God, Thy Father calls Thee! Come forth.**" <u>Death could hold dominion over Him no longer</u>. Jesus arose from the dead, a triumphant conqueror. In solemn awe the angelic host gazed upon the scene. And as Jesus came forth from the sepulcher, <u>those shining angels prostrated themselves to the earth in worship</u>, and hailed Him with songs of victory and triumph.

Satan's angels had been compelled to flee before the bright, <u>penetrating light of the heavenly angels, and</u> **they bitterly complained to their king that their prey had been violently taken from them**, <u>and that He whom they so much hated had risen from the dead</u>. Satan and his hosts had exulted that their power over fallen man had caused the Lord of life to be laid in the grave, but short was their hellish triumph. For as Jesus walked forth from His prison house a majestic conqueror, Satan knew that after a season he must die, and his kingdom pass unto Him whose right it was.

> **He lamented and raged that notwithstanding all his efforts, Jesus had not been overcome**, but had opened a way of salvation for man, and **whosoever would might walk in it and be saved**. (*Early Writings*, pp. 181, 182)

"Satan's angels had been compelled to flee before the bright, penetrating light of the heavenly angels." This same power is available to you and to me. A similar scene will be repeated in your life when you choose to accept the power of God and to not give in to temptation or to be overcome by oppression or affliction. We cannot gain the victory over Satan without help from the host of the Lord. Of the angels of God, Paul wrote: "Are they not all ministering spirits, sent forth to minister for them who shall be heirs of salvation?" (Heb. 1:14). James gave us a promise to claim: "Submit yourselves therefore to God. Resist the devil, and he will flee from you" (James 4:7). The holy angels wait with eager anticipation to minister to us in any and every experience of life so that we may be prepared and preserved for redemption from this world of sin. Such ministry is the work and joy of heaven. If it were necessary, the Lord would send every angel in heaven before letting you be overcome by Satan. Jesus will not allow His blood to have been spilled in vain. So then, "Let us therefore come boldly unto the throne of grace, that we may obtain mercy, and find grace to help in time of need" (Heb. 4:16). What are you waiting for?

Many times you will see, in the Psalms, various warfare prayers that are ready-made to assist you in gaining the victory over sin. Satan usually is not mentioned by name, yet you can readily see how a psalm would apply to him by the context of the statement, indicating that it is of great benefit to use when tempted. Here is a simple question for you: Can you chase a twenty-foot-tall demon? Is Satan scared of you personally? Of course not! But you can be protected and have the help of the Lord to chase Satan and his host away. When I saw those verses, they gave me great joy because that is exactly what I needed for victory: "Submit yourselves therefore to God. Resist the devil, and he will flee from you." A lot of times we look at this verse and wonder how it is to be accomplished. Yet, now you can see through prayer and acting upon your faith that Satan will flee because he is fearful of Jesus and His host, which are commissioned to help you. Some battles with the adversary can be won instantaneously; others require perseverance. Yet, never will we lose when we stay close to Christ.

> To us, as to Peter, the word is spoken, "Satan hath desired to have you, that he may sift you as wheat: but I have prayed for thee, that

> thy faith fail not." Luke 22:31, 32. **Christ will never abandon those for whom He has died.** <u>We may leave Him and be overwhelmed with temptation, but Christ can never turn from one for whom He has paid the ransom of His own life</u>. Could our spiritual vision be quickened, we should see souls bowed under oppression and burdened with grief, pressed as a cart beneath sheaves, and ready to die in discouragement. <u>We should see angels flying quickly to the aid of these tempted ones, **forcing back the hosts of evil that encompass them**, and placing their feet on the sure foundation. **The battles waging between the two armies are as real as those fought by the armies of this world**</u>, and on the issue of the spiritual conflict eternal destinies depend. (*Prophets and Kings*, pp. 175, 176)

Psalm 119:115 must be prayed audibly to be effective because it is a command. If you are in an environment where you are not able to speak aloud, even a whisper under your breath will do. But this may seem strange to people around you, and it may not always be appropriate to speak audibly. Under such circumstances, a prayer in your heart may be as effective. Ezekiel 36:25–27 is particularly effective as a prayer for that circumstance:

> Then will I sprinkle clean water upon you, and ye shall be clean: from all your filthiness, and from all your idols, will I cleanse you. A new heart also will I give you, and a new spirit will I put within you: and I will take away the stony heart out of your flesh, and I will give you an heart of flesh. And I will put my spirit within you, and cause you to walk in my statutes, and ye shall keep my judgments, and do them. (Ezek. 36:25–27)

These words of promise were not originally a prayer, but I quote these words in prayer as I ask our Father in heaven to produce this in my life. I have also put these words in the form of prayer as the promise I am claiming.

Verses 28–30, which follow the promise of cleansing, are promises that can also be claimed for your ministry: "And ye shall dwell in the land that I gave to your fathers; and ye shall be my people, and I will be your God. I will also save you from all your uncleannesses: and I will call for the corn, and will increase it, and lay no famine upon you. And I will multiply the fruit of the tree, and the increase of the field, that ye shall receive no more reproach of famine among the heathen" (Ezek. 36:28–30). God promises to multiply our personal fruit of the Spirit and to increase souls in the harvest of the New Jerusalem. This is righteousness by faith, when we accept this power that God has offered to us through praying and utilizing his promise to the glory of His name for victory over sin. Though we cannot see the power, we live by belief, which God turns into reality.

## Promises from the Writings of Paul

Let us consider Paul's counsel, through the Testimony of Jesus, about fighting the battle of temptation. Since Paul is often called the "apostle of grace," I see great value in understanding how he admonishes us to battle on to victory.

> **In referring to these races as a figure of the Christian warfare**, Paul emphasized the preparation necessary to the success of the contestants in the race—<u>the preliminary discipline, the abstemious diet, the necessity for temperance</u>. "Every man that striveth for the mastery," he declared, "is temperate in all things." The runners put aside every indulgence that would tend to weaken the physical powers, and <u>by severe and continuous discipline, trained their muscles to strength and endurance</u> that, when the day of the contest should arrive, they might put the heaviest tax upon their powers. **How much more important that the Christian, whose eternal interests are at stake, bring appetite and passion under subjection to reason and the will of God!** Never must he allow his attention to be diverted by amusements, luxuries, or ease. All his habits and passions must be brought under the strictest discipline. Reason, enlightened by the teachings of God's word and guided by His Spirit, must hold the reins of control.
>
> <u>And after this has been done</u>, the Christian must put forth **the utmost exertion** in order to gain the victory. In the Corinthian games **the last few strides** of the contestants in the race were made with agonizing effort to keep up undiminished speed. <u>So the Christian, as he nears the goal</u>, **will press onward with even more zeal and determination** than at the first of his course. (*The Acts of the Apostles*, p. 311)

Olympic athletes often credit their diet with being more than fifty percent responsible for their success in competition. How much more should we pay attention to remove refined, processed, and genetically modified (GMO) foods from our diet. When we consider that sugar, white rice, white flour, milk, and chemicals in food, which include preservatives, miscellaneous food additives, and flavorings, can be cancer causing or neurotoxins, we should avoid them to be as fit as possible for the battle because we fight not for a perishable crown but an eternal. As we learned in *Prophets and Kings*, "On the issue of the spiritual conflict eternal destinies depend." As soldiers for Christ, let us continue to look at the Testimony of Jesus and how we are to think about this battle for eternal life and gain more faith and encouragement:

> In the epistle to the Hebrews is pointed out the **single-hearted purpose** that should characterize the Christian's race for eternal life: "Let us lay aside every weight, and the sin which doth so easily beset us, and let us run with patience the race that is set before us, looking unto Jesus the author and finisher of our faith." Hebrews 12:1, 2. Envy, malice, evil thinking, evilspeaking, covetousness—these are weights that the Christian must lay aside if he would run successfully the race for immortality. Every habit or practice that leads into sin and brings dishonor upon Christ must be put away, **whatever the sacrifice**. The blessing of heaven cannot attend any man in violating the eternal principles of right. **One sin cherished is sufficient to work degradation of character and to mislead others**.
>
> The competitors in the ancient games, after they had submitted to **self-denial** and **rigid discipline**, *were not even then sure of the victory*. "Know ye not," Paul asked, "that they which run in a race run all, but one receiveth the prize?" However eagerly and earnestly the runners might strive, the prize could be awarded to but one. One hand only could grasp the coveted garland. Some might put forth the utmost effort to obtain the prize, but as they reached forth the hand to secure it, another, an instant before them, might grasp the coveted treasure.
>
> Such is not the case in the Christian warfare. **Not one who complies with the conditions will be disappointed at the end of the race. Not one who is earnest and persevering will fail of success**. The race is not to the swift, nor the battle to the strong. The weakest saint, as well as the strongest, may wear the crown of immortal glory. All may win who, through the power of divine grace, bring their lives into conformity to the will of Christ. The practice, in the details of life, of the principles laid down in God's word, is too often looked upon as unimportant—a matter too trivial to demand

> attention. But in view of the issue at stake, **nothing is small that will help or hinder**. Every act casts its weight into the scale that determines life's victory or defeat. And the reward given to those who win will be in proportion to the energy and earnestness with which they have striven.
>
> The apostle compared himself to a man running in a race, straining every nerve to win the prize. "I therefore so run," he says, "not as uncertainly; so fight I, not as one that beateth the air: but I keep under my body, *and bring it into subjection*: lest that by any means, when I have preached to others, I myself should be a castaway." That he might not run uncertainly or at random in the Christian race, Paul subjected himself to severe training. The words, "I keep under my body," literally mean to **beat back by severe discipline** the desires, impulses, and passions. (*The Acts of the Apostles*, pp. 312–314)

Without question, the Lord wants us to persevere in obtaining character perfection. The value can be seen in what the Lord is developing in us as we pay careful attention to the smallest of details in God's coaching, not leaving anything undone. We cannot afford to leave an opening for Satan to enter into our lives and weaken us in any way. Therefore, how we spend our time with family and friends, how we eat, what we read, what we do for recreation, the music we listen to, and the work that we do should all be beneficial in some form and should not be a detriment to our entering the kingdom of heaven. We all know from experience that many times in life we have done things that we wish we had not done and that we have left things undone that would have hindered our progress even in the things of the world. Surely it is more important that we not handicap ourselves by our choices from being prepared for the kingdom of heaven. No wonder God, whom we serve through the struggles of life, is increasing our conscientiousness. That is certainly a good character trait to cultivate.

In light of our study, Paul's statement about our going through the struggle with certainty, though the struggle is intense, is most significant. It is certainly worth struggling for something that is certain and of eternal value, considering that the majority of what we have struggled for in this world is very uncertain. Many would do well not to spend so much time training for athletic pursuits when only one competitor can win and even those who win are eventually surpassed by a new champion. On the other hand, time spent in pursuit of the eternal crown will not be lost. To "beat back by severe discipline the desires, impulses and passions," says a lot. Don't be indolent. Don't be deceived by the easy-going life of the world. Salvation is a gift, but character must be developed amidst the pull of the flesh, the world, and Satan. Satan, as a roaring lion, will fight the hardest as we reach the end. Therefore, our struggle requires us to hang on more firmly to God's Word as we near the end. Struggle by faith as Christ struggled for you in the garden of Gethsemane. Though it will be difficult, the victory is guaranteed. There are two types of struggling Christians. Some struggle to maintain the victory by beating back the desires of the flesh. Others struggle emotionally because they have given into temptation when they should have and could have had the victory.

> Paul feared lest, having preached to others, he himself should be a castaway. He realized that if he did not carry out in his life the principles he believed and preached, his labors in behalf of others would avail him nothing. <u>His conversation, his influence, his refusal to yield to self-gratification, must show that his religion **was not a profession merely**</u>, but a daily, living connection with God. One goal he kept ever before him, and strove earnestly to reach—"the righteousness which is of God by faith." Philippians 3:9.
>
> Paul knew that his warfare against evil would not end so long as life should last. <u>Ever he realized the need of putting a strict guard upon himself</u>, that earthly desires might not overcome spiritual zeal. **With all his power he continued to strive against natural inclinations**. Ever he kept before him the ideal to be attained, and this ideal he strove to reach <u>by willing obedience to the law of God</u>. **His words, his practices, his passions**—all were brought under the control of the Spirit of God.
>
> **It was this singlehearted purpose to win the race for eternal life that Paul longed to see revealed in the lives of the Corinthian believers**. <u>He knew that in order to reach Christ's ideal for them</u>, **they had before them a life struggle from which there would be no release**. He entreated them to strive lawfully, day by day seeking for piety and moral excellence. **He pleaded** with them to lay aside every weight and to press forward to the goal of perfection in Christ. (*The Acts of the Apostles*, pp. 314, 315)

Thus, the "apostle of grace" spoke to the early church, and his messages are preserved for us to keep us from falling back into sin as ancient Israel did. Dear reader, rightly understanding what the apostles and prophets were conveying is very important to us. When we understand the battle, as we study the inspired writings, we receive an abundance of strength, power, hope, faith, and assurance that we can indeed be like Christ, without succumbing to lust and not sinning, while living in a body that is under manifold temptations and with a human nature in a sinful flesh-body. Then, and only then, will we truly appreciate and understand the omnipotence of God. Studying the Bible with the understanding that God is omnipotent and that we are to attain to perfection of character converts every promise into a spiritual tool for assistance in the struggle. Then, and only then, does the omnipotence of God appear in the fullness of His glory. Why is that? It is because, with just one look in the mirror of the Ten Commandments and one look in our bathroom mirror, we become instantly aware that only with the power of an omnipotent God can our wretched, miserable, poor, blind, and naked souls—so degraded by sin, so habitually ingrained by cultivation and heredity—break free from the power that calls us so often through our flesh. A theology that does not believe in character perfection is a theology without faith in a powerful God, and it is, in reality, a works-righteousness method of attaining acceptance from God, though perhaps unconscious to the one who holds that belief.

What we are going over in this chapter is "righteousness by faith," right doing, right actions, and right works by depending by faith on the power of what God's Word promises to accomplish in us to obtain the victory whenever we voluntarily exercise our will and choose to follow it. In this you are working in harmony with the will of God. Therefore, you are working with and in His power, which has His guarantee to accomplish that which He intends.

> For as the heavens are higher than the earth, so are my ways higher than your ways, and my thoughts than your thoughts. For as the rain cometh down, and the snow from heaven, and returneth not thither, but watereth the earth, and maketh it bring forth and bud, that it may give seed to the sower, and bread to the eater: So shall my word be that goeth forth out of my mouth: it shall not return unto me void, but it shall accomplish that which I please, and it shall prosper in the thing whereto I sent it. (Isa. 55:9–11)
>
> Being born again, not of corruptible seed, but of incorruptible, by the word of God, which liveth and abideth for ever. But the word of the Lord endureth for ever. And this is the word which by the gospel is preached unto you. (1 Peter 1:23, 25)

Since the Word "abideth for ever" and "endureth for ever," we will not sin so long as the Word resides within us. That is God's promise! That is His guarantee! It is an assurance from God! Wonderful indeed is this! I can speak for myself, and I think that I can speak for others, that our desire is to be perfect. It is a principle that we have by nature, though, unfortunately, it has been perverted by sin. Only in God-given perfection will we be happy with full joy and live the abundant life. So let us go to this fountain of life, which is so rich and life-giving. Remember that the Word of God is the enduring seed. When we get it inside of us, it produces victory over our sinful nature. David wrote: "Thy word have I hid in mine heart, that I might not sin against thee" (Ps. 119:11). John taught: "Whosoever is born of God doth not commit sin; for his seed remaineth in him: and he cannot sin, because he is born of God" (1 John 3:9). There is a work that we are to participate in as Christ strengthens us to keep us in the battle. That work is to memorize Scripture. By it, the Lord will accomplish in our lives that which He pleases. God's promise through Jude is:

"Now unto him that is able to keep you from falling, and to present you faultless before the presence of his glory with exceeding joy, to the only wise God our Saviour, be glory and majesty, dominion and power, both now and ever. Amen" (Jude 24, 25). When God's seed is inside you, Jesus can keep you from falling, and He can maintain His dominion and power in the present and in the future.

## Other Weapons in Our Spiritual Defense

Let us look at other weapons from the Word of God that you can use to defend yourself against temptation. Psalm 51:10–12 is an excellent armament, doubly so because it is a song that can be sung to fill the soul with Scripture about cleansing. I will place in *italics* the words that I have used as I have prayed the verses.

**Psalm 51**
10. "Create in me a clean heart, O God; and renew a right spirit within me."
    *Take away any unclean spirit and give me Thy Holy Spirit.*
11. "Cast me not away from thy presence; and take not thy holy spirit from me."
    *But cast out Satan and his angels away from me and my presence, in the name and blood of Jesus.*
12. "Restore unto me the joy of thy salvation; and uphold me with thy free spirit."
    *Uphold me according to Thy word in which I place my hope.*

Of course, the entire passage is an effective prayer if you have fallen into sin. It emphasizes the mercy of God, which will become oh so apparent as you begin a journey of praying Scripture. David was clearly aware of this and left a record of it for us to learn by it and receive this blessing as he did. Such prayer is suggested in *The Great Controversy:*

> The Bible should never be studied without prayer. <u>The Holy Spirit alone can cause us to feel the importance of those things easy to be understood</u>, or prevent us from wresting truths difficult of comprehension. It is the office of heavenly angels to prepare the heart so to comprehend God's word that we shall be charmed with its beauty, admonished by its warnings, or animated and strengthened by its promises. **We should make the psalmist's petition our own**: "Open Thou mine eyes, that I may behold wondrous things out of Thy law." Psalm 119:18. <u>Temptations often appear irresistible because, through **neglect** of **prayer** and the **study** of the Bible, **the tempted one cannot readily remember God's promises and meet Satan with the Scripture weapons**</u>. But angels are round about those who are willing to be taught in divine things; and in the time of great necessity they will bring to their remembrance the very truths which are needed. Thus "when the enemy shall come in like a flood, the Spirit of the Lord shall lift up a standard against him." Isaiah 59:19. (*The Great Controversy*, pp. 599, 600)

I should take a moment to mention that praying through the Psalms is a very effective method of prayer. Yes, *pray* the psalms—not just read them. *PRAY* them—all 150 of them. All the psalms are not prayers, but the vast majority are. From my experience of learning to pray through them all, I know that you will find promises that are effective tools against the enemy. Their effectiveness can only be realized as you put the verses to use in prayer, claiming each promise according to the context of the Word. With practice and continued use of this method, you will learn to pray effectively any and all Scripture. The Testimony of Jesus admonishes us to use all the promises of Scripture we can claim and that all is material for prayer. This requires learning Scripture through memorization and then asking for the Holy Spirit to give you more understanding as you diligently study God's Word.

Dear reader, have you felt temptations that appear irresistible? The Spirit of Prophecy tells us clearly why this is. It is not because Satan is more powerful than the Almighty. No! It is your neglect of prayer and study of the

Bible, leaving you unable to remember verses that you can use against the devil and his host in achieving victory through God's power. "Temptations often appear irresistible because, through **neglect** of **prayer** and the **study of the Bible**, **the tempted one cannot readily remember God's promises and meet Satan with the Scripture weapons**" (*The Great Controversy*, p. 600). Be resolved with determination that is unyielding to hindrances, excuses, obstacles, or circumstances that you study and memorize the Word of God *regularly*, *systematically*, and *thoroughly*.

"But angels are round about those who are willing to be taught in divine things; and in the time of great necessity they will bring to their remembrance the very truths which are needed. Thus 'when the enemy shall come in like a flood, the Spirit of the Lord shall lift up a standard against him.' Isaiah 59:19" (*The Great Controversy*, p. 600). Is this not just what you need—holy angels all around you protecting you and strengthening you in your time of great necessity under intense temptation? God's angels are the "standard." They form a wall of fire around you—like the ones that encircled Elisha—that neither human beings nor Satan himself can break through. Here is your strength, your power, your victory, which comes through Christ by faith to "keep you from falling" when you willingly utilize the Scripture as your weapon against Satan, temptation, and sin. The Spirit of Prophecy exhorts believers to pray the promises of God:

> **Every promise in the word of God** furnishes us with subject matter for prayer, presenting the **pledged word** of Jehovah as **our assurance**. Whatever spiritual blessing we need, it is our privilege to claim through Jesus. **We may tell the Lord, with the simplicity of a child, exactly what we need**. We may state to Him our temporal matters, asking Him for bread and raiment as well as for the bread of life and the robe of Christ's righteousness. Your heavenly Father knows that you have need of all these things, and you are invited to ask Him concerning them. It is through the name of Jesus that every favor is received. God will honor that name, and will supply your necessities from the riches of His liberality. ...
>
> The gifts of Him who has all power in heaven and earth are in store for the children of God. Gifts so precious that they come to us through the costly sacrifice of the Redeemer's blood; gifts that will satisfy the deepest craving of the heart, gifts lasting as eternity, will be received and enjoyed by all who will come to God as little children. **Take God's promises as your own**, **plead them**

**before Him as His own words**, and you will receive fullness of joy.
(*Thoughts from the Mount of Blessing*, pp. 133, 134)

## My Experience in Expanding My Prayer Time

Most Christians suffer from an anemic prayer life, and praying through the Psalms was the remedy I found to help overcome this ailment. Several years ago, I realized that my five-minute prayer time was not enough. I knew that I needed more spiritual strength, which Scripture presents as only coming through persevering prayer. So I began taking special time for prayer. Having heard the song, "Sweet Hour of Prayer," for many years, I decided I would pray for one hour more than my regular prayer time, which I was patterning after the prophet Daniel's three times a day. In spite of praying three times a day, my total prayer time, adding all three times together, was then only about fifteen minutes. Talk about anemic!

I determined that I would pray through the Psalms to help strengthen my prayer life. At the same time, I decided to have a special period of forty days of prayer. To do this, I divided up the 150 psalms and determined to pray four psalms a day till I had finished. The last three days I chose the favorites I had come across. Not really knowing what I was going to experience, I found myself surprised and thoroughly blessed. On my first attempt at this, I fell into sin in a big way fifteen days into the forty-day period and was very discouraged. For some reason, I knew this was my only hope, and I continued on through the last twenty-five days. After the forty days, I prayed without the Psalms. Then, a few months later, I had another forty-day prayer period and prayed through the Psalms again. After each forty-day period, I saw very encouraging results and victory in different areas of my life in which I had felt I might never overcome. Additionally, I was convicted of things that I had not thought of previously, and I was blessed with a spiritual house-cleaning that I did not expect. I remember once getting up off of my knees and going into my storage room and finding things in boxes to clean out, which I didn't even realize I had, and then throwing those things away while praising God that He was showing me things I needed to get out of my life. Suffice it to say, even without the psalms, my prayers became longer, more fervent, and more specific to the need. Also, my prayers became more salted with the Word of God. I was seeing a definite power in this method of prayer as I was growing spiritually through gaining victory over sins that had been a long struggle. I was drawing closer to the Lord, and the time spent in prayer was indeed sweet, and it was enjoyable to the point that

I wanted to linger longer in prayer. Not only was I seeing personal victory and spiritual growth, but my ministry was clearly getting stronger as well. I was seeing results for people on my prayer list; they were experiencing spiritual growth, conversions, and other things simply through intercession. People were coming to me and telling me that they were seeing the hand of the Lord move for them when I prayed for them. What an encouragement it was for me to see this, and it led me to continue praying in this way.

I should mention that I did not limit my prayers from Scripture to the Psalms. As I studied the Bible, I found numerous other verses that I prayed, as well as Spirit of Prophecy statements, and I would especially pray the prayers of the men and women of the Bible. This experience was extraordinary! When I prayed these prayers of the saints of old, having their similar circumstances and context, I experienced the hand of the Lord in delivering me also. We should not forget that the prayers of the Bible—of Jacob, Hannah, David, Solomon, Jeremiah, Isaiah, Daniel, and others—are the inspired thoughts from the Holy Spirit. Such help is essential. The power these thoughts provide is available to all simply by our asking and complying with the commands of God. It is so wonderful!

What you will discover using this method is that, after the third time through, you will start becoming familiar with some of the psalms that have touched your heart and spoken to your life in an extraordinarily personal way. I found that the Psalms were no longer just chapters with numbers; some of them had my name on them. They fit my experience so well. I then proceeded to memorize these psalms, four in all. With my experience, I recommend that you memorize psalms. How will you know which psalms are especially personal to you? You will have to see. I am sure that God has had a psalm written specifically for each person. After all, God is a personal God.

Many times in praying through the Psalms, my heart was so touched, and the psalm was so personal to me in praying it that I would become so immersed spiritually that I would not want to stop praying. My communion with the Lord was so very sweet! One thing I did not mention is that, in these forty-day periods with an additional hour of prayer, I would get home sometimes at 11 p.m. or later. Having committed to taking this special time for prayer and not wanting to break my commitment, I would pray anyway. Though decidedly sleepy, I would battle through. Yet, amazingly, about forty-five or sometimes fifty minutes or more into prayer, all of a sudden it was as though I was immersed in the Spirit of God, who was leading me in the words to pray and touching my heart in a very personal way. Immense joy! Immense love! That is what I began to experience in prayer, and, oh, how wonderful were the things that I was learning about the character of God and His love and care for me. I was learning to trust Him and have confidence in His Word. This was not dependent on whether I had faith or not, it was dependent on my simply trusting in the word of the Lord. I know that you will have the same experience because the Lord is personal to each of us. Our strength lies in trusting in God's Word, not in our faith. Learn to accept the Word as it is written. The following quotation is another element that has made a tremendous difference in my spiritual life:

> Many who are sincerely seeking for holiness of heart and purity of life seem perplexed and discouraged. <u>They are constantly looking to themselves, and lamenting their lack of faith; and because they have no faith, they feel that they cannot claim the blessing of God.</u> **These persons mistake feeling for faith.** They look above the simplicity of true faith, and thus bring great darkness upon their souls. <u>They should turn the mind from self, to dwell upon the mercy and goodness of God</u> and **to recount His promises**, and **then simply believe that He will fulfill His word.** <u>**We are not to trust in our faith, but in the promises of God**</u>. When we repent of our past transgressions of His law, and resolve to render obedience in the future, <u>**we should believe that God for Christ's sake accepts us, and forgives our sins**</u>. (*The Sanctified Life*, p. 89)

I now regularly use the Psalms in prayer as well as other parts of Scripture, and I particularly enjoy praying the prayers of the great men of the Bible. These prayers, which others already prayed in the Bible, are inspired. Do you know what that means? It means that you are praying in the will of God and that the Holy Spirit will speak those things that you cannot even utter. Furthermore, the Word of God has creative power in it so that what you pray from it will be created and accomplished as you pray in faith.

CHAPTER 13

# Sanctification by Faith

> When we walk with the Lord
> In the light of His word
> What a glory He sheds on our way
> While we do His good will
> He abides with us still
> And with all who will trust and obey
> Trust and obey
> For there's no other way
> To be happy in Jesus
> But to trust and obey.
> —John Henry Sammis[20]

Many times Christian brothers and sisters ask me: What is the will of God? The answer is: His Word! If you are praying in the appropriate context and with the right application, you can ask what you will, and it will be accomplished. The Bible is very clear—the will of God is "your sanctification." Knowing that sanctification is His will is how you can know for a certainty that the Lord is answering your prayers for victory over every sin and for strength to endure every temptation and to overcome every spiritual infirmity that has so weakened your soul. Paul wrote encouragingly:

> Likewise the Spirit also helpeth our infirmities: for we know not what we should pray for as we ought: but the Spirit itself maketh

---

[20] John H. Sammis, "Trust and Obey," 1887, Hymnary, https://1ref.us/1lc (accessed February 18, 2021).

> intercession for us with groanings which cannot be uttered. And he that searcheth the hearts knoweth what is the mind of the Spirit, because he maketh intercession for the saints according to the will of God. (Rom. 8:26–27)

John also wrote: "And this is the confidence that we have in him, that, if we ask any thing according to his will, he heareth us: And if we know that he hear us, whatsoever we ask, we know that we have the petitions that we desired of him" (1 John 5:14, 15).

I must forewarn you—now that you have come to this knowledge and experience that the devil will assault you again and again. Yet, do not be discouraged! Pray again and again. I can say from experience that only when you are striving for the victory do you really understand the mercy of God. As you strive in faith, you will see your wretchedness of soul so very clearly. Especially is this so if you sin after having had victory. What excuse is there for such a failure? There is none! With this knowledge the awakening after sin is committed can be very sobering. As Paul expressed his feelings of unworthiness, you will possibly have the same. But Paul understood more the grace and mercy of God, and this we cannot do until we see our rebellion, a deliberate pushing away of God. But, oh how good our Lord and Saviour is! How patient! How merciful! David knew this well, and he put it on record for us in the Psalms. Take courage, my brother, my sister. Persevere in the battle. Victory is not far off.

I will not go into much detail about my precise method of prayer, but I will say that it follows Jesus' teaching. For details, read the chapter "The Lord's Prayer" in *Thoughts from the Mount of Blessing* and "The Privilege of Prayer" in *Steps to Christ*. These chapters contain the principles of the "science of prayer." I say *science* because the Testimony of Jesus calls it a "divine science." We understand that by definition a science is a method used to accomplish a task that, under the same circumstances, produces the same results every time. Recognizing prayer as a science can change profoundly how you look at your petitions to God. Praying is not guesswork. It's not supposed to be. God has prescribed a method for us to address Him, and He obligates Himself to respond positively each time. "If ye abide in me, and my words abide in you, ye shall ask what ye will, and it shall be done unto you" (John 15:7). Letting Christ's words abide in you is one of the keys to answered prayer, though there are other conditions. The covenant is, in itself, a promise that God has given us to use in breaking free from the bondage of this world in any and every matter that may entangle you.

> Prayer and faith are closely allied, and they need to be studied together. In the prayer of faith there is a **divine science**; it is a science that everyone who would make his lifework a success **must understand**. Christ says, "What things soever ye desire, when ye pray, believe that ye receive them, and ye shall have them." Mark 11:24. **He makes it plain that our asking must be according to God's will**; we must ask for the things that He has **promised**, and whatever we receive must be used in doing His will. The conditions met, the promise is **unequivocal**. (*Education*, pp. 257, 258)

To get an outline of the method I use in prayer, go to my website, and there you can download "The Science of Prayer," from the "Document Downloads" page, for a complete outline of the eight components of the Lord's Prayer. Below I will briefly explain.

I start my prayer with the principle outlined by the Lord in "The Lord's Prayer" (Matt. 6:9–13). I have broken the Lord's Prayer into eight components, according to the Testimony of Jesus explanations, which are the categories of the subtitles. My petitions do not start until verse 13 (component #7), right in the middle of the verse. That is where it is appropriate to petition because all your sins are repented of and confessed, and you are viewed as abiding in Christ and, therefore, considered perfect by God.

I pray through my prayer list, which contains the names of family, friends, and anyone who has asked me to pray for them.

Last of all, I pray through the portions of Scripture that I have determined for the time, and I intersperse my personal needs and requests at this point in the prayer or afterward.

## More Scriptures to Pray

Let's consider some other scriptures that can be used in praying when you are in immediate need against Satan's attacks. First, notice how appropriate the last seven verses of Psalm 40 are to end your petition, with the whole of the psalm being a prayer. When you pray as Christ taught His disciples to pray, this is a most eloquent plea before your Father in heaven. Keep in mind that the Father does not answer our prayers simply and only because He loves us but first for His name's sake, for His mercy's sake, and for His glory. He has created us because He loves us, and He waits to see how we will respond to Him. His love is unchanging, but what we receive from Him varies from person to person according to your relation to Him, your circumstances, your love, your request, your faith, your obedience, your reflecting of His character, your giving to others, and your service for Him and for others for His glory, name, and honor. Everybody doesn't have the same success in prayer, but all pray to the same God as Christians. God the Father loves you as much as He loves Jesus, therefore love is not the deciding factor in why your prayer is received and another's is not. We cannot be proud and think that we are more loved than another or simply more righteous. Please keep in mind the covenant. It's an agreement with a grave penalty if there is a failure. The Father and the Son have their names connected to it, and the word of God is placed above His name—"for thou hast magnified thy word above all thy name" (Ps. 138:2). God has given His word to His creation and upholds it among themselves—the Father, Son, and Holy Spirit—so that it can be depended on every time, for eternity. Therefore, you can depend on it for your needs and requests as each condition is met. What you receive from God versus what another person receives is not God's favoritism but a result of the person's faith—not a lack of power or love from God. God's power and love are constants. Jesus said: "Go thy way, and as thou hast believed, so be it done unto thee" (Matt. 8:13). Your believing and acting upon the Word of God is the determining factor. Knowing this, you can see how David's words are all the more appropriate: "Uphold me according unto thy word" (Ps. 119:116). Based on these principles, let's look at some more scriptures.

**Psalm 40**
11. Withhold not thou thy tender mercies from me, O LORD: let thy lovingkindness and thy truth continually preserve me.
12. For innumerable evils have compassed me about: mine iniquities have taken hold upon me, so that I am not able to look up; they are more than the hairs of mine head: therefore my heart faileth me.
13. Be pleased, O LORD, to deliver me: O LORD, make haste to help me.
14. Let them be ashamed and confounded together that seek after my soul to destroy it; let them be driven backward and put to shame that wish me evil *[Satan and his angels]*.
15. Let them be desolate for a reward of their shame that say unto me, Aha, aha.
16. Let all those that seek thee rejoice and be glad in thee: let such as love thy salvation say continually, The LORD be magnified.
17. But I am poor and needy; yet the LORD thinketh upon me: thou art my help and my deliverer; make no tarrying, O my God.

What a powerful and beautiful prayer! What an aid in spiritual warfare! It underscores our need of mercy and help in the midst of direct spiritual battles, as it points to the innumerable evils that compass us about. Nonetheless, the pleasure of the Lord is in our deliverance from and confounding of Satan and his angels. "Let them be driven backward and put to shame that wish me evil" (Ps. 40:14). Here again we see that the Lord is magnified as He drives back Satan's forces, and He will help us as we acknowledge our poverty and neediness. He will not tarry.

As you utilize a prayer like this, remember that you can intersperse your own words with Scripture, but keep it in the context of the statements and stay close to the wording of the scriptures you use. Using another psalm—Psalm 70—for direct spiritual battle, I will demonstrate below, with words that I would pray italicized.

**Psalm 70**
1. Make haste, O God, to deliver me; make haste to help me, O LORD
   *Thou knowest the trouble I have. Thou seest my enemies and the work of Satan.*
2. Let them be ashamed and confounded that seek after my soul: let them be turned backward, and put to confusion, that desire my hurt.
   *Let Satan and His angels and wicked men be turned backward and put to confusion.*
3. Let them be turned back for a reward of their shame that say, Aha, aha.
4. Let all those that seek thee rejoice and be glad in thee: and let such as love thy salvation say continually, Let God be magnified.
   *Let me rejoice in Thine salvation and continually praise Thy name. Be magnified, Father, in delivering me.*
5. But I am poor and needy: make haste unto me, O God: thou art my help and my deliverer; O LORD, make no tarrying.
   *Lord, Thou knowest that I am spiritually poor and that I am temporally needy of deliverance. Make haste and hear my cry.*

Remember that there are great promises in many parts of the Bible for use in prayer. The idea is that you take the words as written and form them into a request if they are not already a direct promise. If they can be stated verbatim as they read, simply ask the Father to fulfill that which He has already stated that He will do. The Holy Spirit will lead your mind to fill in your own words according to your circumstances and needs. Wherever I am reading or studying in the Bible, I now make a prayer and use it as a request based on my current circumstances and needs, keeping it in harmony with the context, circumstances, and conditions in my life. Thus, my study is filled with prayer and the Holy Spirit leads in the direction I should go because the words have originated from Him.

Second Samuel 22 is another wonderful prayer, especially for those needing victory in their battles with the world and the devil. It is clearly also an ultimate victory prayer—even a salvational prayer—which you can see in verses 40–43 when applied to the devil and his followers. It is their end result. I like praying those verses in conjunction with Psalm 110:1; Romans 16:20; and Hebrews 10:13. I definitely recommend such a prayer for those who realize their need in faithfully striving to develop the character of Christ. The Lord has not reserved all the blessings for the final victory. He wants you to have triumphs all along the way. As you learn to pray 2 Samuel 22, you will see that it is easy to intersperse your own words, applying the verses to the particular situation you may be encountering.

**2 Samuel 22**
1. And David spake unto the LORD the words of this song in the day that the LORD had delivered him out of the hand of all his enemies, and out of the hand of Saul:
2. And he said, The LORD is my rock, and my fortress, and my deliverer;
   *Be Thou my foundation and make me strong against the work of the enemy.*
3. The God of my rock; in him will I trust: he is my shield, and the horn of my salvation, my high tower, and my refuge, my saviour; thou savest me from violence.
   *Keep Thy word to me, Father, and save me from violence; shield me and protect me, for I trust in Thee.*
4. I will call on the LORD, who is worthy to be praised: so shall I be saved from mine enemies.
   *I have called on Thee because Thou art a covenant-keeping God.*
5. When the waves of death compassed me, the floods of ungodly men made me afraid;
   *Men have made me afraid, but increase my faith in Thee and take away my fear of all but Thee.*
6. The sorrows of hell compassed me about; the snares of death prevented me;
7. In my distress I called upon the LORD, and cried to my God: and he did hear my voice out of his temple, and my cry did enter into his ears.

*Let my cry enter into Thine ears because of the righteousness of Christ, for I have no righteousness except through Him.*

8. Then the earth shook and trembled; the foundations of heaven moved and shook, because he was wroth.
9. There went up a smoke out of his nostrils, and fire out of his mouth devoured: coals were kindled by it.
10. He bowed the heavens also, and came down; and darkness was under his feet.
11. And he rode upon a cherub, and did fly: and he was seen upon the wings of the wind.
12. And he made darkness pavilions round about him, dark waters, and thick clouds of the skies.
13. Through the brightness before him were coals of fire kindled.
14. The LORD thundered from heaven, and the most High uttered his voice.
15. And he sent out arrows, and scattered them; lightning, and discomfited them.
    *Shoot Thine arrows at Satan and his angels that they may be scattered and that their work may be destroyed in the name and blood of Jesus.*
16. And the channels of the sea appeared, the foundations of the world were discovered, at the rebuking of the LORD, at the blast of the breath of his nostrils.
17. He sent from above, he took me; he drew me out of many waters;
    *Deliver me out of the multitude of people in this world given over to sin; deliver me from this flood of iniquity.*
18. He delivered me from my strong enemy, and from them that hated me: for they were too strong for me.
    *Remember Satan is too strong for me; I need Thy arm of deliverance.*
19. They prevented me in the day of my calamity: but the LORD was my stay.
20. He brought me forth also into a large place: he delivered me, because he delighted in me.
    *Provide for me a large safe place of deliverance from the enemy.*
21. The LORD rewarded me according to my righteousness: according to the cleanness of my hands hath he recompensed me.
    *Reward me, Father in heaven, according to Christ's righteousness. Hear my prayer. Let my sins be cleansed by the blood of Jesus that I may appear clean before Thee in Him.*

22. For I have kept the ways of the LORD, and have not wickedly departed from my God.
*Lord, I have not turned away from keeping Thy commandments. Remember to hear my prayer for Thy mercy's sake.*
23. For all his judgments were before me: and as for his statutes, I did not depart from them.
24. I was also upright before him, and have kept myself from mine iniquity.
*Let Jesus be my righteousness and my keeper.*
25. Therefore the LORD hath recompensed me according to my righteousness; according to my cleanness in his eye sight.
*Recompense me according to Christ's righteousness and not according to what I deserve in my own works.*
26. With the merciful thou wilt shew thyself merciful, and with the upright man thou wilt shew thyself upright.
27. With the pure thou wilt shew thyself pure; and with the froward thou wilt shew thyself unsavoury.
28. And the afflicted people thou wilt save: but thine eyes are upon the haughty, that thou mayest bring them down.
*Bring down the proud of the world, and let them not triumph over me for Thy name's sake. Remember to glorify Thy name to the world.*
29. For thou art my lamp, O LORD: and the LORD will lighten my darkness.
30. For by thee I have run through a troop: by my God have I leaped over a wall.
31. As for God, his way is perfect; the word of the LORD is tried: he is a buckler to all them that trust in him.
*Father, make my way perfect as Thy way is perfect that I might be like Thee, for I trust in Thee.*
32. For who is God, save the LORD? and who is a rock, save our God?
*Father, there is no other god. Therefore, I look to Thee alone. Be my God.*
33. God is my strength and power: and he maketh my way perfect.
34. He maketh my feet like hinds' feet: and setteth me upon my high places.
*Make my steps sure that I slip not into sin.*
35. He teacheth my hands to war; so that a bow of steel is broken by mine arms.
*Teach me to fight against Satan with Thy Word for Thy glory.*
36. Thou hast also given me the shield of thy salvation: and thy gentleness hath made me great.
*I thank Thee for being gentle with me though I do not deserve Thy mercy.*
37. Thou hast enlarged my steps under me; so that my feet did not slip.

38. I have pursued mine enemies, and destroyed them; and turned not again until I had consumed them.
*Make me faithful in fully surrendering and obtaining complete, thorough victory over Satan and all his host. Let the Holy Spirit lead me and convince me of all the sin in my life of which I may yet be unaware until all of Satan's strongholds be broken in my life.*
39. And I have consumed them, and wounded them, that they could not arise: yea, they are fallen under my feet.
40. For thou hast girded me with strength to battle: them that rose up against me hast thou subdued under me.
*I thank Thee for the strength Thou hast given me. I accept it and will go forward in faith believing that Thou wilt keep me victorious.*
41. Thou hast also given me the necks of mine enemies, that I might destroy them that hate me.
*Let Jesus' foot be in my foot that my victory over Satan will be sure, his neck be broken and his power destroyed in my life.*
42. They looked, but there was none to save; even unto the LORD, but he answered them not.
43. Then did I beat them as small as the dust of the earth, I did stamp them as the mire of the street, and did spread them abroad.
44. Thou also hast delivered me from the strivings of my people, thou hast kept me to be head of the heathen: a people which I knew not shall serve me.
*Deliver me, Lord, from the confusion of the people and their strife. Convict them and convert them that they may serve me as I teach them Thy Word.*
45. Strangers shall submit themselves unto me: as soon as they hear, they shall be obedient unto me.
*Let their hearts be soft to receive the Word that I speak unto them; let the Holy Spirit speak through me that they may be converted.*
46. Strangers shall fade away, and they shall be afraid out of their close places.
47. The LORD liveth; and blessed be my rock; and exalted be the God of the rock of my salvation.
48. It is God that avengeth me, and that bringeth down the people under me,
*Father, I leave it to Thee to avenge me. Be glorified.*
49. And that bringeth me forth from mine enemies: thou also hast lifted me up on high above them that rose up against me: thou hast delivered me from the violent man.

50. Therefore I will give thanks unto thee, O LORD, among the heathen, and I will sing praises unto thy name.
51. He is the tower of salvation for his king: and sheweth mercy to his anointed, unto David, and to his seed for evermore.

The passage above is a sample of how I have prayed using the psalms to help frame my words, staying very close to that which the Lord has already promised. Then I know for sure that He will hear my prayer, as I also understand that He first hears my prayer for the glory of His name to keep the covenant.

Psalm 143 is particularly appropriate for those who may feel the frustration and weariness of a protracted battle in the afflictions, troubles, obstacles, and trials of life. Its conclusion includes four especially key principles that should be understood in the science of prayer and salvation:

1. "Teach me to do thy will." *The Lord especially wants us to repent but more so to change.*
2. "For thou art my God." *This is saying, in effect: I look only to Thee for salvation from any and all things. I have no other gods before me. A "god," by biblical definition, is an idol or something man-made that we believe in or that we feel we must do in order to save us or make a situation or our experience better.*
3. "For thy name's sake." *This means to God's credit a keeper of His word.*
4. "For thy righteousness' sake." *This means for the vindication of His righteous character, the keeping of His good name as a fair God who only does right.*

The last two of these principles are why God keeps His word to us. It is not just because He loves us that He answers our prayers. It is of the utmost importance that He keep His name holy and that He keep His covenant and His Word. Understanding these principles gives us the confidence that we can continually place our trust in Him and that, with patience, we can wait for the fulfilling of His Word to us.

## Psalm 143
1. Hear my prayer, O LORD, give ear to my supplications: in thy faithfulness answer me, and in thy righteousness.
   *Continue Thy faithfulness in keeping Thy Word and Thy covenant to me. Because of Jesus' righteousness and blood, hear my prayer, for I have no righteousness outside of Him.*

2. And enter not into judgment with thy servant: for in thy sight shall no man living be justified.
   *Lord, let me not be judged in my righteousness, or I will only deserve condemnation. Thou hast given us Christ and hast applied His righteousness to my name that Thou mayest have pleasure in my redemption.*
3. For the enemy hath persecuted my soul; he hath smitten my life down to the ground; he hath made me to dwell in darkness, as those that have been long dead.
4. Therefore is my spirit overwhelmed within me; my heart within me is desolate.
   *Lord, I am weary and weak, but let not my strength fail. Let the Holy Spirit reside in my heart.*
5. I remember the days of old; I meditate on all thy works; I muse on the work of thy hands.
6. I stretch forth my hands unto thee: my soul thirsteth after thee, as a thirsty land. Selah.
7. Hear me speedily, O LORD: my spirit faileth: hide not thy face from me, lest I be like unto them that go down into the pit.
   *Lord, I am weary and weak, but let not my strength fail. Let the Holy Spirit reside in my heart.*
8. Cause me to hear thy lovingkindness in the morning; for in thee do I trust: cause me to know the way wherein I should walk; for I lift up my soul unto thee.
   *Father, renew my strength for this new day. Open my eyes in Thy Word and Testimony that I may know the way that Thou wouldest have me to walk. Let it be clear to me.*
9. Deliver me, O LORD, from mine enemies: I flee unto thee to hide me.
   *Deliver me from Satan; hide me from the work of my enemies.*
10. Teach me to do thy will; for thou art my God: thy spirit is good; lead me into the land of uprightness.
    *Teach me daily to do Thy will and give me of Thy good spirit that I may have no evil spirit controlling me.*
11. Quicken me, O LORD, <u>for thy name's sake</u>: <u>for thy righteousness' sake</u> bring my soul out of trouble.
12. And of thy mercy cut off mine enemies, and destroy all them that afflict my soul: for I am thy servant.
    *Father, let me not be slow in living a holy life. Help me to be instant in following Thy will that Thou mayest be glorified. Be justified in delivering me out of all my troubles by leading me to truly walk as Christ walked.*

The underlined statements in verse 11 are why God keeps His word to us—it is not just because He loves us that He answers our prayers. It is of the utmost importance that He keep His name holy and that He keep His covenant and word. These are the seal that certifies that we can continually place our trust in Him.

## Special Examples

In Psalm 62 and 120 below, there are verses that are direct commands, which are implements for your offense against the devil and his dominion. Remember that the armor of God has six pieces, five being defensive and only one being offensive. That offensive piece of armor is the sword of the Spirit, which represents the Word of God. We must appreciate it for what it is and use it for the victory that Christ has secured for us. Not using it for its intended use is an insult to Christ, for He Himself said, "Man shall not live by bread alone, but by every word that proceedeth out of the mouth of God" (Matt. 4:4). Psalm 119 in its entirety is about the word of God, so there is special significance and power in praying this psalm overall in that it uplifts and exalts the Word to be used in all aspects of our lives. Thus, the Word of God itself admonishes us to depend on it. This is the science of salvation, the science of victory. As you ask God to keep that which He has already covenanted to do according to the terms of the covenant, your redemption is guaranteed—not by your reaching down into your inner being for strength but by a firm mental purpose, a resolve to depend on the Word by acting on it because that is what it says and not because you feel like it. In this way is the victory gained and God is glorified.

"Wherewithal shall a young man cleanse his way? by taking heed thereto **according to thy word**" (Ps. 119:9). "Let thy mercies come also unto me, O LORD, even thy salvation, **according to thy word**" (Ps. 119:41). "So shall I have wherewith to answer him that reproacheth me: **for I trust in thy word**" (Ps. 119:42). "**Remember the word** unto thy servant, upon which thou hast caused me to hope" (Ps. 119:49). "I am afflicted very much: quicken me, O LORD, **according unto thy word**" (Ps. 119:107). "Thou art my hiding place and my shield: **I hope in thy word**. Depart from me, ye evildoers: for I will keep the commandments of my God. Uphold me **according unto thy word**, that I may live: and let me not be ashamed of my hope. Hold thou me up, and I shall be safe: and I will have respect unto thy statutes continually" (Ps. 119:114–117). "Order my steps **in thy word**: and let not any iniquity have dominion over me" (Ps. 119:133). "Plead my cause, and deliver me: quicken me **according to thy word**" (Ps. 119:154). "Let my supplication come before thee: deliver me **according to thy word**" (Ps. 119:170).

From these verses flow the blessings of God's covenant that He wants you to have, and it is your privilege to ask for cleansing from sin, mercy and salvation from present trials, an answer to the reproaches of Satan, an admonishment from God to remember that which He has already promised us, victory from affliction, a place of hiding and a shield, sustaining power, a promise that no sin or demon may have dominion over you, and the intercession of Jesus. These are promises from God from the covenant itself that He has already proclaimed will occur which can be a reality in your personal life when you believe:

> I will abide by My own word, I have obligated Myself to fulfill these requests and even stronger terms. You may demand its fulfillment from Me, for I have made a blood covenant with you which I will not renege on that you may know without a doubt that it is impossible for Me to lie.

Now look at what God has given to you according to your need, in Psalm 62 and Psalm 120, and note especially the third verse in both psalms. Your need is your highest qualification for making a request—especially for victory over sin and iniquity, abominations in your life, transgressions, the world, and Satan. These are ready-made, inspired prayers.

## Psalm 62
1. Truly my soul waiteth upon God: from him cometh my salvation.
2. He only is my rock and my salvation; he is my defence; I shall not be greatly moved.
3. How long will ye imagine mischief against a man? ye shall be slain all of you: as a bowing wall shall ye be, and as a tottering fence.
4. They only consult to cast him down from his excellency: they delight in lies: they bless with their mouth, but they curse inwardly. Selah.
5. My soul, wait thou only upon God; for my expectation is from him.
6. He only is my rock and my salvation: he is my defence; I shall not be moved.

## Psalm 120
1. In my distress I cried unto the LORD, and he heard me.
2. Deliver my soul, O LORD, from lying lips, and from a deceitful tongue.

3. What shall be given unto thee? or what shall be done unto thee, thou false tongue?
4. Sharp arrows of the mighty, with coals of juniper.
5. Woe is me, that I sojourn in Mesech, that I dwell in the tents of Kedar!
6. My soul hath long dwelt with him that hateth peace.
7. I am for peace: but when I speak, they are for war.

Both of these psalms directly address Satan. Thus, from God's point of view, they are commands, demands, requests, or promises to deliver you in the battle against Satan, sin, and temptation. Certain portions of Scripture seem especially effective in gaining the victory, and these are two of my favorite scriptures to use in prayer because I have seen results from them when other scriptures may not deliver as quickly. As you begin to use the Word of God as He intended, you will discover that, in some encounters with Satan, you need to be much more direct. These two psalms above could be used under such circumstances. Overall, the more you systematically and consistently study the Word, the more you will find the keys to victory and the more you will learn the specific verses for the exact circumstances you are in. This will have the affect of giving you a speedier deliverance. "Blessed be the LORD my strength, which teacheth my hands to war, and my fingers to fight" (Ps. 144:1).

We are not to hold converse with the devil. However, commanding him in the authority, name, and blood of Jesus Christ is our privilege and duty. Keep in mind also that we have a part to play and conditions that we must fill to rightly expect, request, demand, and realize the victory that God has promised and will grant us to the glory of His name.

## Praying the Words of Peter to Partake of the Divine Nature

We have looked at the words of Paul, "the apostle of grace." Let us now look at the words of inspiration given through Peter, a man who struggled with controlling his impulses, that we may have an even better understanding of the work to be done in obtaining victory over our human nature, lusts, impulses, temptation, and sin.

> Simon Peter, a servant and an apostle of Jesus Christ, to them that have obtained like precious faith with us through the righteousness of God and our Saviour Jesus Christ: Grace and peace be

multiplied unto you through the knowledge of God, and of Jesus our Lord, According as his divine power hath given unto us all things that pertain unto life and godliness, through the knowledge of him that hath called us to glory and virtue: Whereby are given unto us exceeding great and precious promises: that by these ye might be partakers of the divine nature, having escaped the corruption that is in the world through lust. And beside this, giving all diligence, add to your faith virtue; and to virtue knowledge; and to knowledge temperance; and to temperance patience; and to patience godliness; and to godliness brotherly kindness; and to brotherly kindness charity. For if these things be in you, and abound, they make you that ye shall neither be barren nor unfruitful in the knowledge of our Lord Jesus Christ. (2 Peter 1:1–8)

We may obtain the precious faith needed for salvation "through the righteousness of God." The strength is not from us but "according as his divine power hath given unto us all things"—not some things, not most things but "all things that pertain unto life and godliness." We will not be able to blame God that something was lacking.

Whatever is lacking in your life spiritually, I believe it is now easy for you to see that it is simply due to your not accepting and applying that which is provided for your benefit. Be faithful and apply all that God has provided, and you will see the power of the Lord lead you to victory in your life. The life that Peter is talking about in verse 3 is not life in heaven but eternal life that comes from the "born again" experience, which must be established here on earth before the close of probation before the second coming of Christ in a world with demons and alluring sin.

You may have mourned because you have a human nature, cumbered with hereditary and cultivated tendencies to sin, and you may have even excused yourself, saying, "I am only human," yet God offers you to partake of His divine nature. It is true that with only a human nature we cannot overcome sin, but I ask: Does a divine nature sin? Absolutely not! It can never sin. Neither does a human nature connected to a divine nature sin. This truth is one of the "exceeding great and precious promises" that God has offered you. Will you accept it? By faith, you can receive it and let the smile of God shine upon you. It is your privilege to request, allow, and accept this nature. Then, because of your choice, God can enforce against Satan all that is necessary for you to be kept free from sin. Like no other experience of mankind, this victory will vindicate the name of the Lord because it will bear a stark contrast to Satan's experience of "the mystery of iniquity." It will reveal the power of God to keep mankind unsullied under manifold temptations, which Lucifer did not face when he sinned. It will show that those who choose to place implicit trust and faith in the Lord will be kept from falling though we are weaker than Satan. Bear in mind that Satan will get to test the finished product—human beings re-created in the image of God, experiencing continuous victory in a world of sin. Victorious humanity becomes an incomprehensible mystery to Satan and his angels, for, in the pure and holy environment of heaven, he never experienced the deception, coercion, and harassment that he employs to tempt people to sin. Yet, now he sees a people who will not sin under any circumstance or condition. The grandest testimony is that the evidence of the transforming power of God will stand up to the most powerful being that God ever created, who first accused and rebelled against Him, as he is allowed to harass, tempt, afflict, persecute, and torture them to the utmost. However, they do not sin, demonstrating that Lucifer or anyone else has no excuse for sinning and falling from grace. John wrote: "Whosoever is born of God doth not commit sin; for his seed remaineth in him: and he cannot sin, because he is born of God" (1 John 3:9).

"Satan **had claimed** that it was impossible for man to obey God's commandments; and in our own strength it is true that we cannot obey them. But Christ came in the form of humanity, and by His perfect obedience **He proved that humanity and divinity combined can obey every one of God's precepts**" (*Christ's Object Lessons*, p. 314). Our objective in this struggle is to obtain the character of Christ, to connect our human nature with the divine nature. That connection is the key to victory. You must be resolute in maintaining that connection by perseverance, diligence, and endurance. Though we may be "partakers of the divine nature," you still must struggle unto victory as Christ struggled in Gethsemane. May our struggles be in maintaining the victorious life—not with guilt and remorse for giving into temptation—knowing there is a better way.

## Climbing *Peter's* Ladder

The Testimony of Jesus comments on the beginning of Peter's second epistle:

> These words are full of instruction, and strike the keynote of victory. The apostle presents before the believers the ladder of Christian progress, every step of which represents advancement in

the knowledge of God, and in the climbing of which there is to be no standstill. Faith, virtue, knowledge, temperance, patience, godliness, brotherly kindness, and charity are the rounds of the ladder. We are saved by climbing round after round, mounting step after step, to the height of Christ's ideal for us. Thus He is made unto us wisdom, and righteousness, and sanctification, and redemption.

God has called His people to **glory** and **virtue**, and these will be manifest in the lives of all who are truly connected with Him. Having become partakers of the heavenly gift, they are to go unto perfection, being "kept by the power of God through faith." 1 Peter 1:5. **It is the glory of God to give His virtue to His children**. He desires to see men and women reaching the highest standard; and when by faith they lay hold of the power of Christ, **when they plead** His unfailing promises, and claim them as their own, when **with an importunity that will not be denied** they seek for the power of the Holy Spirit, **they will be made complete in Him**. (*The Acts of the Apostles*, p. 530)

The Lord is clear that you are "kept by the power of God, through faith." This is a set dependence on that which God has stated to you in His Word—not a dependence based on feeling or circumstance. You are justified by faith; you are righteous by faith. Keep the Word of God in mind. Hold firmly to it with importunity because God has promised and because He is a faithful covenant-keeping God. Ignore your feelings and know that the Holy Spirit and the holy angels are with you to help you through the struggle against temptation and sin. Notice that a ladder must be climbed rung by rung. You cannot ascend the next rung of the ladder until you have climbed past the rung before. Of the characteristics to be acquired, the first is ***diligence***, which is a key principle in the science of prayer. The next rung in the "ladder of sanctification" is *faith*. To ascend the ladder, you must do so "with an importunity that will not be denied." Faith does not come by osmosis or by passive acquisition but, rather, by diligence.

Next comes *virtue*, and then, in order to continue growing, you must have ***knowledge***. What kind of knowledge? Truth! Wisdom! Wisdom is a type of learning that is gained by applying truth so that you might live righteously in a wicked world. James wrote: "If any of you lack wisdom, let him ask of God, that giveth to all men liberally, and upbraideth not; and it shall be given him. But let him ask in faith, nothing wavering" (James 1:5, 6). Through the circumstances of life, the Lord is leading you to the highest standard these cause you to lay firm hold, like Jacob, on the power of Christ. Those who do so "with an importunity that will not be denied ... will be made complete." It is a certainty. Remember what Jesus said about God's response to the entreaties of His elect, "I tell you that he will avenge them speedily" (Luke 18:8). The Lord knows that you have an immense battle to fight against the foe of all souls, but He will not leave you to be defeated when you persevere. You can and will have victory when you recognize how utterly dependent you are on the sustaining power of the Holy Spirit, choosing to remain connected to the Lord by faith.

After knowledge comes *temperance*, which includes moderation in that which is good and complete abstinence in that which is harmful. This principle is crucial in choosing the food you eat. The connection between what we eat and whether we go to heaven or hell is that our food affects our brain, and our brain controls our body. When we put substances into our body that cause it to malfunction, we greatly hinder our ability to live a righteous life. Remember that the principle of temperance applies to our rest, sleep, exercise, study, work, play, and fellowship. Every area of life needs to have the proper balance as God requires.

Only with temperance can you and will you have *patience*. Impatience is a direct result of intemperance. When you do not sleep enough or you work too much or you take too much time with one project so that you are late for the next and then have to hurry, it inevitably affects your progress on the ladder of sanctification. So does what you eat. A simple analogy of this comes from the fact that animals are not patient when it comes to eating, and, as the saying goes, "we are what we eat." We are to be like God, not like a beast. Thus, it is not a good time to be eating meat of any kind—whether pig meat, which was never appropriate to eat or and even chicken—when you should be preparing for translation and growing in faith. Being chicken and having faith are the opposite of each other.

Having acquired patience, we can actually be *godly*, which means being like God. This transformation of character does not take place in the perfect, pure, and holy environment of heaven but here in this wicked world. As Paul wrote to Titus: "For the grace of God that bringeth salvation hath appeared to all men, Teaching us that, denying ungodliness and worldly lusts, we should live soberly, righteously, and godly, in this present world" (Titus 2:11, 12). Since "the grace [or power] of God ... hath appeared to all men," everyone can be godly. That is a promise. No one will be able to accuse God of withholding the power, grace, or ability to live like God, for God has "given unto us all things that pertain unto life and godliness."

This means everything that is needed to be like God. What more could you ask for?

Interestingly enough, the ladder has further rungs to be ascended. Next up from godliness are **brotherly kindness** and **charity**. We talk frequently about charity (or love), not realizing that it is the last rung of the ladder. When we have charity, we already have the eight preceding characteristics. We cannot, in truth, have charity without being like God, for God is love, and godliness precedes brotherly kindness, which precedes charity. The Bible is replete with admonitions on this subject.

> Then said he also to him that bade him, When thou makest a dinner or a supper, call not thy friends, nor thy brethren, neither thy kinsmen, nor thy rich neighbours; lest they also bid thee again, and a recompense be made thee. But when thou makest a feast, call the poor, the maimed, the lame, the blind: And thou shalt be blessed; for they cannot recompense thee: for thou shalt be recompensed at the resurrection of the just. (Luke 14:12–14)
>
> Ye have heard that it hath been said, An eye for an eye, and a tooth for a tooth: But I say unto you, That ye resist not evil: but whosoever shall smite thee on thy right cheek, turn to him the other also. And if any man will sue thee at the law, and take away thy coat, let him have thy cloke also. And whosoever shall compel thee to go a mile, go with him twain. Give to him that asketh thee, and from him that would borrow of thee turn not thou away. Ye have heard that it hath been said, Thou shalt love thy neighbour, and hate thine enemy. But I say unto you, Love your enemies, bless them that curse you, do good to them that hate you, and pray for them which despitefully use you, and persecute you; that ye may be the children of your Father which is in heaven: for he maketh his sun to rise on the evil and on the good, and sendeth rain on the just and on the unjust. For if ye love them which love you, what reward have ye? do not even the publicans the same? And if ye salute your brethren only, what do ye more than others? do not even the publicans so? (Matt. 5:38–47)

To be a brother even to an enemy or a stranger that we do not know—that is biblical "brotherly kindness." The characteristic of "brotherly kindness" means treating a person the way that person would like to be treated, according to their personal physical and spiritual needs, taking into consideration their personality and not exactly the way that we ourselves would want to be treated. The Lord would have us manifest His true character to others. He would have us see to it that they are cared for and strengthened for the kingdom of heaven.

Paul wrote: "Let nothing be done through strife or vainglory; but in lowliness of mind let each esteem other better than themselves. Look not every man on his own things, but every man also on the things of others" (Phil. 2:3, 4). "Let every one of us please his neighbour for his good to edification" (Rom. 15:2). "Love worketh no ill to his neighbour: therefore love is the fulfilling of the law" (Rom. 13:10). When the man told Jesus that to love God "with all the heart, and with all the understanding, and with all the soul, and with all the strength, and to love his neighbour as himself, is more than all whole burnt offerings and sacrifices," Jesus responded, "Thou art not far from the kingdom of God" (Mark 12:33, 34).

These are immensely wonderful verses in the light of a world of selfishness. The kingdom of heaven is made up of holy angels and unfallen beings. Who are they? We are told by inspiration that they are beings that look after the needs of others, and their personal needs are cared for not by themselves but by someone else. Therefore, you and I, who look after the needs of those around us and not ourselves, will be judged as fit citizens to adopt into heavenly culture. This sustains life—theirs and ours, the receiver and the giver. As Jesus said, when you have done this, you are "not far from the kingdom of God."

First Corinthians 13 makes more sense in the light of Second Peter chapter 1. If we have missed a rung in the ladder, we will have a counterfeit. What we will have may look like charity, but, in reality, it is devoid of the Holy Spirit who must be inside us, controlling the process. As Paul declares, we must "live in the Spirit" and "walk in the Spirit" (Gal. 5:25). Consider what charity encompasses:

> Though I speak with the tongues of men and of angels, and have not charity, I am become as sounding brass, or a tinkling cymbal. And though I have the gift of prophecy, and understand all mysteries, and all knowledge; and though I have all faith, so that I could remove mountains, and have not charity, I am nothing. And though I bestow all my goods to feed the poor, and though I give my body to be burned, and have not charity, it profiteth me nothing. Charity suffereth long, and is kind; charity envieth

not; charity vaunteth not itself, is not puffed up, doth not behave itself unseemly, seeketh not her own, is not easily provoked, thinketh no evil; rejoiceth not in iniquity, but rejoiceth in the truth. (1 Cor. 13:1–6)

We may program ourselves to do works of beneficence, but unless we actually have the fruit of the Spirit that includes love, it will be of no profit to us. It is the motive that gives meaning. Many of the elements of charity are in the heart and in the mind. Our feelings and thoughts and actions must be in harmony with one another. We must not do things just to *look* good. Envy, pride (being "puffed up"), and evil thinking are heart and mind issues. Let me put it another way: Unless we are giving ourselves to God and to others willingly and cheerfully, with joy, peace and rejoicing, our actions mean nothing to God, and they profit us nothing.

"Rejoice, O young man, in thy youth; and let thy heart cheer thee in the days of thy youth, and walk in the ways of thine heart, and in the sight of thine eyes: but know thou, that for all these things God will bring thee into judgment" (Eccl. 11:9). The angels cheerfully carry out all of God's commands with a heart of love, truly desiring to help the fallen, decrepit, and wretched human beings that we are. When we allow the Holy Spirit with the holy angels to abide with us, we too will have such a disposition as we carry out the work God has given us, cheerfully representing Him in every experience. "Then Paul, after that the governor had beckoned unto him to speak, answered, Forasmuch as I know that thou hast been of many years a judge unto this nation, I do the more cheerfully answer for myself" (Acts 24:10). Paul spent many nights in chains in rat-infested, insect-filled prison cells with no running water to wash away human waste, yet we never hear of him complaining but only cheerfully suffering for the cross of Calvary.

## Looking unto Jesus

"For the preaching of the cross is to them that perish foolishness; but unto us which are saved it is the power of God" (1 Cor. 1:18). "But God forbid that I should glory, save in the cross of our Lord Jesus Christ, by whom the world is crucified unto me, and I unto the world" (Gal. 6:14). We may read these verses without allowing their deep significance to penetrate our minds. Yet, being crucified means self-sacrifice, giving ourselves for the benefit of someone else with no thought of personal return. Sometimes it means suffering unjustly. Such a sacrifice is foolishness to the world, for the world values self-exaltation, as we learn in Daniel 8, which portrays each succeeding kingdom exalting itself above the previous. Notice how our Saviour lived out these principles in His youth:

> Christ was not exclusive, and He had given special offense to the Pharisees by departing in this respect from their rigid rules. <u>He found the domain of religion fenced in by high walls of seclusion, **as too sacred a matter for everyday life**</u>. These walls of partition He overthrew. In His contact with men He did not ask, What is your creed? To what church do you belong? <u>He exercised His helping power in behalf of all who needed help</u>. Instead of secluding Himself in a hermit's cell in order to show His heavenly character, He labored earnestly for humanity. He inculcated the principle that Bible religion does not consist in the mortification of the body. <u>He taught that pure and undefiled religion is not meant only for set times and special occasions. At all times and in all places He manifested a loving interest in men, and shed about Him the light of a **cheerful piety**</u>. All this was a rebuke to the Pharisees. **It showed that religion does not consist in selfishness, and that their morbid devotion to personal interest was far from being true godliness**. This had roused their enmity against Jesus, so that they tried to enforce His conformity to their regulations.
>
> <u>Jesus worked to relieve every case of suffering that He saw. He had little money to give, but He often denied Himself of food in order to relieve those who appeared more needy than He. His brothers felt that His influence went far to counteract theirs. He possessed a tact which none of them had, or desired to have</u>. When they spoke harshly to poor, degraded beings, Jesus sought out these very ones, and spoke to them words of encouragement. To those who were in need He would give a cup of cold water, and would quietly place His own meal in their hands. **As He relieved their sufferings, the truths He taught were associated with His acts of mercy, and were thus riveted in the memory**.
>
> All this displeased His brothers. Being older than Jesus, they felt that He should be under their dictation. They charged Him with thinking Himself superior to them, and reproved Him for setting Himself above their teachers and the priests and rulers of the

people. **Often they threatened and tried to intimidate Him; but He passed on, making the Scriptures His guide.**

Jesus loved His brothers, and treated them with **unfailing kindness**; but they were jealous of Him, and manifested the most decided unbelief and contempt. They could not understand His conduct. Great contradictions presented themselves in Jesus. He was the divine Son of God, and yet a helpless child. The Creator of the worlds, the earth was His possession, and yet poverty marked His life experience at every step. He possessed a dignity and individuality wholly distinct from earthly pride and assumption; **He did not strive for worldly greatness, and in even the lowliest position He was content**. This angered His brothers. They could not account for His constant serenity under trial and deprivation. They did not know that for our sake He had become poor, that we "through His poverty might be rich." 2 Cor. 8:9. They could understand the mystery of His mission no more than the friends of Job could understand his humiliation and suffering.

Jesus was misunderstood by His brothers because He was not like them. His standard was not their standard. In looking to men they had turned away from God, and they had not His power in their lives. **The forms of religion which they observed could not transform the character**. They paid "tithe of mint and anise and cummin," but omitted "the weightier matters of the law, judgment, mercy, and faith." Matthew 23:23. The example of Jesus was to them a continual irritation. He hated but one thing in the world, and that was sin. **He could not witness a wrong act without pain which it was impossible to disguise**. Between the formalists, whose sanctity of appearance concealed the love of sin, and a character in which zeal for God's glory was always paramount, the contrast was unmistakable. Because the life of Jesus condemned evil, He was opposed, both at home and abroad. His unselfishness and integrity were commented on with a sneer. His forbearance and kindness were termed cowardice.

Of the bitterness that falls to the lot of humanity, there was no part which Christ did not taste. There were those who tried to cast contempt upon Him because of His birth, and even in His childhood He had to meet their scornful looks and evil whisperings.

> If He had responded by an impatient word or look, if He had conceded to His brothers by even one wrong act, He would have failed of being a perfect example. Thus He would have failed of carrying out the plan for our redemption. **Had He even admitted that there could be <u>an excuse for sin</u>, Satan would have triumphed, and the world would have been lost.** This is why the tempter worked to make His life as trying as possible, that He might be led to sin. (*The Desire of Ages*, pp. 86–88)

A life like that of Jesus means having a life that is transformed, and, as it is transformed, it transforms the lives of those around us. In no other way can we be victorious in our ministry to others. Live what you read in the Word and in the Testimony of Jesus. Let the mind of Christ be in you as you let God use you to manifest His character of love to the people around you. Be patient in affliction, suffering, and reproaches and in every trial and insult. This will strengthen you as it works to transform the hard hearts around you. The religion of Christ not only transforms you personally, but it transforms those around you. Act in faith as you pray, believing that God has given you His grace to be manifested in your character, though you may feel or sense nothing. Carry out what you are convicted to do and your strength in that area will increase. When you experience sanctification, the glory of God will be seen in you.

We must look to Jesus: "Looking unto Jesus the author and finisher of our faith; who for the joy that was set before him endured the cross, despising the shame, and is set down at the right hand of the throne of God" (Heb. 12:2). The mind of Christ was focused on the joy that the redeemed would have in heaven. That motivation led Him to endure the trials of this world, which all will experience when they live for the glory of God. The grace of God enables us to minister in cheerfulness:

> Having then gifts differing according to <u>the grace that is given</u> to us, whether prophecy, let us prophesy according to the proportion of faith; or ministry, let us wait on our ministering: or he that teacheth, on teaching; or he that exhorteth, on exhortation: he that giveth, let him do it with simplicity; he that ruleth, with diligence; he that sheweth mercy, with cheerfulness. Let love be without dissimulation. Abhor that which is evil; cleave to that which is good. Be kindly affectioned one to another with brotherly love; in honour preferring one another. (Rom. 12:6–10)

The Lord is asking us to carry out His calling with cheerfulness, knowing that others will be saved because of our steadfastness in maintaining the principles of the Word and in not deviating from God's commandments:

> Every man according as he purposeth in his heart, so let him give; not grudgingly, or of necessity: for God loveth a cheerful giver. And God is able to make all grace abound toward you; that ye, always having all sufficiency in all things, may abound to every good work: (As it is written, He hath dispersed abroad; he hath given to the poor: his righteousness remaineth for ever. Now he that ministereth seed to the sower both minister bread for your food, and multiply your seed sown, and increase the fruits of your righteousness;) Being enriched in every thing to all bountifulness, which causeth through us thanksgiving to God. (2 Cor. 9:7–11)
>
> <u>Through trial and persecution the **glory**—the **character**—of God is revealed in His chosen ones</u>.... They follow Christ through sore conflicts; they endure self-denial and experience bitter disappointments; but thus they learn the guilt and woe of sin, and they look upon it with abhorrence. Being partakers of Christ's sufferings, they can look beyond the gloom to the glory, saying, "I reckon that the sufferings of this present time are not worthy to be compared with the glory which shall be revealed in us" (Rom. 8:18). (*The Acts of the Apostles*, pp. 576, 577)

Keep in mind that, normally speaking, difficult experiences are not pleasant, but as you purpose in your heart to act without complaining and with cheerfulness, the Lord has obligated Himself to give you the right spirit. Christ's life in you will be as bread for your spiritual life, nurturing that life and sowing seed that will bear fruit unto eternal life in others around you, increasing the fruit of the Spirit in your own life. Is this not the main objective of the plan of salvation and the covenant? As we receive God's enrichment, your life will become more abundant, though it may be with trial, affliction or suffering for the cross of Christ. Through these painful experiences, we will have cause for much thanksgiving and praise to God.

## Lessons from Peter

The entire book of First Peter is about this experience and how suffering amidst these difficult experiences leads us to bring glory to God. Normally when we think of the glory of God, we first think of something shining like the sun. Yet, this is not the main way that God's glory is manifested in the world. Few realize that, in praying to bring glory to God, the best way to do so is by showing God's character to their fellow man. Showing His glory in its fullness with the brilliancy of the manifestation of light would kill us and everyone else. Yet, through the way we live, fallen human beings can see the character of God contrasted with the character of the devil and of the world by seeing Christians living without sin, though confronted with difficult experiences. Then, by "beholding," people will "be changed" (2 Cor. 3:8). This demonstration is why God needs fallen sinful human beings to be co-laborers with Him in the redemption of others. Please read the entire book of First Peter when you have time, keeping in mind the process of revealing the glory of God, and then see what power the Lord has for your life.[21] You already know that your day by day and moment by moment experiences can be very trying and that your utilization of Scripture at each encounter is the key to your success. Notice some of the distinct sections of First Peter that bring these experiences out:

**1 Peter 1:22**
Seeing ye have purified your souls in obeying the truth through the Spirit unto unfeigned love of the brethren, see that ye love one another with a pure heart fervently.

Actually allowing this love into our lives is what helps to purify us. If you have asked the Lord to purify you, this is the process.

**1 Peter 2:12–23**
Having your conversation honest among the Gentiles: that, whereas they speak against you as evildoers, they may by your good works, which they shall behold, glorify God in the day of visitation. Submit yourselves to every ordinance of man for the Lord's sake: whether it be to the king, as supreme; or unto governors, as unto them that are sent by him for the punishment of evildoers, and for the praise of them that do well. For so is the will of God, that with well doing ye may put to silence the ignorance of foolish men: As free, and not using your liberty for a cloke of maliciousness, but as

---

[21] Go to my website, Revelation of H.E.$^2$M.$^2$ and there listen to the entire catalog of studies (accessed July 15, 2021). www.revelationofhem.org

the servants of God. Honour all men. Love the brotherhood. Fear God. Honour the king. Servants, be subject to your masters with all fear; not only to the good and gentle, but also to the froward. For this is thankworthy, if a man for conscience toward God endure grief, suffering wrongfully. For what glory is it, if, when ye be buffeted for your faults, ye shall take it patiently? but if, when ye do well, and suffer for it, ye take it patiently, this is acceptable with God. For even hereunto were ye called: <u>because Christ also suffered for us, leaving us an example, that **ye should follow his steps**: **Who did no sin**, neither was guile found in his mouth: Who, when he was reviled, reviled not again; when he suffered, he threatened not; but committed himself to him that judgeth righteously</u>.

This is a beautiful picture of the glory of God in sinful but transformed human beings who manifest the character of the Lord. What a promise we have from the Lord that we will be spoken of as evildoers! And who will do so? It may be family, spouse, parents, children, relatives, or friends. Yet, because you remain steadfast and faithful under the trial, those who talk about you will glorify God when they are saved because they personally reviled you, yet they saw the character of Christ manifested through you. Knowing that such will be the case gives us hope and motivates us to submit to human ordinances when they do not conflict with the commandments of God. Let God be your judge. He is faithful and righteous, though mankind is not.

**1 Peter 3:8–18**
Finally, be ye all of one mind, having compassion one of another, love as brethren, be pitiful, be courteous: Not rendering evil for evil, or railing for railing: but contrariwise blessing; knowing that ye are thereunto called, that ye should inherit a blessing. For he that will love life, and see good days, let him refrain his tongue from evil, and his lips that they speak no guile: Let him eschew evil, and do good; let him seek peace, and ensue it. For the eyes of the Lord are over the righteous, and his ears are open unto their prayers: but the face of the Lord is against them that do evil. And who is he that will harm you, if ye be followers of that which is good? But and if ye suffer for righteousness' sake, happy are ye: and be not afraid of their terror, neither be troubled; but sanctify the Lord God in your hearts: and be ready always to give an answer

to every man that asketh you a reason of the hope that is in you with meekness and fear: Having a good conscience; that, whereas they speak evil of you, as of evildoers, they may be ashamed that falsely accuse your good conversation in Christ. For it is better, if the will of God be so, that ye suffer for well doing, than for evil doing. For Christ also hath once suffered for sins, the just for the unjust, that he might bring us to God, being put to death in the flesh, but quickened by the Spirit.

The power that is available to you through prayer and that you utilize by faith is to have compassion, love, pity, and courtesy in the midst of evil, railings, and reviling. When people see you act in such an unexpected way, it shows that something else is possible besides an angry response. This contrast is what the Lord needs us to demonstrate to the world. It allows the people of the world to decide whether to accept or to reject the character of God in their life. Until this aspect of the character of God is seen in its fullness, the Lord cannot return. We have feared to live in the humility that Peter described because we have not wanted to be humiliated and have preferred to stand for our rights with the assumption that God will not sustain us when we are threatened. That is why we fight back, and fighting back is, in reality, a demonstration of our lack of faith in God's sustaining us and in His glorifying Himself through the experience. Notice that God has promised that no one can harm us as we follow that which is good. This is the "better" way that will "bring us (and others) to God." This is the power of the gospel in our life and in the lives of those to whom we are witnessing. It is transforming and redeeming.

### 1 Peter 4:8–14
And above all things have fervent charity among yourselves: for charity shall cover the multitude of sins. Use hospitality one to another without grudging. As every man hath received the gift, even so minister the same one to another, as good stewards of the manifold grace of God. If any man speak, let him speak as the oracles of God; if any man minister, let him do it as of the ability which God giveth: that God in all things may be glorified through Jesus Christ, to whom be praise and dominion for ever and ever. Amen. Beloved, think it not strange concerning the fiery trial which is to try you, as though some strange thing happened unto you: But rejoice, inasmuch as ye are partakers of Christ's sufferings; that,

when his glory shall be revealed, ye may be glad also with exceeding joy. If ye be reproached for the name of Christ, happy are ye; for the spirit of glory and of God resteth upon you: on their part he is evil spoken of, but on your part he is glorified.

Brothers and sisters, Peter is describing the love and experience that the Lord needs you to have to prepare you for His kingdom and to bring others into the kingdom through your living testimony. When others see God's glory through you, manifesting patience, love, and forgiveness, it will transform the hearts of family, friends, associates, and even enemies. Peter speaks clearly that we are not to think it strange that trials should come, but we should rejoice that we have suffered for the Lord's sake and that souls will be redeemed through our suffering.

**1 Peter 5:10**
But the God of all grace, who hath called us unto his eternal glory by Christ Jesus, after that ye have suffered a while, make you perfect, stablish, strengthen, settle you.

Interestingly enough, this is the experience that perfects you as you go through it, that establishes you immovably in the truth to stand firmly for the Lord, that makes you stronger, and that settles you to receive the seal of God. Notice the process:

**Christ desires nothing so much** as to redeem His heritage from the dominion of Satan. But before we are delivered from Satan's power without, we must be delivered from his power within. **The Lord permits trials in order that we may be cleansed from earthliness,** from selfishness, from harsh, unchristlike traits of character. **He suffers the deep waters of affliction to go over our souls** in order that we may know Him and Jesus Christ whom He has sent, in order that we may have deep heart longings to be cleansed from defilement, and may come forth from the trial **purer, holier, happier**. Often we enter the furnace of trial with our souls darkened with selfishness; but if patient under the crucial test, we shall come forth reflecting the divine character. When His purpose in the affliction is accomplished, "He shall bring forth thy righteousness as the light, and thy judgment as the noonday." Ps. 37:6.

> There is **no danger** that the Lord will neglect the prayers of His people. **The danger is** that in temptation and trial they will become discouraged, and fail to persevere in prayer. (*Christ's Object Lessons*, pp. 174, 175)

Beware of the danger of discouragement, for it is one of the tools the devil frequently uses when he is being defeated. His aim is to discourage you in the midst of your gaining the victory over him. He attempts to make life miserable for you spiritually and possibly physically. Remember Job? We have no indication how long his affliction lasted, but one thing is obvious—the devil was defeated as he tried to continuously discourage the victorious-living Job to get him to give up and surrender. Don't throw victory into the jaws of defeat. Don't fall prey to Satan's deception. The more victorious you become, the more assaults you will have to endure. Yet, the hand of the Almighty will sustain you and not leave you to the power of the enemy.

> **Every manifestation of God's power for His people** arouses the enmity of Satan. **Every time God works in their behalf,** Satan with his angels works with renewed vigor to compass their ruin. He is jealous of all who make Christ their strength. His object is to instigate evil, and when he has succeeded, throw all the blame upon the tempted ones. He points to their filthy garments, their defective characters. He presents their weakness and folly, their sins of ingratitude, their unlikeness to Christ, which have dishonored their Redeemer. All this he urges as an argument proving his right to work his will in their destruction. **He endeavors to affright their souls with the thought that their case is hopeless**, that the stain of their defilement **can never be washed away.** He hopes so to destroy their faith that they will **yield fully** to his temptations, and turn from their allegiance to God. (*Christ's Object Lessons*, p. 168)

One objective of the assaults of Satan is to destroy our faith and cause us to "yield fully" to him after his protracted assault. He only needs one success out of a thousand or more attempts. Your defects, your sin, your defilement can be washed away, which causes Satan's great fear. His work is largely to get humans to die in their sins so that he doesn't have to burn for all the evil he has influenced them to commit. Perseveringly depend on the Word of the Lord and not on your feelings or on circumstances. Remember that Christ is able to save to the uttermost. Dear reader, as you are well aware by now, the battle to live as a Christian is not easy. Yet, just because so many are in rebellion or deceived does not mean that you also must fall for the lie of the devil that your sin cannot be cleansed and that you can never attain to complete, continual victory.

Strange as it may seem, one of the things that has motivated me is the fact that the possibility of one extreme is in itself evidence of the possibility of the other extreme. I saw this first, when I was a child, in reading Genesis 6:5, which says, "And God saw that the wickedness of man was great in the earth, and that every imagination of the thoughts of his heart was only evil continually." If man can be continually evil in thought and action, that is evidence that mankind can be continually righteous with thoughts constantly pure and holy.

Take heart, dear friend, the God of grace offers you continual victory in a mind stayed on Christ, living in the Spirit. "For though we walk in the flesh, we do not war after the flesh: (For the weapons of our warfare are not carnal, but mighty through God to the pulling down of strong holds;) Casting down imaginations, and every high thing that exalteth itself against the knowledge of God, and bringing into captivity every thought to the obedience of Christ" (2 Cor. 10:3–5). Grasp this truth by faith. If you only believe *after* you have accomplished something, then you did not have faith. However, true righteousness by faith is belief in the power of God in His Word to accomplish that which He says *before* you have the victory and *before* you see the results. Believe first, then act on that belief, even going a step further in directly utilizing the covenant. Put your dependence in that which God has promised. Your "own faith" is not the most important factor, but what God has said and what He has promised you. These are what you are to act on.

> Many who are sincerely seeking for holiness of heart and purity of life seem perplexed and discouraged. They are constantly looking to themselves, and lamenting their lack of faith; and because they have no faith, they feel that they cannot claim the blessing of God. These persons mistake feeling for faith. They look above the simplicity of true faith, and thus bring great darkness upon their souls. They should turn the mind from self, to dwell upon the mercy and goodness of God and to recount His promises, and then **simply believe that He will fulfill His word.** We are not to trust in our faith, but in the promises of God. When we repent of our past transgressions of His law, and resolve to render obedience in the future, we should believe that God for Christ's sake accepts us, and forgives our sins.

> Darkness and discouragement will sometimes come upon the soul and threaten to overwhelm us, but we should not cast away our confidence. We must keep the eye fixed on Jesus, **feeling or no feeling**. We should seek to faithfully perform every known duty, and **then calmly rest in the promises of God**. (*The Sanctified Life*, p. 89)

## Faithfulness

Trust in God's Word in doing what God has commanded, as stated above, is the key to utilizing God's Word and covenant promises for our redemption from temptation and sin. The question is: What does the Word of God say? Act on what it says and not on either your feeling faith or not feeling it. Simply take God at His word, feeling it or not. Accept His Word and utilize it, and you will see the victory and the manifestation of God in your life.

> If we receive the witness of men, the witness of God is greater: for this is the witness of God which he hath testified of his Son. He that believeth on the Son of God hath the witness in himself: he that believeth not God hath made him a liar; because he believeth not the record that God gave of his Son. And this is the record, that God hath given to us eternal life, and this life is in his Son. He that hath the Son hath life; and he that hath not the Son of God hath not life. These things have I written unto you that believe on the name of the Son of God; that ye may know that ye have eternal life, and that ye may believe on the name of the Son of God. (1 John 5:9–13)

It is clear from this that, in receiving the Word of God, we will witness in our own personal life God's transforming power. Often we receive the witness or word of human beings without question, while we hesitate in receiving God's word. Why question God ever? Men have failed you, while the sum total of evidence is that God has never failed you.

"Lift up your eyes on high, and behold who hath created these things, that bringeth out their host by number: he calleth them all by names by the greatness of his might, for that he is strong in power; not one faileth" (Isa. 40:26). If more people would take time to meditate on the creation of the Lord, as Isaiah said, then they would readily see God's faithfulness—especially in the stars, which are so predictable that we use them to tell time. When have they ever failed to be in the place that we expected them?

Never! Consider their size and the speed at which they travel. Is not the Creator and God who sustains all the vast, starry heavens, also able to sustain you—little you—when you put your trust in Him? Behold the heavens with the trillions of stars, planets, and moons all orbiting at amazingly high velocities, yet none of them collides with another or fails to keep precise place and time.

> The Saviour manifested divine compassion toward the Syrophenician woman. His heart was touched as He saw her grief. He longed to give her an immediate assurance that her prayer was heard; but He desired to teach His disciples a lesson, and for a time He seemed to neglect the cry of her tortured heart. <u>When her faith had been made manifest,</u> He spoke to her words of commendation and sent her away with the precious boon she had asked. The disciples never forgot this lesson, and it is placed on record to show the result of **persevering prayer.**
> 
> <u>It was Christ Himself who put into that mother's heart the persistence which would not be repulsed.</u> **It was Christ who** gave the pleading widow courage and determination before the judge. **It was Christ who,** centuries before, in the mysterious conflict by the Jabbok, had inspired Jacob with the same persevering faith. **And the confidence which He Himself had implanted, He did not fail to reward.** (*Christ's Object Lessons*, p. 175)

## Perseverance

Take courage—take courage and persevere with an importunity that will not be denied. Do not let go of Christ until you are blessed with transformation of character. Dearly beloved, it is the love of God that allows us to go through so much that is painful because the suffering and affliction are for our good. They will deliver us from the love of the world so that we can see the value of eternal life. It will be worth it all. Sometimes when you pray a scripture for victory, your petition will be answered immediately. However, many times it will not. Either way, hold firm your faith. It is God's purpose to develop and reveal unbreakable faith in you so that angels, demons, and those around you will see it to God's glory. As you develop faith that will not break, you will also have developed a character like Christ's. Christ Himself puts the desire in you to persevere. Perseverance is a gift direct from heaven, which He will not fail to reward. God has put the desire in your heart to be like Him. However, He cannot and will not force you. He cannot and will not accept a forced obedience. So He waits for you to yield yourself to the Spirit's urging and make God's desire your own desire. Does temptation not work the same way but in reverse? Let the mind of faith develop and mature in you to the glory of God.

> Having received the faith of the gospel, the next work of the believer is to add to his character virtue, and thus cleanse the heart and prepare the mind for the reception of the knowledge of God. This knowledge is the foundation of all true education and of all true service. **It is the only real safeguard against temptation**; and it is this alone that can make one like God in character. Through the knowledge of God and of His Son Jesus Christ, are given to the believer "all things that pertain unto life and godliness." **No good gift is withheld from him who sincerely desires to obtain the righteousness of God**. (*Acts of Apostles*, pp. 530, 531)

Notice, in the statement above, that the believer has a work to do. It is of special importance that you prepare your mind to receive the knowledge of God, which is truth for the salvation of your soul. There are four different outcomes in the parable of the sower and the seed in Matthew 13, yet the seed is always the same. The seed is the Word of God. The soil into which it is cast represents the heart—your heart. Whether you bear fruit depends not on the seed but on the condition of the soil, the heart. You must let the mind of Christ be in you and let God's Word be your guide, and then you will bear fruit.

## The Growth of the Plant

The work we are to do is that of sowing. To have a successful crop, simply casting the seed to the earth is not enough. If the seed is cast on hard, crusted, and unbroken soil, whatever moisture it receives will quickly dry up and any sprouting plant will die immediately. The soil must be broken up. That is, the heart must be softened so that moisture can be retained and the growth that has commenced can continue. Nature demonstrates to us this lesson and need of persistence in the soft dust of the earth being able to maintain a constant moist environment. Even though the application of water is momentary the growth is continual. The soil can be amended if needed. To do so requires testing the soil to determine whether there is a lack or over-abundance of necessary nutrients. If the soil has the necessary nutrients, then also the pH of the soil must be correct, and there must be adequate sun and water (none of which would be enough by itself), and the environment must be perfect for abundant growth and plentiful fruit. As the Testimony of Jesus says: "… **no good gift is withheld from him who sincerely desires to obtain the righteousness of God.**" Depend on the Word that God has given. Pray it back to Him. Ask Him, with a perseverance that will not be denied, to fulfill that which He has already promised. To do so is your life now and eternally. Wrestle with the Lord as Jacob wrestled the angel, knowing that the Lord is only delaying so you will persevere and gain strength, fortitude, and a true change of mind to be resolute in righteousness. Jesus died to provide you righteousness. He will not turn you away empty-handed.

Therefore, personal Bible study and prayer is critical to your development. When you have prayed and studied, you can go forth doing what the Word declares, and you will be transformed. Yet, before you see the results, you need to receive the Word in faith, believing in its power to transform. That is what Abraham did, and it is what Paul describes in Romans. Believe that God will give you the victory even though you are indeed a sinner. Your past is of no concern; victory is not prevented by what you have done. Victory is only prevented by a lack of faith and application of the offered promises of God that He presents to you.

Wait with patience for the effects of the power of the Word. We have a part to do that prepares the way for God's work in our heart, transforming us supernaturally. It is a work that we cannot do for ourselves; we must patiently wait for the power of God to be evident. A seed planted does not instantaneously grow into a mature plant.

> The parable of the seed reveals that God is at work in nature. <u>The seed has in itself a germinating principle, a principle that God Himself has implanted</u>; yet if left to itself the seed would have no power to spring up. Man has his part to act in promoting the growth of the grain. He must prepare and enrich the soil and cast in the seed. He must till the fields. **But there is a point beyond which he can accomplish nothing**. No strength or wisdom of man can bring forth from the seed the living plant. Let man put forth his efforts to the utmost limit, he must still depend upon One who has connected the sowing and the reaping by wonderful links of His own omnipotent power.

There is life in the seed, there is power in the soil; but **unless an infinite power is exercised day and night, the seed will yield no returns**. The showers of rain must be sent to give moisture to the thirsty fields, the sun must impart heat, electricity must be conveyed to the buried seed. The life which the Creator has implanted, He alone can call forth. <u>Every seed grows, every plant develops,</u> **by the power of God**.

"As the earth bringeth forth her bud, and as the garden causeth the things that are sown in it to spring forth, so the Lord God will cause righteousness and praise to spring forth." Isaiah 61:11. <u>As in the natural, so in the spiritual sowing; the teacher of truth must seek to prepare the soil of the heart</u>; he must sow the seed; but the power that alone can produce life is from God. There is a point beyond which human effort is in vain. While we are to preach the word, we can not impart the power that will quicken the soul, and cause righteousness and praise to spring forth. In the preaching of the word there must be the working of an agency beyond any human power. Only through the divine Spirit will the word be living and powerful to renew the soul unto eternal life. This is what Christ tried to impress upon His disciples. He taught that it was nothing they possessed in themselves which would give success to their labors, but that <u>it is the miracle-working power of God which gives efficiency to His own word</u>.

The work of the sower is **a work of faith**. <u>The mystery of the germination and growth of the seed he cannot understand</u>. But he has **confidence** in the agencies by which God causes vegetation to flourish. In casting his seed into the ground, he is apparently throwing away the precious grain that might furnish bread for his family. But he is only <u>giving up a present good for a larger return</u>. He casts the seed away, expecting to gather it manyfold in an abundant harvest. **So Christ's servants are to labor, expecting a harvest from the seed they sow**. (*Christ's Object Lessons*, pp. 63–65)

The above passages can be applied to personal consecration as well as to evangelism. It may appear that you do not have time to pray and study the Word of God every morning before leaving your home. It may seem fruitless today because so many things need to be done, and the day never seems to have enough hours. Yet, once again you must remember the principle of faith in doing what God has asked you to do. When you seek "first the kingdom of God and His righteousness," you will see God's hand supernaturally arranging every matter of your life.

> The good seed may for a time lie unnoticed in a cold, selfish, worldly heart, giving no evidence that it has taken root; but afterward, as the Spirit of God breathes on the soul, the hidden seed springs up, and at last bears fruit to the glory of God. In our lifework we know not which shall prosper, this or that. This is not a question for us to settle. We are to do our work, and leave the results with God. "In the morning sow thy seed, and in the evening withhold not thine hand." Ecclesiastes 11:6. God's great covenant declares that "while the earth remaineth, seed-time and harvest … shall not cease." Genesis 8:22. In the confidence of this promise the husbandman tills and sows. Not less confidently are we in the spiritual sowing to labor, **trusting His assurance**, "So shall My word be that goeth forth out of My mouth; it shall not return unto Me void, but it shall accomplish that which I please, and it shall prosper in the thing whereto I sent it." Isaiah 55:11. "He that goeth forth and weepeth, bearing precious seed, shall doubtless come again with rejoicing, bringing his sheaves with him." Psalm 126:6.
>
> The germination of the seed represents the beginning of spiritual life, and the development of the plant is a beautiful figure of Christian growth. As in nature, so in grace; there can be no life without growth. **The plant must either grow or die**. As its growth is silent and imperceptible, but continuous, so is the development of the Christian life. At every stage of development our life may be perfect; yet if God's purpose for us is fulfilled, there will be continual advancement. **Sanctification is the work of a lifetime**. As our opportunities multiply, our experience will enlarge, and our knowledge increase. We shall become strong to bear responsibility, and our maturity will be in proportion to our privileges. (*Christ's Object Lessons*, pp. 65, 66)

If you are not growing spiritually, you are dead. We are to be continually drawing from the stores of heaven to sustain us day by day. Trust that the Word will accomplish that which God said that His Word would accomplish, and it will. Walk in faith, knowing that God fulfills His Word to you as you believe it and live it, even though you do not feel or see that which has been promised. We received Christ by faith, and we must live by faith. When we come to Christ for the first time, it is completely an act of faith. Yet, you must never move beyond faith and begin to work on your own. Sanctification is also and always an act of faith. Accept that you are to live a life of cooperation, action, and works by faith in response to the Word and the promises that you are claiming to obtain victory. Sanctification is the work of a lifetime because it is continuous, not because you reach a point at which you can stop growing. We are ever reaching higher in drawing nearer and becoming more like God day by day. Keep in mind that your growth is guaranteed based on the type of seed planted. Therefore, as we allow that seed to be the Word of God, we will grow into the measure of the stature of Jesus Christ. This is the assurance—only be patient and persevere. Walk by faith, not by sight. Remember that growth is silent and imperceptible, and that perfection can be attained at each stage. Perfection is not only full maturity.

> The plant grows by receiving that which God has provided to sustain its life. It sends down its roots into the earth. It drinks in the sunshine, the dew, and the rain. It receives the life-giving properties from the air. **So the Christian is to grow by co-operating with the divine agencies.** Feeling our helplessness, we are to improve all the opportunities granted us to gain a fuller experience. As the plant takes root in the soil, so we are to take deep root in Christ. As the plant receives the sunshine, the dew, and the rain, **we are to open our hearts to the Holy Spirit**. The work is to be done "not by might, nor by power, but by My Spirit, saith the Lord of hosts." Zech. 4:6. If we keep our minds stayed upon Christ, He will come unto us "as the rain, as the latter and former rain unto the earth." Hosea 6:3. As the Sun of Righteousness, He will arise upon us "with healing in His wings." Mal. 4:2. We shall "grow as the lily." We shall "revive as the corn, and grow as the vine." Hosea 14:5, 7. By **constantly** relying upon Christ as our personal Saviour, we shall grow up into Him in all things who is our head. (*Christ's Object Lessons*, pp. 66, 67)

The Holy Spirit convicts of sin, of righteousness, and of judgment to come. Because the first two steps, conviction of sin and of righteousness, prepare you for judgment, you need to pay particular attention to them. As you pray and study, you must allow your heart to be sensitive to the impressions of the Holy Spirit pointing you to the confirmation of the Word and the Testimony of Jesus. Neglecting to do that which you are impressed to do impedes growth and will eventually cause your death. As the growth of a plant can be stunted without the proper elements, so will you not advance in growth if you fail to do the little things that God calls you to do day by day.

Many get impatient and want to bear three full ears of corn almost overnight. Yet, when we look at nature, we see a progression of growth. A blade of grass, which is what a cornstalk is in the beginning, could not stand up under the weight of three full ears of corn. We must grow first, and, in time, the supernatural power of God will bring forth fruit. Our part is to trust that the promises of God will bear fruit in us—in time.

God will not forget the work that He is doing in you. Be as patient with yourself as God is patient with you. "Being confident of this very thing, that he which hath begun a good work in you will perform it until the day of Jesus Christ" (Phil. 1:6). The life in the plant comes from God. The spiritual life begun in your heart is from God as well. The mortal life was given to us without our participation, but the spiritual life requires your personal will and co-operation.

> The change of heart by which we become children of God is in the Bible spoken of as birth. Again, it is compared to the germination of the good seed sown by the husbandman. In like manner those who are just converted to Christ are, "as new-born babes," to "grow up" to the stature of men and women in Christ Jesus. 1 Peter 2:2; Ephesians 4:15. Or like the good seed sown in the field, they are to grow up and bring forth fruit. Isaiah says that they shall "be called trees of righteousness, the planting of the Lord, that He might be glorified." Isaiah 61:3. So from natural life, illustrations are drawn, to help us better to understand the mysterious truths of spiritual life.
>
> Not all the wisdom and skill of man can produce life in the smallest object in nature. It is only through the life which God Himself has imparted, that either plant or animal can live. So it is **only through the life from God that spiritual life is begotten in the hearts of men**. Unless a man is "born from above," he cannot become a partaker of the life which Christ came to give. John 3:3, margin. (*Steps to Christ*, p. 67)

Keep in mind that you are receiving the power of God by faith. Yes, you have made a choice to accept it and to work with it, but you need to remember that the power that transforms your life by faith does not come by more strenuous work on your part. Recognize that you may have to battle fiercely but that your tenacity should be based on the fact that you are depending on the Word, "being fully persuaded that" God's word will "perform" God's will. Believe that you have received the power. The power to grow comes from God.

> As with life, so it is with growth. It is God who brings the bud to bloom and the flower to fruit. It is by His power that the seed develops, "first the blade, then the ear, after that the full corn in the ear." Mark 4:28. And the prophet Hosea says of Israel, that "he shall grow as the lily." "They shall revive as the corn, and grow as the vine." Hosea 14:5, 7. And Jesus bids us "consider the lilies how they grow." Luke 12:27. The plants and flowers grow not by their own care or anxiety or effort, **but by receiving that which God has furnished to minister to their life.** <u>The child cannot, by any anxiety or power of its own, add to its stature. No more can you, by anxiety or effort of yourself, secure spiritual growth.</u> The plant, **the child, grows by receiving from its surroundings that which ministers to its life**—<u>air, sunshine, and food</u>. What these gifts of nature are to animal and plant, **such is Christ to those who trust in Him**. He is their "everlasting light," "a sun and shield." Isaiah 60:19; Psalm 84:11. He shall be as "the dew unto Israel." "He shall come down like rain upon the mown grass." Hosea 14:5; Psalm 72:6. He is the living water, "the Bread of God ... which cometh down from heaven, and giveth life unto the world." John 6:33.
>
> In the matchless gift of His Son, <u>God has encircled the whole world with an atmosphere of **grace as real as the air** which circulates around the globe.</u> All who choose to breathe this life-giving atmosphere **will live and grow up to the stature of men and women** in Christ Jesus. (*Steps to Christ*, pp. 67, 68)

The difference between the natural world and our spiritual growth is that, with regard to spiritual growth, you must choose to willfully breathe and benefit from God's full grace before grace's full power takes effect in your life. Grace is like the air. It is always there. Our struggle is to stay with the choice of utilizing the full benefit. Why? Because the flesh, which is the human nature, may feel like doing something else; and, yes, you may not see your soul growing closer to the Lord and, yes, you may not feel stronger and, yes, you will feel more temptations. Yet, nonetheless, you have the power from God's "atmosphere of grace" that will sustain you in a life of victory over every temptation.

> As the flower turns to the sun, that the bright beams may aid in perfecting its beauty and symmetry, **so should we turn** to the Sun of Righteousness, that heaven's light may shine upon us, that our character may be developed into the likeness of Christ. (*Steps to Christ*, p. 68)

To allow the atmosphere of grace to have its effect, you must stay in prayer, in meditation, and in Bible study, focused on the Lord and His way. This is how we "abide in Christ." Enoch walked with God because he prayed "without ceasing." Turn your mind back to Christ through prayer, meditation about Him, and memorization of the Word for power in the battle when you have temptations. Breathe spiritually through these elements. These exercises keep you connected to Christ, who, of course, keeps you alive.

> Jesus teaches the same thing when He says, "Abide in Me, and I in you. As the branch cannot bear fruit of itself, except it abide in the vine; no more can ye, except ye abide in Me.… Without Me ye can do nothing." John 15:4, 5. You are just as dependent upon Christ, in order to live a holy life, as is the branch upon the parent stock for growth and fruitfulness. Apart from Him you have no life. You have no power to resist temptation or to grow in grace and holiness. **Abiding in Him, you may flourish. Drawing your life from Him, you will not wither nor be fruitless. You will be like a tree planted by the rivers of water.**
> Many have an idea that they must do some part of the **work alone**. They have trusted in Christ for the forgiveness of sin, **but now they seek by their own efforts to live aright.** *But every such effort must fail.* Jesus says, "Without Me ye can do nothing." Our growth in grace, our joy, our usefulness,—**all depend upon our union with Christ**. It is by **communion** with Him, daily, hourly,—by abiding in Him,—**that we are to grow in grace**. He is not only the Author, but the Finisher of our faith. It is Christ first and last and always. He is to be with us, not only at the beginning and the end of our course, but at every step of the way. David says, "I have set the Lord always before me: because He is at my right hand, I shall not be moved." Psalm 16:8. (*Steps to Christ*, pp. 68, 69)

It is true that we must work, yet not alone; it is always with Christ—at every moment. Work, believing and consciously knowing that He is with you as He has promised. Yet, you can receive His promise only as you receive it by faith, and then it will be accomplished. Attempting to live the Christian life without Christ is why so many experience failure. Too much of the time, too many believe that victory is not possible because they are not having victory. Remember, Christ has never lost a battle with Satan, and He never will. Commit yourself to Him by faith. The problem is disconnection from Christ, the Vine, which brings a cessation of breathing, a cutting off of the breath of spiritual life, the conscious utilization of the atmosphere of grace. If we do not notice when it is interrupted, of course a need for a remedy is not noticed or seems impossible, for Christ is the only remedy. Therefore, commit yourself by faith to Him in every work, in every activity; consciously abide in Him moment by moment, and, yes, in the struggle with your nature, resist the urge to follow your own way, difficult though it may be.

> Do you ask, "**How am I to abide in Christ**?" In the same way as you received Him at first. "As ye have therefore received Christ Jesus the Lord, so walk ye in Him." "The just shall live **by faith**." Colossians 2:6; Hebrews 10:38. You gave yourself to God, to be His wholly, to serve and obey Him, and you took Christ as your Saviour. You could not yourself atone for your sins or change your heart; but having given yourself to God, **you believe** that He for Christ's sake did all this for you. By faith you became Christ's, and by faith you are to grow up in Him—by giving and taking. You are to give all,—your heart, your will, your service,—give yourself to Him to obey all His requirements; and **you must take all**,—Christ, the fullness of all blessing, to abide in your heart, to be your strength, your righteousness, your everlasting helper,—to give you power to obey. (*Steps to Christ*, pp. 69, 70)

This truth is too easily overlooked. When we come to Christ, it is by faith. In Colossians 2:6, Paul is saying that we are to walk and work in Christ by the same manner of faith that we exercised in coming to Christ. The only difference is that, instead of believing that He receives you and forgives you, you must believe that He has strength and power for you to overcome every temptation and that the victory is already yours by the power that He can rightly give you through His victory on the cross. Then you act on that faith. When you act *without faith*, you will surely fall. However, when you act *in faith,* praying continually—especially the commands and promises of Scripture—you will be victorious. By this means we are to abide in Christ. To give all your heart, will, and service to God is to give up your choice, your ideas, your methods, and your feelings. You are committing to surrender to all of God's requirements. If He doesn't say to do something, then you don't do it. It is to live by the letter and spirit of the covenant. Notice what you are to take from Christ: a full blessing, Jesus into your heart, and His strength, which leads you into righteousness and everlasting help, giving you more than sufficient power to be able to obey.

## Dwelling on Christ

Consecrate yourself to God in the morning; make this your very first work. **Let your prayer be**, 'Take me, O Lord, as wholly Thine. I lay all my plans at Thy feet. Use me today in Thy service. Abide with me, and let all my work be wrought in Thee.' **This is a daily matter**. Each morning consecrate yourself to God for that day. Surrender all your plans to Him, to be carried out or given up as His providence shall indicate. Thus day by day you may be giving your life into the hands of God, and thus your life will be molded more and more after the life of Christ.

A life in Christ is a life of restfulness. There may be no ecstasy of feeling, but there should be an abiding, peaceful trust. Your hope is not in yourself; it is in Christ. Your weakness is united to His strength, your ignorance to His wisdom, your frailty to His enduring might. So you are not to look to yourself, not to let the mind dwell upon self, but look to Christ. **Let the mind dwell upon His love, upon the beauty, the perfection, of His character. Christ in His self-denial, Christ in His humiliation, Christ in His purity and holiness, Christ in His matchless love**—*this is the subject for the soul's contemplation*. **It is by loving Him, copying Him, depending wholly upon Him, that you are to be transformed into His likeness.** (*Steps to Christ*, pp. 70, 71)

I do not believe that it is possible to overstate our need of dwelling continually on Christ and His attributes. Such focus is the overlooked secret to victory. By beholding we become "changed into the same image from glory to glory, even as by the Spirit of the Lord" (2 Cor. 3:18). This is where the struggle is—keeping the mind on Christ and not on the things of the world, on ourselves or on other people. Memorization of the Word—especially the Gospels, the epistles, and the psalms—will help us to keep focused on Christ. God, in His goodness, has even given us that prayer to pray the first thing in the morning—that all we do is surrendered to Him. These are not simply suggestions of God. He knew that these weapons and tools would be essential to your obtaining the victory.

> Jesus says, "Abide in Me." These words convey the idea of rest, stability, confidence. Again He invites, "Come unto Me, ... and I will give you rest." Matthew 11:28. The words of the psalmist express the same thought: "Rest in the Lord, and wait patiently for Him." And Isaiah gives the assurance, "In quietness and in confidence shall be your strength." Psalm 37:7; Isaiah 30:15. This rest is not found in inactivity; for in the Saviour's invitation the promise of rest is united with the call to labor: "Take My yoke upon you: ... and ye shall find rest." Matthew 11:29. <u>The heart that rests most fully upon Christ will be most earnest and active in labor for Him.</u>
> 
> When the mind dwells upon self, it is turned away from Christ, the source of strength and life. Hence it is **Satan's constant effort to keep the attention diverted** <u>from the Saviour and thus prevent the union and communion of the soul with Christ.</u> The **pleasures** of the world, life's **cares** and **perplexities** and **sorrows**, the **faults** <u>of others,</u> or <u>your own</u> faults and imperfections—**to any or all of these he will seek to divert the mind.** Do not be misled by his devices. Many who are really conscientious, and who desire to live for God, he too often leads to dwell upon their own faults and weaknesses, and thus by separating them from Christ he hopes to gain the victory. <u>We should not make self the center and indulge anxiety and fear as to</u> **whether we shall be saved.** <u>All this turns the soul away from the Source of our strength.</u> **Commit the keeping of your soul to God, and trust in Him. Talk and think of Jesus. Let self be lost in Him. Put away all doubt; dismiss your fears**. Say with the apostle Paul, "I live; yet not I, but Christ liveth in me: and the life which I now live in the flesh I live by the faith of the Son of God, who loved me, and gave Himself for me." Galatians 2:20. **Rest in God. He is able to keep that which you have committed to Him. If you will leave yourself in His hands, He will bring you off more than conqueror through Him that has loved you.** (*Steps to Christ*, pp. 71, 72)

Incredible! "If you will leave yourself in His hands," you will be "more than conqueror." "Put away all doubt." "Commit the keeping of your soul to God." Fantastic! These are the secrets of victory. Don't ever think about your faults, your imperfections and the faults and imperfections of others. That is a trap, a snare of Satan to take your mind off of Christ. Focusing on pleasure, sorrows, and perplexities can accomplish the same thing. You must keep the Almighty Saviour in your heart and mind, and, though you have experiences and things to overcome, He will bear you up upon His wings and keep you in His hands through the protection of the angels, who are ministering spirits.

## Mind Training

Train your mind to dwell on Christ and His Word and believe every word of it. Such training is sanctification by faith, and it is your assurance and guarantee of salvation. Do not let Satan divert your attention. Pray for strength, and stay focused in faith. If you are thinking about Jesus and not about yourself or other sinners, you will not have the sad experience of the man who is drawn away by his own lustful thoughts, for this results in sin and then death (James 1:14, 15). Because we tend to act on whatever we are thinking, follow the counsel of Paul in "forgetting those things which are behind" (Phil. 3:13). In other words, don't dwell on your past or the past of others. Live in the present and look forward to the glorious future that God has for you. In exercising the mind to focus on Jesus, you will gradually grow strong spiritually like the muscles of a bodybuilder. Notice what the Testimony of Jesus says about this:

> If we would develop a character which God can accept, **we must form correct habits in our religious life**. Daily prayer is **as essential** to growth in grace, and even to spiritual life itself, as is temporal food to physical well-being. We should **accustom ourselves** to often lift the thoughts to God in prayer. **If the mind wanders, we must bring it back; by persevering effort, habit will finally make it easy**. We cannot for **one moment** separate ourselves from Christ with safety. **We may have His presence to attend us at every step, but only by observing the conditions which He has Himself laid down**. (*Messages to Young People*, pp. 114, 115)

When Christ took human nature upon Him, He bound humanity to Himself by a tie of love that can never be broken by any power **save the choice of man himself.** <u>Satan will constantly present allurements to induce us to break this tie—to choose to separate ourselves from Christ.</u> **Here is where we need to watch, to strive, to pray, that nothing may entice us to** *choose* **another master; for we are always free to do this. But let us keep our eyes fixed upon Christ, and He will preserve us. Looking unto Jesus, we are safe. Nothing can pluck us out of His hand.** In constantly beholding Him, we 'are changed into the same image from glory to glory, even as by the Spirit of the Lord.' 2 Corinthians 3:18. (*Steps to Christ*, p. 72)

We can have Christ constantly with us but only by observing the habits He has set before us to develop. Learn to pray without ceasing and to persevere by bringing the mind back into focus on Christ after it wanders. Let it be your custom to lift up your thoughts to God in prayer. To keep your mind on Christ and not on self or on others, you must follow what the Scriptures tell you to do. "Thy word have I hid in mine heart, that I might not sin against thee" (Ps. 119:11). "The law of his God is in his heart; none of his steps shall slide" (Ps. 37:31). Memorization is an aid and a necessity in obtaining the victory.[22] Having God's Word in the heart and mind is part of the covenant agreement (Heb. 8:10). Remember, God will keep His Word to you as you cooperate with Him. Your part is to choose to put Scripture in your mind and to keep your mind focused on Him and not on the things of the world. The Word of God has a transforming power that you can count on.

"Being born again, not of corruptible seed, but of incorruptible, by the word of God, which liveth and abideth for ever" (1 Peter 1:23). "Whosoever is born of God doth not commit sin; for his seed remaineth in him: and he cannot sin, because he is born of God" (1 John 3:9). The Word is incorruptible, so when you take it inside, you will experience a new birth that "abideth for ever." Then, as the Word remains in you through continual meditation upon it, it will accomplish that which God intended—overcoming sin, commandment keeping, sanctification, and holiness. "So shall my word be that goeth forth out of my mouth: it shall not return unto me void, but it shall accomplish that which I please, and it shall prosper in the thing whereto I sent it" (Isa. 55:11).

---

[22] See "EFFECTIVE BIBLE STUDY AND SPIRITUAL GROWTH," available at https://1ref.us/1kr (accessed February 17, 2021).

## CHAPTER 14

# Faith to Follow

> Footprints of Jesus
> Leading the way,
> Footprints of Jesus
> By night and by day,
> I know if I follow
> My life will be sweet,
> For I am saved,
> Oh yes, by His wounded feet.
> — Lucie Eddie Campbell[23]

As we conclude this subject, we must stop and look at what the apostle Paul wrote about "Abraham our father of faith." Consider that Paul said that Abraham was "fully persuaded" to believe. I would like for you to consider how Abraham was "persuaded," in the words of Paul. Persuaded about what? We must know what this was because, as Abraham's children, we are saved under the same covenant and must also come to the point of being persuaded as he was. I have no doubt that, to be persuaded as Abraham was, we will likewise be saved as he was. Let us open our minds to what the Holy Spirit has revealed to us regarding Abraham in Romans 4. Therefore, let us, in like manner, be "fully persuaded."

Romans 4:1. What shall we say then that Abraham our father, as pertaining to the flesh, hath found?

---

[23] Lucie Eddie Campbell, "Footprints of Jesus," Hymnary, https://1ref.us/1ld (accessed February 18, 2021).

2. For if Abraham were justified by works, he hath whereof to glory; but not before God.
3. For what saith the scripture? Abraham believed God, and it was counted unto him for righteousness.

Here Paul carries our minds back to Genesis 15:6 where God counted Abraham righteous for believing something that had not yet happened. Simply put, when one makes up his mind to accept what God has promised, God counts that frame of mind as righteous, though the person has, as yet, taken no physical action.

The Lord had brought Abraham forth to view the stars as an indication of His ability to keep His promise to make Abraham's seed as numberless as the stars. The Lord also reminded Abraham that He had brought him out of Ur. In His faithfulness, God gave Abraham evidence that He could be trusted in something yet future, something unseen and unrealized as of yet. "Lift up your eyes on high, and behold who hath created these things, that bringeth out their host by number: he calleth them all by names by the greatness of his might, for that he is strong in power; not one faileth" (Isa. 40:26). Since the Lord can create and keep these giant stars and planets functioning and orbiting at immense speeds in perfect time, certainly He can handle any smaller issue.

Abraham was persuaded that He was righteous because God had said he was, making his righteousness a reality, though not because of what Abraham had done. Abraham believed in the promise that God gave him that God would forgive him and cleanse him and thereafter supply the fact of righteousness through the merits of Christ—justification by Christ's death taking the place of Abraham's death.

Keep in mind that as soon as you believe God, you are righteous. That occurs before any physical action. Your righteousness is based on faith in God and His power and not on what you can do without His power, but with His power.

4. Now to him that worketh is the reward not reckoned of grace, but of debt.
5. But to him that worketh not, but believeth on him that justifieth the ungodly, his faith is counted for righteousness.

Abraham believed before the fact, that is, before the works were accomplished. Such belief is righteousness by faith. Like Abraham, we too can only be counted righteous by believing before the fact of the works. Because of the evidence he already had in his life, Abraham was resolved to trust God, and God made a covenant with him there. It could not be by faith if we are led to believe after we see the work completed.

6. Even as David also describeth the blessedness of the man, unto whom God imputeth <u>righteousness without works,</u>
7. Saying, Blessed are they whose iniquities are forgiven, and whose sins are covered.
8. Blessed is the man to whom the Lord will not impute sin.

Is this not the blessing that you need—"righteousness without works"? What a God we serve, that He is able to justly impute righteousness to us! Such righteousness is not something that He can simply declare, it must be *a reality* for Him to be a just God in the legal sense. His law was actually broken, so someone must really die. Also, righteousness must be literally accomplished through the works of Jesus. Then, when we acknowledge by faith what Jesus can do, Christ's righteousness can be literally accounted to the person for justification. As you have a real righteousness and a literal death of Christ substituting for your death, God must give you a literal righteousness, and this is through your taking in the Seed, the Word of God. In nature, seeds only reproduce what they are; they don't change into a different plant.

What am I saying? For God to be legally and truly just, He cannot take fallen men or women to heaven who have only been forgiven but who have no real righteousness imputed or imparted to them. In other words, God cannot take redeemed men to heaven who will eventually be devils all over again. They have to have real righteousness—in the past, in the present, and forever. Thus, the plan of salvation is an actual restoration. The redeemed will not have rubber stamped righteousness. There will be quantifiable evidence one way or another. So, when Abraham believed—though no works were yet seen—those works would eventually be evidenced. "To declare, I say, at this time his righteousness: that he might be just, and <u>the justifier of him</u> which believeth in Jesus" (Rom. 3:26). Faith is the seed that eventually leads to the reality of works. More on this in a moment.

Consider the stars. NASA, the American space agency, has charted the stars and the position of the other objects in space. They know years ahead of time where each one will be. With this knowledge, they can send a spacecraft into space at 17,000+ mph (27,000+ kph) and precisely accomplish a mission. In like manner, when you resolve to follow God, He knows that you will be living righteously. Then, ultimately, His imputed righteousness will be not only given to you, but you will have become a living representation of the character of God.

Remember that the seed is the Word of God. A seed planted will eventually grow into the variety of plant that it is by nature. Therefore, when you believe and when the seed, which is the Word, is planted in you, God can justifiably say that you are righteous on two accounts—on account of Jesus' life and death, as well as on account of your future actions that will be manifested, validating God's accounting of the past. In other words, you believe that God keeps His promise in forgiving you and cleansing you of your past sins; you believe that Christ's righteousness is applied to your account; and you believe that you have power to live victoriously over every temptation of Satan. This righteousness is a living reality, not just a declaration. It is true justice in having made a truly just person—you—that God "might be just, and the justifier of him which believeth in Jesus" (Rom. 3:26). God is "just," but the word, "justifier" refers to God's work in you to make you literally righteous. I must, needs be, especially clear on this point. In other words, God as "justifier" re-creates an individual who performs actions that are actually righteous and just continuously based on their own wills. So based on them not performing these works by instinct but still having a choice to do other than that but they don't, they vindicate the name of God against the claim of Satan that he was created inferior and couldn't keep God's law or that he was forced and hadn't really chosen to do so. The literal evidence that God produces is not in Himself but His creation and we who partake of this, which is imparted righteousness, cannot claim merit because it is only a demonstration of the power of God through you or I not us producing something independent of God. In the final judgment scene, God can therefore present the redeemed as being just because they have been justified and because God through Christ has not taken forgiven sinners into a holy environment to continue living like devils. They are sanctified. Then, like the stars in their paths and like seeds that are planted, their future behavior is already known. As in the natural, so in the spiritual—the law is unvarying. In nature, everyone understands there is a cause and effect. Now, back to Romans 4:

9. Cometh this blessedness then upon the circumcision only, or upon the uncircumcision also? for we say that faith was reckoned to Abraham for righteousness.
10. How was it then reckoned? when he was in circumcision, or in uncircumcision? Not in circumcision, but in uncircumcision.

11. And he received the sign of circumcision, a seal of the righteousness of the faith which he had yet being uncircumcised: that he might be the father of all them that believe, though they be not circumcised; that righteousness might be imputed unto them also:
12. And the father of circumcision to them who are not of the circumcision only, but who also walk in the steps of that faith of our father Abraham, which he had being yet uncircumcised.

Verse 9, which contrasts uncircumcision (the symbol of sin) and circumcision (the symbol of righteousness), indicates that you can partake of God's righteousness while still a sinner. That is the "blessedness" that David is talking about. Do you believe this? That is what is at stake. Obviously, Abraham saw the covenant of God as God's promise to actually make him a righteous man—not in declaration or word only, but in his actual life and living example—a living truth. No matter how degraded, depraved, or sinful a person may be, he or she can have this "blessedness" by believing in the redeeming God—even while still a sinner and without circumcision (that is, by being good by working their way into God's favor or through ceremonial rites).

13. For the promise, that he should be the heir of the world, was not to Abraham, or to his seed, through the law, but through the righteousness of faith.
14. For if they which are of the law be heirs, faith is made void, and the promise made of none effect:

If you could earn your way into God's favor, then there would be no need for a covenant or the plan of redemption. No faith would be needed—just hard work and sweat.

15. Because the law worketh wrath: for where no law is, there is no transgression.
16. Therefore it is of faith, that it might be by grace; to the end the promise might be sure to all the seed; not to that only which is of the law, but to that also which is of the faith of Abraham; who is the father of us all,
17. (As it is written, I have made thee a father of many nations,) before him whom he believed, even God, who quickeneth the dead, and calleth those things which be not as though they were.

We have the promise from God that we will also be heirs of the world with Abraham through faith that God will make you righteous. The Almighty is able to quicken the dead, that is, those who are dead in sin, and to call something that is not as though it were and that will eventually be a living reality. Though you are apparently spiritually dead with no righteousness in you—like a dead battery without an electrical charge—do not worry, God can resurrect you. He is the Living God, the Creator and giver of life.

18. Who against hope believed in hope, that he might become the father of many nations, according to that which was spoken, So shall thy seed be.
19. And being not weak in faith, he considered not his own body now dead, when he was about an hundred years old, neither yet the deadness of Sarah's womb:
20. He staggered not at the promise of God through unbelief; but was strong in faith, giving glory to God;

Abraham believed against hope. You must also believe against hope, though the world has many temptations to offer and your past is filled with numerous failures. Don't be stymied by your mental or physical condition; they are not a factor to the Lord. As Abraham "staggered not at the promise of God," you too must be strong in faith. To stagger not is to not waver, to not be weak-kneed. Abraham considered only God's power, not his physical capability or his past performance. If you have no faith, pray and ask the Creator to create faith—saving faith—in you. Your dependence is to be in God's power, not your own capabilities. We are kept by the power of God (1 Peter 1:5).

21. And being fully persuaded that, what he had promised, he was able also to perform.

If you will be saved, you must be persuaded about the same thing about which Abraham was persuaded—that God has literally forgiven him, has really died in his place, has really given him righteousness to his account, and has literally given him power to live victoriously continually—no matter the temptation or circumstance. You must be persuaded that God is "able also to perform" that which He has already promised. The Greek word here says, in one portion of the definition: "to fill one with any thought, conviction, or inclination to make one certain." Abraham was certain; he was filled with the assurance that God would redeem him and his posterity. This filled his thoughts. We need our thoughts filled with the certainty of the saving grace of God in our personal lives. Keep fresh in your mind the blessings that He has already provided you and the victories He has already given you. Even if you have not known the Lord before, His grace has sustained you to this day. He has kept Satan from destroying you many times. He will continue acting in faithfulness toward you, as you consent, until you become a finished product ready for redemption. Choose now this day to believe; put your hand in God's hand and let Him fulfill His Word in you for His glory.

22. And therefore it was imputed to him for righteousness.
23. Now it was not written for his sake alone, that it was imputed to him;
24. **But for us also**, to whom it shall be imputed, **if we believe on him that raised up Jesus our Lord from the dead**;
25. Who was delivered for our offences, and was raised again for our justification.

"Therefore!" Let the Holy Spirit persuade you also into a settled belief, for Abraham's story was not just for himself. Though you may have been a deceived, deluded and rebellious sinner, Paul declares that Abraham's story is for you. "It shall be imputed, if we believe." If God can raise physically dead flesh from the grave and spiritually dead flesh in human minds, then, quite naturally, He can redeem a person who is persuaded with a mind that is made up to believe that God's grace is sufficient to redeem. Let this be your thought. Let the mind of Christ be in you. Romans chapter 5 picks up Paul's commentary:

Romans 5:1 Therefore being justified by faith, we have peace with God through our Lord Jesus Christ:
2. By whom also we have access by faith into this grace wherein we stand, and rejoice in hope of the glory of God.
3. And not only so, but we glory in tribulations also: knowing that tribulation worketh patience;
4. And patience, experience; and experience, hope:
5. And hope maketh not ashamed; because the love of God is shed abroad in our hearts by the Holy Ghost which is given unto us.
6. For when we were yet without strength, **in due time Christ died for the ungodly**.

Christ knows that, left to yourself, you are without strength, but this is a key point in the great controversy. By accepting His offer of justification and grace (which is His power for you), you will receive a new spiritual life and, by continual dependence on Christ, you will defeat Satan in every trial. Therefore, you can be truly "justified by faith" and you can "have peace with God." As verse 2 says, the way to access this grace (or power) is by faith. Therefore, you can "rejoice in hope of the glory of God," having joy in the midst of trials and temptations, knowing that the grace of God will not fail you but will continually sustain you and give you increasing strength.

## Jesus' Example

Notice the methods you can utilize to obtain the victory—especially, the example of the Saviour Himself.

> "Man shall not live by bread alone, but by every word of God." Often the follower of Christ is brought where he cannot serve God and carry forward his worldly enterprises. **Perhaps it appears that obedience to some plain requirement of God will cut off his means of support.** Satan would make him believe that he must sacrifice his conscientious convictions. **But the only thing in our world upon which we can rely is the word of God**. "Seek ye first the kingdom of God, and His righteousness; and all these things shall be added unto you." Matt. 6:33. Even in this life it is not for our good to depart from the will of our Father in heaven. When we learn the power of His word, we shall not follow the suggestions of Satan in order to obtain food or to save our lives. **Our only questions will be, What is God's command? and what His promise? Knowing these, we shall obey the one, and trust the other.** (*The Desire of Ages*, p. 121)
>
> Of the bitterness that falls to the lot of humanity, there was no part which Christ did not taste. There were those who tried to cast contempt upon Him because of His birth, and even in His childhood He had to meet their scornful looks and evil whisperings. If He had responded by an impatient word or look, if He had conceded to His brothers by even one wrong act, He would have failed of being a perfect example. Thus He would have failed of carrying out the plan for our redemption. Had He even admitted that there could be **an excuse for sin**, Satan would have triumphed, and the

world would have been lost. This is why the tempter worked to make His life as trying as possible, that He might be led to sin.

But to every temptation He had one answer, **"It is written."** He rarely rebuked any wrongdoing of His brothers, but <u>He had a word from God to speak to them</u>. Often He was accused of cowardice for refusing to unite with them in some forbidden act; but His answer was, It is written, "The fear of the Lord, that is wisdom; and to depart from evil is understanding." Job 28:28.

There were some who sought His society, feeling at peace in His presence; but many avoided Him, because they were rebuked by His stainless life. Young companions urged Him to do as they did. He was bright and cheerful; they enjoyed His presence, and welcomed His ready suggestions; <u>but they were impatient at His</u> **scruples**, and pronounced Him narrow and strait-laced. Jesus answered, **It is written, "Wherewithal shall a young man cleanse his way? by taking heed thereto according to Thy word." "Thy word have I hid in mine heart, that I might not sin against Thee."** Psalm 119:9, 11.

Often He was asked, Why are you bent on being so singular, so different from us all? **It is written**, He said, "Blessed are the undefiled in the way, who walk in the law of the Lord. Blessed are they that keep His testimonies, and that seek Him with the whole heart. They also do no iniquity; they walk in His ways." Psalm 119:1–3.

When questioned why He did not join in the frolics of the youth of Nazareth, He said, **It is written**, "<u>I have rejoiced</u> in the way of Thy testimonies, as much as in all riches. <u>I will meditate</u> in Thy precepts, and have respect unto Thy ways. I will delight myself in Thy statutes; <u>I will not forget</u> Thy word." Psalm 119:14–16.

Jesus did not contend for His rights. Often His work was made unnecessarily severe because He was willing and uncomplaining. Yet He did not fail nor become discouraged. He lived above these difficulties, as if in the light of God's countenance. He did not retaliate when roughly used, but bore insult patiently.

Again and again He was asked, Why do You submit to such despiteful usage, even from Your brothers? **It is written**, He said, "My son, <u>forget not</u> My law; but let thine heart keep My commandments: for length of days, and long life, and peace, shall they add to thee. Let not mercy and truth forsake thee: bind them about thy neck; <u>write them upon the table of thine heart</u>: so shalt thou find favor and good understanding in the sight of God and man." Proverbs 3:1–4. (*The Desire of Ages*, pp. 88, 89)

Jesus rejoiced in the Word; He meditated on the Word; He did not forget the Word, for He memorized it and kept it ever in His mind. "If any man serve me, let him follow me; and where I am, there shall also my servant be: if any man serve me, him will my Father honour" (John 12:26). This was His dependence; this is to be your dependence too. In depending on the Word as Jesus depended on the Word, you too will have victory.

> The Saviour took upon Himself the **infirmities of humanity** and lived a sinless life, that men might have <u>**no fear** that because of the weakness of human nature they could not overcome</u>. Christ came to make us **"partakers of the divine nature,"** and <u>His life declares that humanity, combined with divinity</u>, **does not commit sin**. (*The Ministry of Healing*, p. 180)

Fear not, dear sinner, you also have a human nature as did Christ. A person who is persuaded has no fear. Let the mind of Christ be in you. It is a mind of faith, as His was a mind without fear, seeking help from His Father in heaven. The secret of living a sinless life is to connect your humanity with divinity and partake of the divine nature through His precious promises (2 Peter 1:4). Christ's life "<u>declares that humanity, **combined** with divinity, **does not commit sin**</u>." Remember that the seed, or the Word of God, kept in the mind and heart, only produces righteousness. It never produces sin. No corn seed has ever produced a tobacco plant. In like manner, the Word of God will never produce a sinner when its principles are taken inside the soul and believed and lived.

> When Christ bowed his head and died, **he bore the pillars of Satan's kingdom with him to the earth.** He vanquished Satan **in the same nature** over which in **Eden Satan obtained the victory**. <u>**The enemy was overcome by** Christ in **his human nature**</u>. The power of the Saviour's Godhead was hidden. **He overcame in human nature, relying upon God for power**. This is the privilege of all. **In proportion to our faith will be our victory**. (*The Youth's Instructor*, April 25, 1901, par. 11)

This is tremendous! Satan's kingdom is rubble. Christ overcame, not as God or as the Almighty, but simply as a man like you, using His Father's divine power, not His own personal divinity. He was utilizing God the Father's power in human nature in the same way that you must use it to overcome in your struggles with temptation. "As thou hast believed, so be it done unto thee" (Matt. 8:13). If you believe, you will have the victory. If you don't believe, you will be defeated by Satan. Your nature, when depending on God and His covenant, is stronger than Satan and all his host of demons. Be persuaded and believe. Accept the righteousness of Christ. Accept the victory and the gift of salvation.

> **Prayer** is heaven's ordained means of success in the conflict with sin and the development of Christian character. **The divine influences that come in answer to the prayer of faith will accomplish in the soul of the supplicant all for which he pleads.** For the pardon of sin, for the Holy Spirit, for a Christlike temper, for wisdom and strength to do His work, for **any gift** He has promised, we may ask; and the promise is, "Ye shall receive." (*The Acts of the Apostles*, p. 564)
>
> The record of Christ's contest with Satan was chronicled **for the help and encouragement of the people of God today.** In this contest Christ worked **no miracle** and gave **no sign.** His only dependence was **God** and **his word**. In the future, Satan is to come down with great power, to work signs and wonders. He will bring down fire from heaven in the presence of his devotees, and, to those who have allowed themselves to be led away from the only true foundation,—**the word of God,**—will give proof of his authority. He will deceive if possible the very elect. Those who are standing firm upon the word of the everlasting God will meet Satan with the weapon with which Christ met him,—**"it is written."** This will be of **more power** than the working of miracles. The people of God will conquer through the Holy Spirit's working, which is stronger than miracles or aught else. It is from the Lord that we are to obtain power. (*The Southern Watchman*, March 1, 1904, Art. B, par. 39)

## Final Words

Prayer is the key and the appointed method of success. Utilized to its utmost and every gift of God in any and every need to achieve godliness, and then God will provide for your born-again experience as you pray the Word by faith, particularly the KJV, which is based on the manuscripts of the Textus Receptus. I use the KJV because Satan will probably quote from the modern translations, which have been altered to suit his false doctrines. Abraham made a covenant with the Lord, recognizing that the Lord is a faithful, covenant-keeping God. It is apparent that he trusted God to work in him and redeem him from sin. We cannot repeat this enough—you can depend on the Lord to help you at every step of the battle. The struggle is to keep your hand in His hand, your mind on His Word. God and His Word are to be your dependence—your only dependence! Meet Satan and every temptation with "It is written." Doing so is more powerful "<u>than the working of miracles.</u>" His Word will conquer Satan and his host of demons—"The people of God will conquer through the Holy Spirit's working, which is stronger than miracles or aught else." To depend on the Word of God is of greater value than miracles. Imagine that! In reality, transformation of character through the Word is the working out of the greatest miracle that can be performed. It is your victory, your salvation, and your eternal redemption. Make the choice today to accept the covenant—God's guarantee—and accept the God of heaven, the Creator, Redeemer, and Saviour as your one and only God.

The Lord has His portion of the covenant that He is committed to complete. Yet, of supreme importance to you, is the part that He has committed to you. Yet, He will also help you with your part every step of the way. Give Him your hand, your mind, and your body, and let Him help you.

> Fear thou not; for I am with thee: be not dismayed; for I am thy God: I will strengthen thee; yea, I will help thee; yea, I will uphold thee with the right hand of my righteousness. Behold, all they that were incensed against thee shall be ashamed and confounded: they shall be as nothing; and they that strive with thee shall perish. Thou shalt seek them, and shalt not find them, even them that contended with thee: they that war against thee shall be as nothing, and as a thing of nought. For I the LORD thy God will hold thy right hand, saying unto thee, Fear not; I will help thee. Fear not, thou worm Jacob, and ye men of Israel; I will help thee, saith the LORD, and thy redeemer, the Holy One of Israel. (Isa. 41:10–14)

Let us look at a few concluding statements from the Testimony of Jesus:

> Through the measure of His grace furnished to the human agent, not one need miss heaven. <u>Perfection of character is attainable by every one who strives for it</u>. This is made the **very foundation of the new covenant of the gospel**. The law of Jehovah is the

tree; the gospel is the fragrant blossoms and fruit which it bears. (*Selected Messages*, vol. 1, pp. 211, 212)

God desires us to choose the heavenly in place of the earthly. He opens before us the possibilities of a heavenly investment. He would give encouragement to our loftiest aims, security to our choicest treasure. (*Christ's Object Lessons*, p. 374)

Do not neglect secret prayer. <u>Plead as earnestly as you would if your **mortal life** were at stake</u>. Remain before God until unutterable longings for salvation are begotten within you, and the sweet evidence is obtained of pardoned sin. <u>Do not lay off your armor or leave the battle-field until you have obtained the victory, and can triumph in your Redeemer</u>. (*Signs of the Times*, May 1, 1884, par. 9)

We should study the Bible more that we may become familiar with the promises of God; then when Satan comes in, flooding the soul with his temptations, as he surely will, we may meet him with, "It is written." We may be shut in by the promises of God, which will be as a wall of fire about us. We want to know how to exercise faith. Faith "is the gift of God," but the power to exercise it is ours. If faith lies dormant, it is no advantage to us; but in exercise, it holds all blessings in its grasp. It is the hand by which the soul takes hold of the strength of the Infinite. It is the medium by which human hearts, renewed by the grace of Christ, are made to beat in harmony with the great Heart of love. Faith plants itself on the promises of God, and claims them as surety that he will do just as he said he would. Jesus comes to the sinful, helpless, needy soul, and says, "What things soever ye desire, when ye pray, believe that ye receive them, and ye shall have them." Believe; claim the promises, and praise God that you do receive the things you have asked of him, and when your need is greatest, you will experience his blessing and receive special help. (*Signs on the Times*, May 22, 1884, par. 3)

The new covenant is therefore a guarantee about a group in the last generation, the 144,000, that you are called to be a part of, by the generation in which you are born—a group that represent the fullness of the work of the seed of the Word and the gospel to redeem and fully restore fallen man. Therefore, God's Word affirms that His promises are not to a special few people but that the last church, though Laodicean in their condition, can get this victory as a group but that you particularly can personally be a part of that group. The only question is, "Do you and will you believe in God's power to accomplish this in you and those around you?" The covenant, which is in reality the Bible as a whole, has everything you need for victory. Study it over and over. Memorize it again and again. Pray it without ceasing, and see the glory of the Lord in your own life and allow His name to be vindicated through your reclamation and redemption from Satan and sin. Simply depend on every part of the Bible to accomplish in your life that which God has purposed for it, and you will not fail. It has God's guarantee, and you can count on it. The Lord Himself has staked His life for eternity on that blood covenant. Do not forget that His falling or failing at any point still would require an execution of the second death, from which there is no resurrection, for the failure to fulfill what He committed to do. "He that believeth on the Son of God hath the witness in himself" (1 John 5:10). I pray that you will make a commitment today to surrender anew to the Lord and, by faith, to grasp all the promises of the Word that you will have this witness in your life.

> The rainbow round about the throne is an **assurance** that God is true, that in Him is no variableness, neither shadow of turning. **We have sinned against Him, and are undeserving of His favor**; yet He Himself has put into our lips that most wonderful of pleas, "**Do not abhor us, for Thy name's sake; do not disgrace the throne of Thy glory; remember, break not Thy covenant with us**." Jeremiah 14:21. When we come to him confessing our unworthiness and sin, **He has pledged Himself to give heed to our cry**. The honor of His throne is staked for the fulfillment of His word unto us. (*Christ's Object Lessons*, p. 148)
>
> Now the God of peace, that brought again from the dead our Lord Jesus, that great shepherd of the sheep, through the blood of the everlasting covenant, Make you perfect in every good work to do his will, working in you that which is wellpleasing in his sight, through Jesus Christ; to whom be glory for ever and ever. Amen. (Heb. 13:20, 21)

# Bibliography

## Books

Andreasen, M. L. *The Book of Hebrews.* Washington, DC: Review and Herald Publishing Association, 1948.

White, Ellen G. *The Acts of the Apostles.* Mountain View, CA: Pacific Press Publishing Association, 1911.

———. *Christ's Object Lessons.* Washington, DC: Review and Herald Publishing Association, 1900.

———. *Counsels on Diet and Foods.* Washington, DC: Review and Herald Publishing Association, 1938.

———. *The Desire of Ages.* Mountain View, CA: Pacific Press Publishing Association, 1898.

———. *Early Writings.* Washington, DC: Review and Herald Publishing Association, 1882.

———. *Education.* Mountain View, CA: Pacific Press Publishing Association, 1903.

———. *God's Amazing Grace.* Washington, DC: Review and Herald Publishing Association, 1973.

———. *The Great Controversy.* Mountain View, CA: Pacific Press Publishing Association, 1911.

———. *Messages to Young People.* Hagerstown, MD: Review and Herald Publishing Association, 1930.

———. *The Ministry of Healing.* Mountain View, CA: Pacific Press Publishing Association, 1905.

———. *Patriarchs and Prophets*. Washington, DC: Review and Herald Publishing Association, 1890.

———. *Prophets and Kings*. Mountain View, CA: Pacific Press Publishing Association, 1917.

———. *The Sanctified Life*. Washington, DC: Review and Herald Publishing Association, 1937.

———. *Selected Messages*. Book 1. Washington, DC: Review and Herald Publishing Association, 1958.

———. *The SDA Bible Commentary*. Vol. 7. Washington, DC: Review and Herald Publishing Association, 1957.

———. *The Spirit of Prophecy*. Vol. 1. Battle Creek, MI: Seventh-day Adventist Publishing Association, 1870.

———. *The Spirit of Prophecy*. Vol. 3. Battle Creek, MI: Seventh-day Adventist Publishing Association, 1878.

———. *Spiritual Gifts*. Vol. 3. Battle Creek, MI: Seventh-day Adventist Publishing Association, 1864.

———. *Steps to Christ*. Mountain View, CA: Pacific Press Publishing Association, 1892.

———. *Testimonies for the Church*. Vol. 2. Mountain View, CA: Pacific Press Publishing Association, 1871.

———. *Testimonies for the Church*. Vol. 4. Mountain View, CA: Pacific Press Publishing Association, 1881.

———. *Testimonies to Ministers and Gospel Workers*. Mountain View, CA: Pacific Press Publishing Association, 1923.

———. *Thoughts from the Mount of Blessing*. Mountain View, CA: Pacific Press Publishing Association, 1896.

## Magazine Articles

White, Ellen G. *Review and Herald,* May 6, 1875. EGW Writings.org. https://1ref.us/1l9 (accessed February 18, 2021).

———. *Review and Herald,* January 27, 1903. EGW Writings.org. https://1ref.us/1l3 (accessed February 18, 2021).

———. *Signs of the Times,* March 14, 1878. EGW Writings.org. https://1ref.us/1l8 (accessed February 18, 2021).

———. *Signs of the Times,* May 1, 1884. EGW Writings.org. https://1ref.us/1le (accessed February 18, 2021).

———. *Signs of the Times,* May 22, 1884. EGW Writings.org. https://1ref.us/1lf (accessed February 18, 2021).

———. *Signs of the Times,* April 15, 1886. EGW Writings.org. https://1ref.us/1l7 (accessed February 18, 2021).

———. *Signs of the Times,* June 12, 1901. EGW Writings.org. https://1ref.us/1l5 (accessed February 18, 2021).

———. *The Southern Watchman,* March 1, 1904. EGW Writings.org. https://1ref.us/1la (accessed February 18, 2021).

———. *The Youth's Instructor,* March 1, 1872. EGW Writings.org. https://1ref.us/1l4 (accessed February 18, 2021).

———. *The Youth's Instructor,* April 25, 1901. EGW Writings.org. https://1ref.us/1l6 (accessed February 18, 2021).

## Music

Burg, Carolina Sandell. "Children of the Heavenly Father." 1855. Hymnary. https://1ref.us/1l0 (accessed February 18, 2021).

Campbell, Lucie Eddie. "Footprints of Jesus." Hymnary. https://1ref.us/1ld (accessed February 18, 2021).

Ellington, A. D. "Like Jesus." 1931. Hymnary. https://1ref.us/1kt (accessed February 17, 2021).

Elliot, Charlotte. "Just As I Am, Without One Plea." Hymnary. https://1ref.us/1kz (accessed February 17, 2021).

"Fairest Lord Jesus." 17th century German. Hymnary. https://1ref.us/1l1 (accessed February 18, 2021).

Havergal, Frances R. "Live Out Thy Life within Me." Hymnary. https://1ref.us/1lb (accessed February 18, 2021).

Lemmel, Helen H. "Turn Your Eyes Upon Jesus." 1922. Hymnary. https://1ref.us/1kv (accessed February 17, 2021).

Luther, Martin. "A Mighty Fortress." 1529. Hymnary. https://1ref.us/1ku (accessed February 17, 2021).

Mote, Edward. "My Hope Is Built on Nothing Less." 1834. Hymnary. https://1ref.us/1kx (accessed February 17, 2021).

Pollard, Adelaide. "Have Thine Own Way, Lord." 1906. Hymnary. https://1ref.us/1kw (accessed February 17, 2021).

Sammis, John H. "Trust and Obey." 1887. Hymnary. https://1ref.us/1lc (accessed February 18, 2021).

Watts, Isaac. "Psalm 5." 1806. Hymnary. https://1ref.us/1ky (accessed February 17, 2021).

Wesley, Charles. "Love Divine, All Loves Excelling." 1747. Hymnary. https://1ref.us/1l2 (accessed February 18, 2021).

## ASPECT Books
www.ASPECTBooks.com

We invite you to view the complete
selection of titles we publish at:
**www.ASPECTBooks.com**

We encourage you to write us
with your thoughts about this,
or any other book we publish at:
**info@ASPECTBooks.com**

ASPECT Books' titles may be purchased in
bulk quantities for educational, fund-raising,
business, or promotional use.
**bulksales@ASPECTBooks.com**

Finally, if you are interested in seeing
your own book in print, please contact us at:
**publishing@ASPECTBooks.com**

We are happy to review your manuscript at no charge.

www.ingramcontent.com/pod-product-compliance
Lightning Source LLC
Chambersburg PA
CBHW071655160426
43195CB00012B/1477